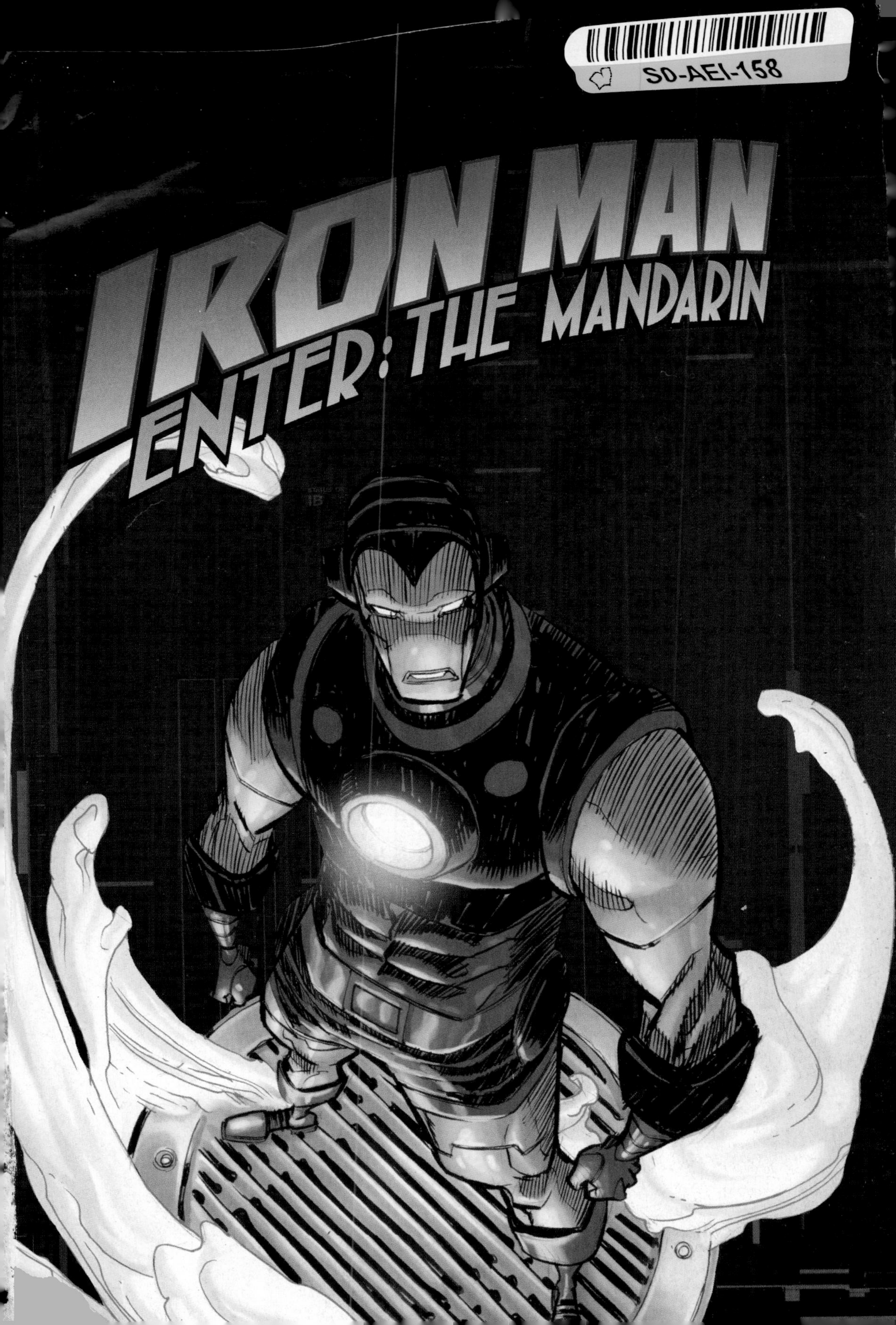
IRON MAN
ENTER: THE MANDARIN

IRON MAN
ENTER: THE MANDARIN

WRITER: Joe Casey
ARTIST: Eric Canete
COLORS: Dave Stewart
LETTERS: Comicraft
ASSISTANT EDITOR: Thomas Brennan
EDITOR: Stephen Wacker

Based on Tales of Suspense #50 -55
by Stan Lee and Don Heck

COLLECTION EDITOR: Cory Levine
EDITORIAL ASSISTANT: Jody LeHeup
ASSISTANT EDITOR: John Denning
EDITORS, SPECIAL PROJECTS: Jennifer Grünwald & Mark D. Beazley
SENIOR EDITOR, SPECIAL PROJECTS: Jeff Youngquist
SENIOR VICE PRESIDENT OF SALES: David Gabriel
PRODUCTION: Jerron Quality Color & Jerry Kalinowski

EDITOR IN CHIEF: Joe Quesada
PUBLISHER: Dan Buckley

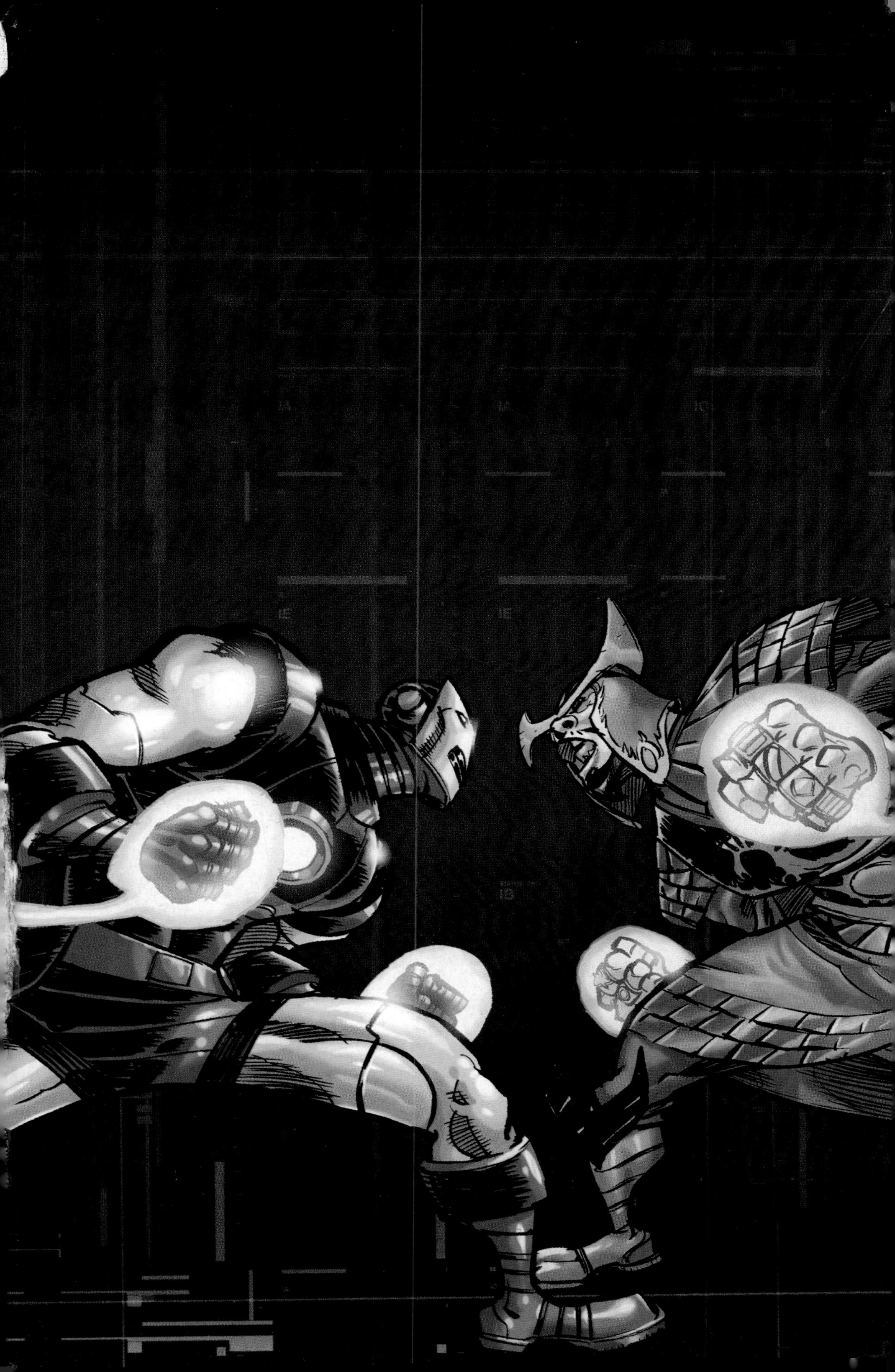

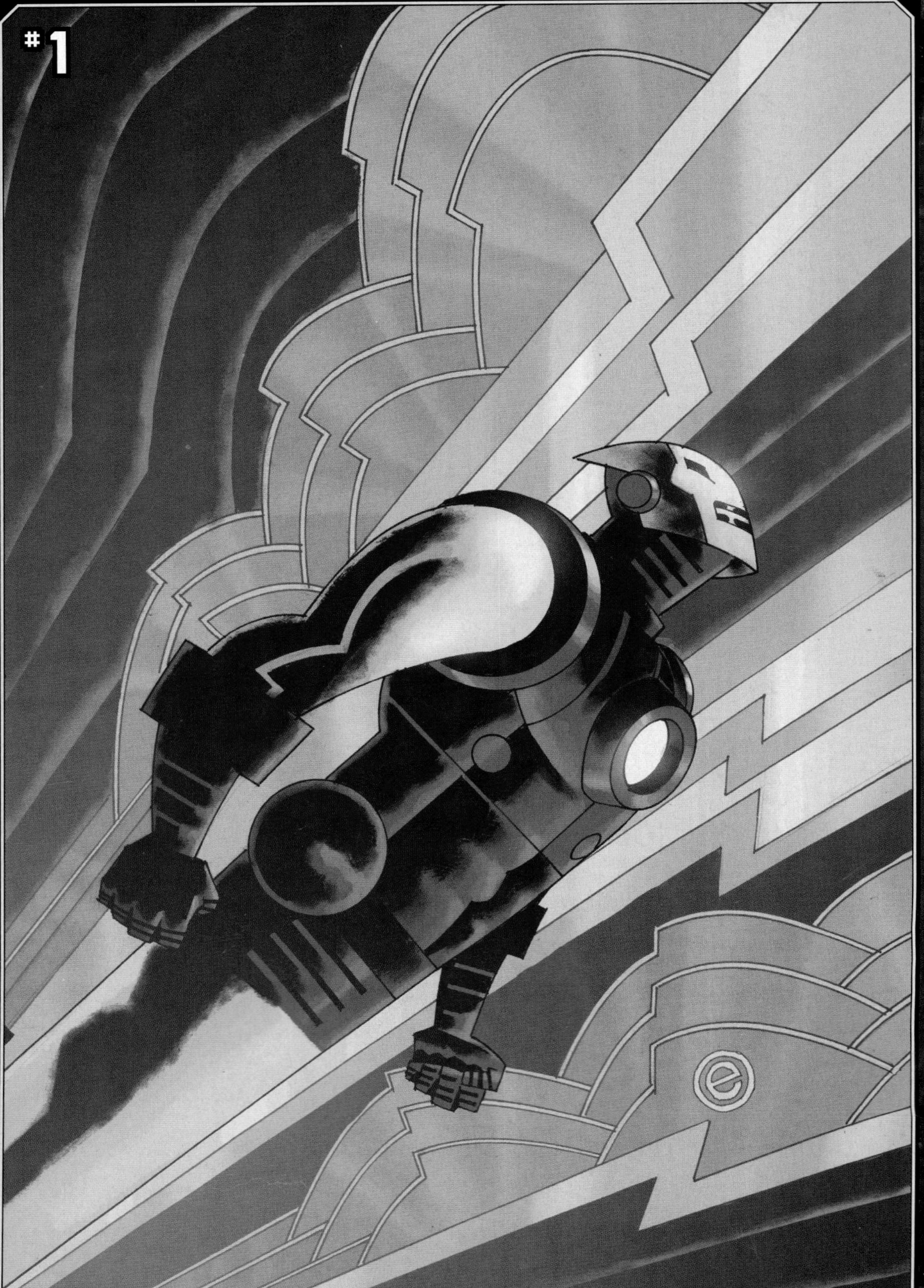

#1

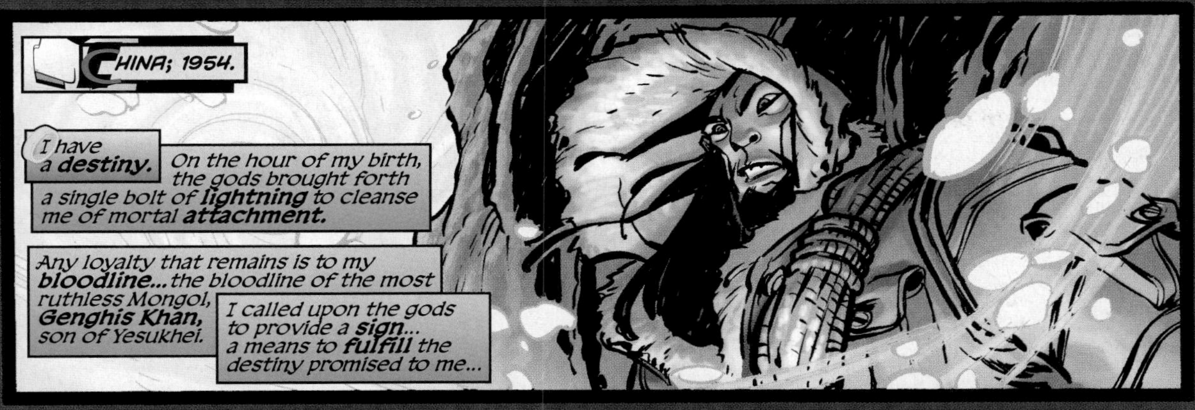
CHINA; 1954.
I have a destiny. On the hour of my birth, the gods brought forth a single bolt of lightning to cleanse me of mortal attachment.
Any loyalty that remains is to my bloodline... the bloodline of the most ruthless Mongol, Genghis Khan, son of Yesukhei.
I called upon the gods to provide a sign... a means to fulfill the destiny promised to me...

ENTER THE MANDARIN

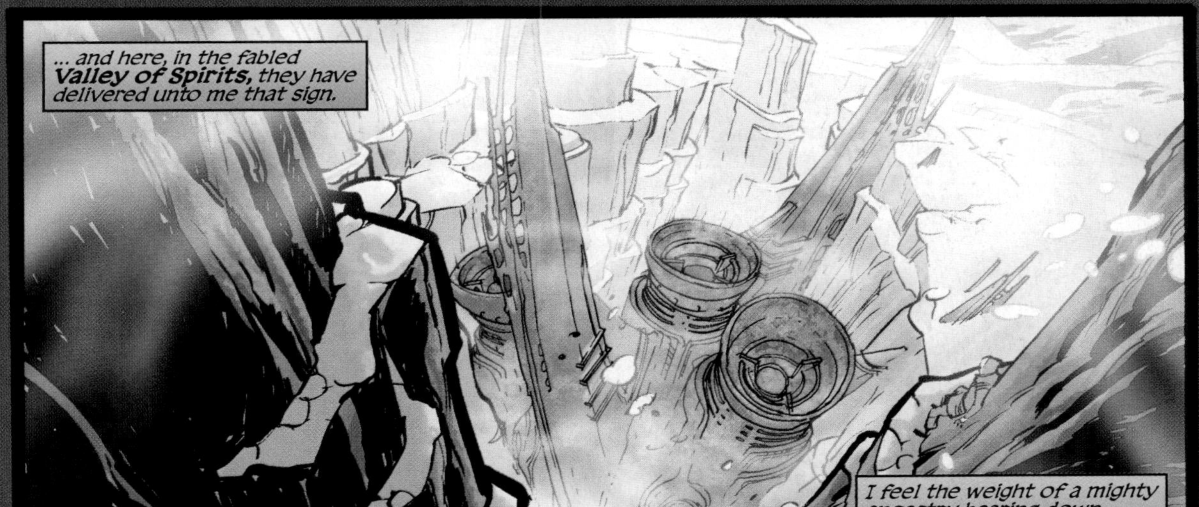
... and here, in the fabled Valley of Spirits, they have delivered unto me that sign.
I feel the weight of a mighty ancestry bearing down upon my shoulders... pushing me to continue.

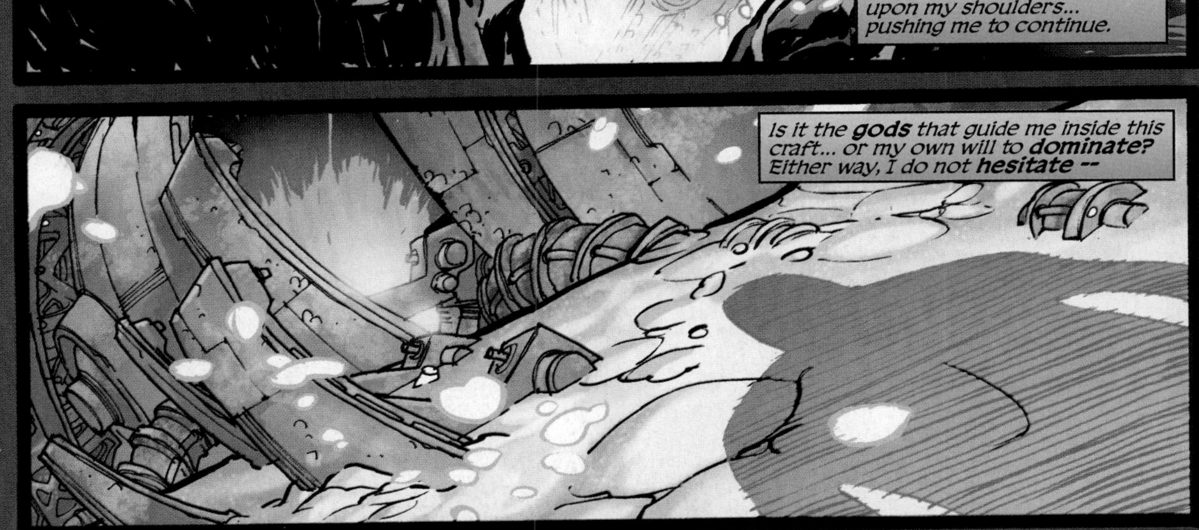
Is it the gods that guide me inside this craft... or my own will to dominate? Either way, I do not hesitate --

--and I am duly **punished** for my arrogance.

The **true nature** of this discovery becomes obvious to me. A **crippled vessel**... fallen from the **stars**...

A **lesser** man would surely be **felled** by this alien attack, meant to burn the **brain** from your skull. But I am **not** such a man...

... and I am only driven **forward**... to the **source** of this assault.

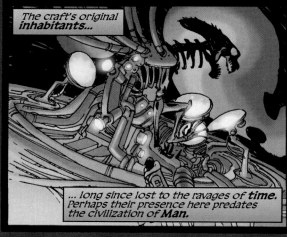

The craft's original **inhabitants**...

... long since lost to the ravages of **time**. Perhaps their presence here predates the civilization of **Man.**

I ascend to the **zenith**... emanating such **power** that I can **taste** it on my tongue. I can feel it **dancing** up my spine.

So **alien**... and yet so **familiar**...

...calling out to me...

...singing **hymns** in my **name**...

...that sound like the end of the world.

->HHNNN...<-

->...NNNTTT...<-

-- DISENGAGE EXTERNAL AC SYSTEMS///////// 01 01 01 011 ///////// COMPLETE

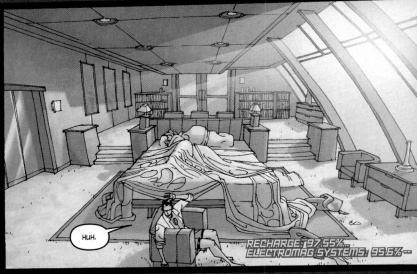

HUH.

RECHARGE: 97.55%--
ELECTROMAG. SYSTEMS: 95.6%--

...SURE, IT'S A SHOW FOR THE STOCKHOLDERS. WHAT ISN'T? BUT, AT THE SAME TIME, IT'S A CHANCE FOR THE EMPLOYEES TO SUIT UP AND FEAST LIKE KINGS. IT'S GOOD FOR MORALE. WE CAN'T ALL BE *SUPERMODELS* TWENTY-FOUR SEVEN, VERONICA.

SAYS *PEOPLE'S* SEXIEST BILLIONAIRE, TWO YEARS RUNNING...

...BUT I WON'T HOLD YOUR BOURGEOIS SYMPATHIES AGAINST YOU. HOW 'BOUT DINNER AT EL MOROCCO TONIGHT? MAYBE AFTERWARDS, WE'LL GET *ALL* YOUR CLOTHES OFF...

YOU WANNA FEAST LIKE A *KING*, MR. STARK--

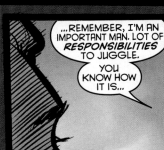

HOLD IT. I'M STILL WRAPPING MY HEAD AROUND YOU USING THE WORD "*BOURGEOIS*" IN A SENTENCE. BUT LET'S PLAY IT BY EAR, MISS VOGUE...

...REMEMBER, I'M AN IMPORTANT MAN. LOT OF *RESPONSIBILITIES* TO JUGGLE.

YOU KNOW HOW IT IS...

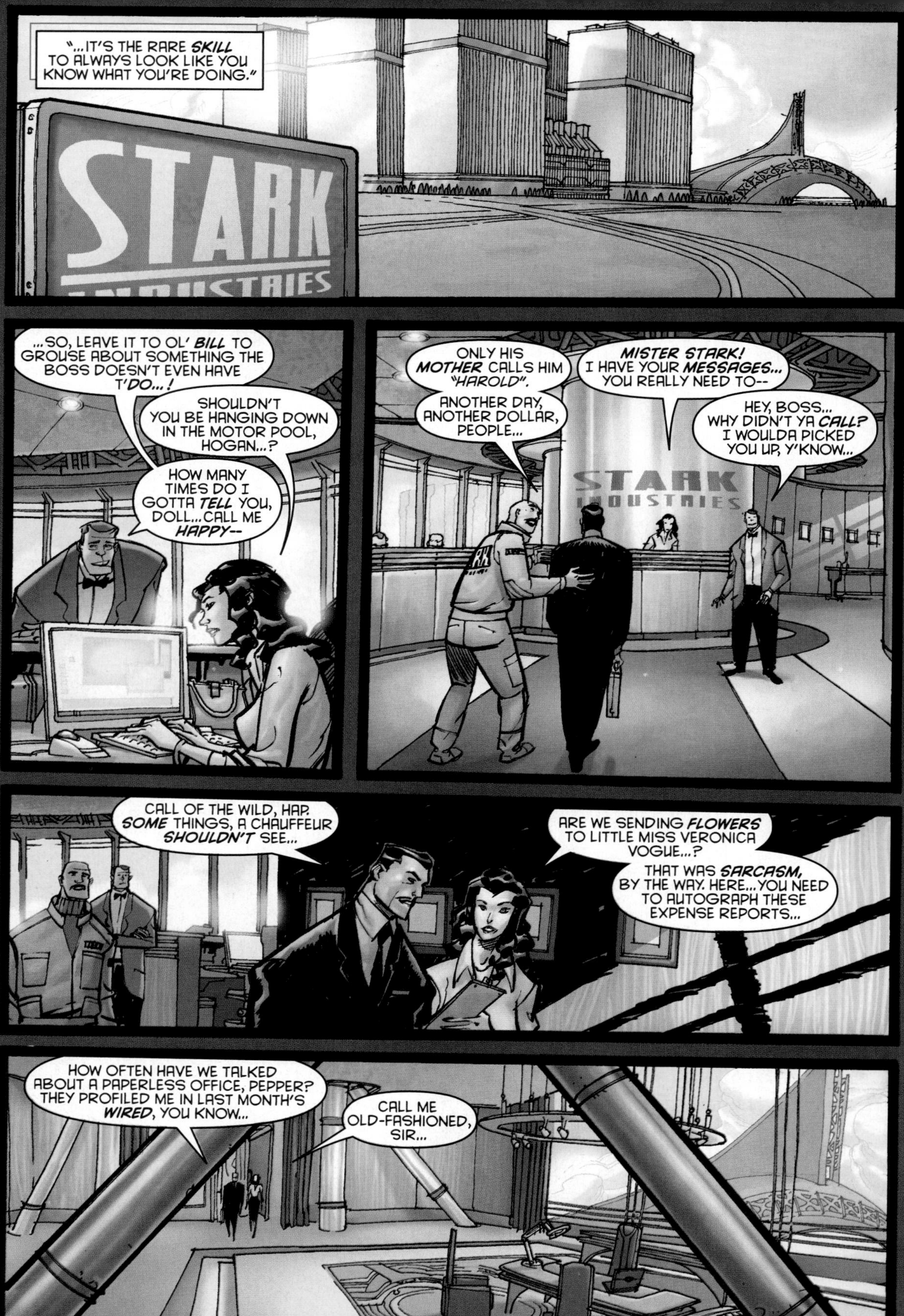
"...IT'S THE RARE SKILL TO ALWAYS LOOK LIKE YOU KNOW WHAT YOU'RE DOING."
STARK INDUSTRIES
...SO, LEAVE IT TO OL' BILL TO GROUSE ABOUT SOMETHING THE BOSS DOESN'T EVEN HAVE T'DO...!
SHOULDN'T YOU BE HANGING DOWN IN THE MOTOR POOL, HOGAN...?
HOW MANY TIMES DO I GOTTA TELL YOU, DOLL...CALL ME HAPPY--
ONLY HIS MOTHER CALLS HIM "HAROLD".
ANOTHER DAY, ANOTHER DOLLAR, PEOPLE...
MISTER STARK! I HAVE YOUR MESSAGES... YOU REALLY NEED TO--
HEY, BOSS... WHY DIDN'T YA CALL? I WOULDA PICKED YOU UP, Y'KNOW...
STARK INDUSTRIES
CALL OF THE WILD, HAP. SOME THINGS, A CHAUFFEUR SHOULDN'T SEE...
ARE WE SENDING FLOWERS TO LITTLE MISS VERONICA VOGUE...?
THAT WAS SARCASM, BY THE WAY. HERE...YOU NEED TO AUTOGRAPH THESE EXPENSE REPORTS...
HOW OFTEN HAVE WE TALKED ABOUT A PAPERLESS OFFICE, PEPPER? THEY PROFILED ME IN LAST MONTH'S WIRED, YOU KNOW...
CALL ME OLD-FASHIONED, SIR...

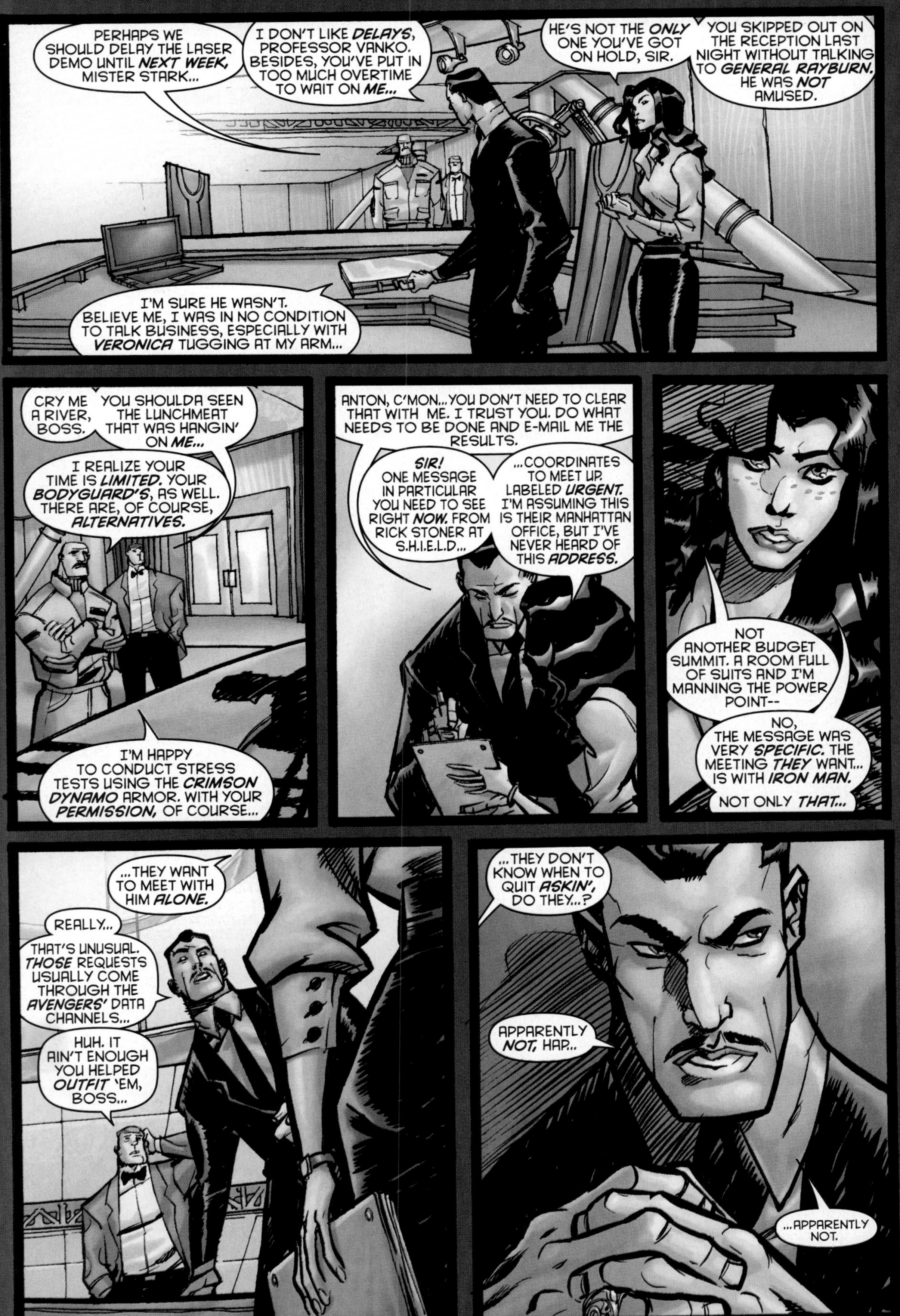
PERHAPS WE SHOULD DELAY THE LASER DEMO UNTIL NEXT WEEK, MISTER STARK...
I DON'T LIKE DELAYS, PROFESSOR VANKO. BESIDES, YOU'VE PUT IN TOO MUCH OVERTIME TO WAIT ON ME...
HE'S NOT THE ONLY ONE YOU'VE GOT ON HOLD, SIR.
YOU SKIPPED OUT ON THE RECEPTION LAST NIGHT WITHOUT TALKING TO GENERAL RAYBURN. HE WAS NOT AMUSED.
I'M SURE HE WASN'T. BELIEVE ME, I WAS IN NO CONDITION TO TALK BUSINESS, ESPECIALLY WITH VERONICA TUGGING AT MY ARM...
CRY ME A RIVER, BOSS.
YOU SHOULDA SEEN THE LUNCHMEAT THAT WAS HANGIN' ON ME...
I REALIZE YOUR TIME IS LIMITED. YOUR BODYGUARD'S, AS WELL. THERE ARE, OF COURSE, ALTERNATIVES.
I'M HAPPY TO CONDUCT STRESS TESTS USING THE CRIMSON DYNAMO ARMOR. WITH YOUR PERMISSION, OF COURSE...
ANTON, C'MON...YOU DON'T NEED TO CLEAR THAT WITH ME. I TRUST YOU. DO WHAT NEEDS TO BE DONE AND E-MAIL ME THE RESULTS.
SIR! ONE MESSAGE IN PARTICULAR YOU NEED TO SEE RIGHT NOW. FROM RICK STONER AT S.H.I.E.L.D...
...COORDINATES TO MEET UP. LABELED URGENT. I'M ASSUMING THIS IS THEIR MANHATTAN OFFICE, BUT I'VE NEVER HEARD OF THIS ADDRESS.
NOT ANOTHER BUDGET SUMMIT. A ROOM FULL OF SUITS AND I'M MANNING THE POWER POINT--
NO, THE MESSAGE WAS VERY SPECIFIC. THE MEETING THEY WANT... IS WITH IRON MAN.
NOT ONLY THAT...
...THEY WANT TO MEET WITH HIM ALONE.
REALLY...
THAT'S UNUSUAL. THOSE REQUESTS USUALLY COME THROUGH THE AVENGERS' DATA CHANNELS...
HUH. IT AIN'T ENOUGH YOU HELPED OUTFIT 'EM, BOSS...
...THEY DON'T KNOW WHEN TO QUIT ASKIN', DO THEY...?
APPARENTLY NOT, HAP...
...APPARENTLY NOT.

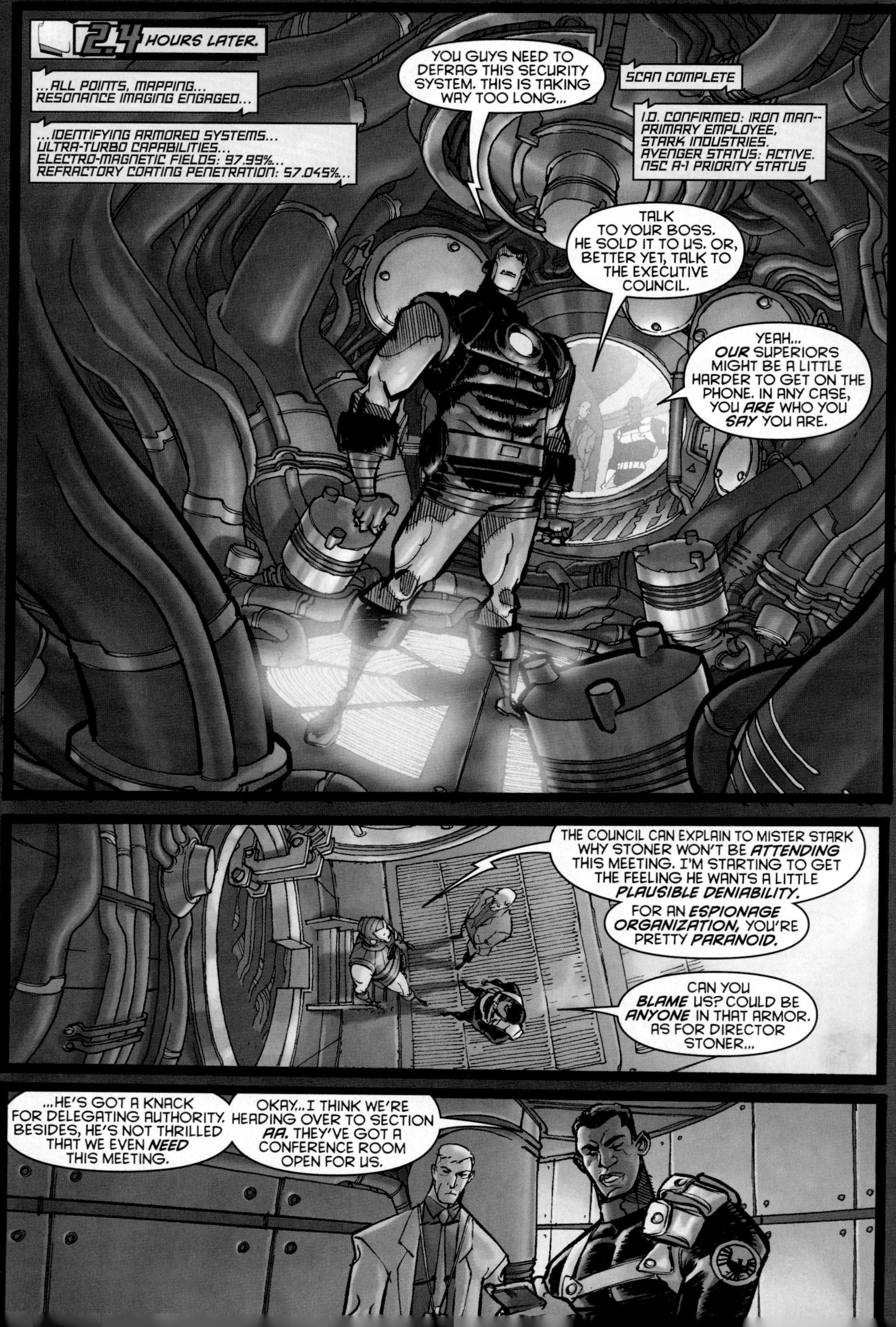
2.4 HOURS LATER.
...ALL POINTS, MAPPING... RESONANCE IMAGING ENGAGED...
...IDENTIFYING ARMORED SYSTEMS... ULTRA-TURBO CAPABILITIES... ELECTRO-MAGNETIC FIELDS: 97.99%... REFRACTORY COATING PENETRATION: 57.045%...
YOU GUYS NEED TO DEFRAG THIS SECURITY SYSTEM. THIS IS TAKING WAY TOO LONG...
SCAN COMPLETE
I.D. CONFIRMED: IRON MAN-- PRIMARY EMPLOYEE, STARK INDUSTRIES. AVENGER STATUS: ACTIVE. NSC A-1 PRIORITY STATUS
TALK TO YOUR BOSS. HE SOLD IT TO US. OR, BETTER YET, TALK TO THE EXECUTIVE COUNCIL.
YEAH... OUR SUPERIORS MIGHT BE A LITTLE HARDER TO GET ON THE PHONE. IN ANY CASE, YOU ARE WHO YOU SAY YOU ARE.
THE COUNCIL CAN EXPLAIN TO MISTER STARK WHY STONER WON'T BE ATTENDING THIS MEETING. I'M STARTING TO GET THE FEELING HE WANTS A LITTLE PLAUSIBLE DENIABILITY.
FOR AN ESPIONAGE ORGANIZATION, YOU'RE PRETTY PARANOID.
CAN YOU BLAME US? COULD BE ANYONE IN THAT ARMOR. AS FOR DIRECTOR STONER...
...HE'S GOT A KNACK FOR DELEGATING AUTHORITY. BESIDES, HE'S NOT THRILLED THAT WE EVEN NEED THIS MEETING.
OKAY... I THINK WE'RE HEADING OVER TO SECTION AA. THEY'VE GOT A CONFERENCE ROOM OPEN FOR US.

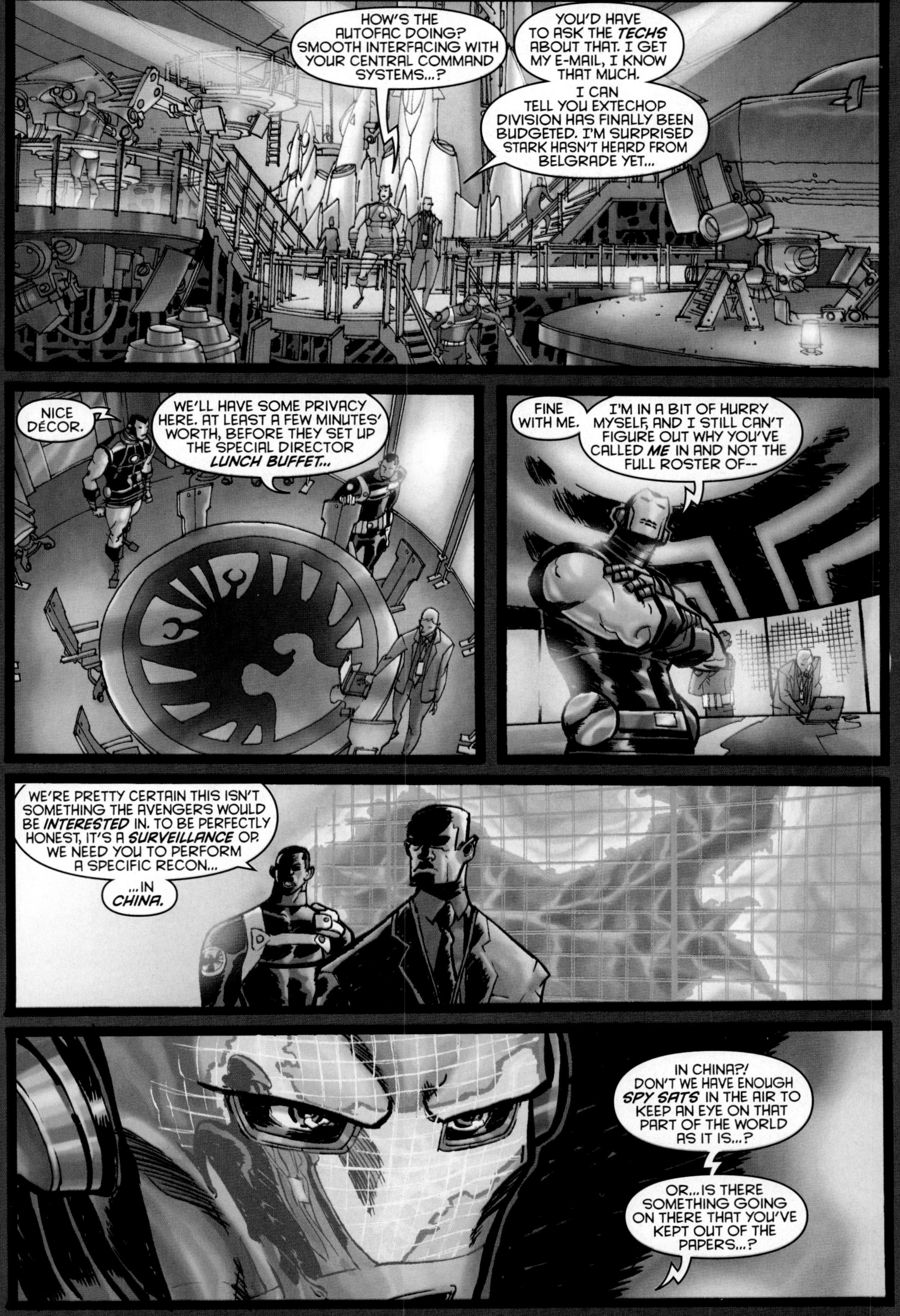
HOW'S THE AUTOFAC DOING? SMOOTH INTERFACING WITH YOUR CENTRAL COMMAND SYSTEMS...?
YOU'D HAVE TO ASK THE *TECHS* ABOUT THAT. I GET MY E-MAIL, I KNOW THAT MUCH.
I CAN TELL YOU EXTECHOP DIVISION HAS FINALLY BEEN BUDGETED. I'M SURPRISED STARK HASN'T HEARD FROM BELGRADE YET...
NICE DÉCOR.
WE'LL HAVE SOME PRIVACY HERE. AT LEAST A FEW MINUTES' WORTH, BEFORE THEY SET UP THE SPECIAL DIRECTOR *LUNCH BUFFET...*
FINE WITH ME.
I'M IN A BIT OF HURRY MYSELF, AND I STILL CAN'T FIGURE OUT WHY YOU'VE CALLED *ME* IN AND NOT THE FULL ROSTER OF--
WE'RE PRETTY CERTAIN THIS ISN'T SOMETHING THE AVENGERS WOULD BE *INTERESTED* IN. TO BE PERFECTLY HONEST, IT'S A *SURVEILLANCE* OP. WE NEED YOU TO PERFORM A SPECIFIC RECON...
...IN *CHINA.*
IN CHINA?! DON'T WE HAVE ENOUGH *SPY SATS* IN THE AIR TO KEEP AN EYE ON THAT PART OF THE WORLD AS IT IS...?
OR...IS THERE SOMETHING GOING ON THERE THAT YOU'VE KEPT OUT OF THE PAPERS...?

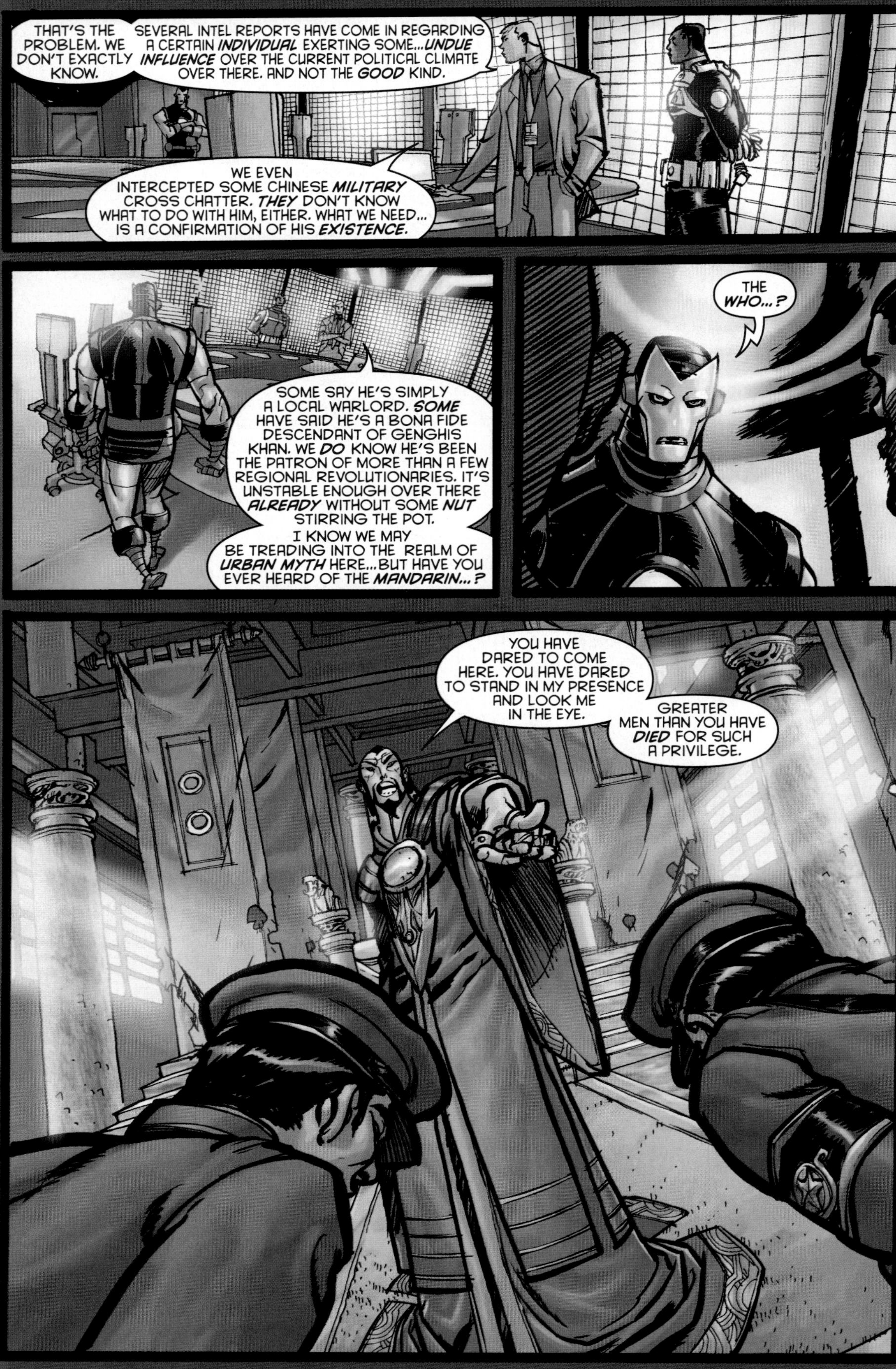

THAT'S THE PROBLEM. WE DON'T EXACTLY KNOW.
SEVERAL INTEL REPORTS HAVE COME IN REGARDING A CERTAIN INDIVIDUAL EXERTING SOME... UNDUE INFLUENCE OVER THE CURRENT POLITICAL CLIMATE OVER THERE. AND NOT THE GOOD KIND.
WE EVEN INTERCEPTED SOME CHINESE MILITARY CROSS CHATTER. THEY DON'T KNOW WHAT TO DO WITH HIM, EITHER. WHAT WE NEED... IS A CONFIRMATION OF HIS EXISTENCE.
SOME SAY HE'S SIMPLY A LOCAL WARLORD. SOME HAVE SAID HE'S A BONA FIDE DESCENDANT OF GENGHIS KHAN. WE DO KNOW HE'S BEEN THE PATRON OF MORE THAN A FEW REGIONAL REVOLUTIONARIES. IT'S UNSTABLE ENOUGH OVER THERE ALREADY WITHOUT SOME NUT STIRRING THE POT.
I KNOW WE MAY BE TREADING INTO THE REALM OF URBAN MYTH HERE... BUT HAVE YOU EVER HEARD OF THE MANDARIN...?
THE WHO...?
YOU HAVE DARED TO COME HERE. YOU HAVE DARED TO STAND IN MY PRESENCE AND LOOK ME IN THE EYE.
GREATER MEN THAN YOU HAVE DIED FOR SUCH A PRIVILEGE.

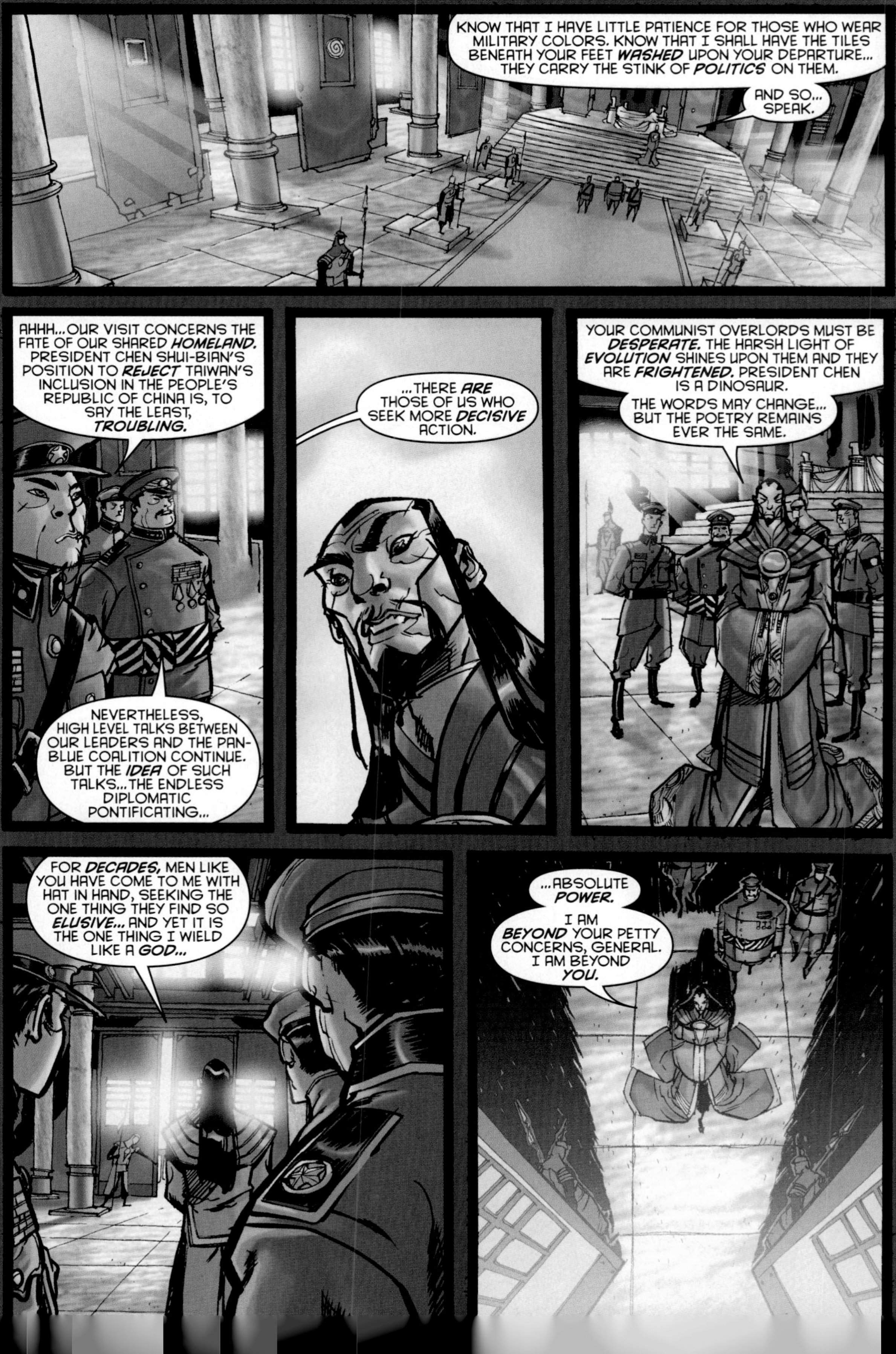
KNOW THAT I HAVE LITTLE PATIENCE FOR THOSE WHO WEAR MILITARY COLORS. KNOW THAT I SHALL HAVE THE TILES BENEATH YOUR FEET WASHED UPON YOUR DEPARTURE... THEY CARRY THE STINK OF POLITICS ON THEM.
AND SO... SPEAK.
AHHH...OUR VISIT CONCERNS THE FATE OF OUR SHARED HOMELAND. PRESIDENT CHEN SHUI-BIAN'S POSITION TO REJECT TAIWAN'S INCLUSION IN THE PEOPLE'S REPUBLIC OF CHINA IS, TO SAY THE LEAST, TROUBLING.
NEVERTHELESS, HIGH LEVEL TALKS BETWEEN OUR LEADERS AND THE PAN-BLUE COALITION CONTINUE. BUT THE IDEA OF SUCH TALKS...THE ENDLESS DIPLOMATIC PONTIFICATING...
...THERE ARE THOSE OF US WHO SEEK MORE DECISIVE ACTION.
YOUR COMMUNIST OVERLORDS MUST BE DESPERATE. THE HARSH LIGHT OF EVOLUTION SHINES UPON THEM AND THEY ARE FRIGHTENED. PRESIDENT CHEN IS A DINOSAUR.
THE WORDS MAY CHANGE... BUT THE POETRY REMAINS EVER THE SAME.
FOR DECADES, MEN LIKE YOU HAVE COME TO ME WITH HAT IN HAND, SEEKING THE ONE THING THEY FIND SO ELUSIVE... AND YET IT IS THE ONE THING I WIELD LIKE A GOD...
...ABSOLUTE POWER.
I AM BEYOND YOUR PETTY CONCERNS, GENERAL. I AM BEYOND YOU.

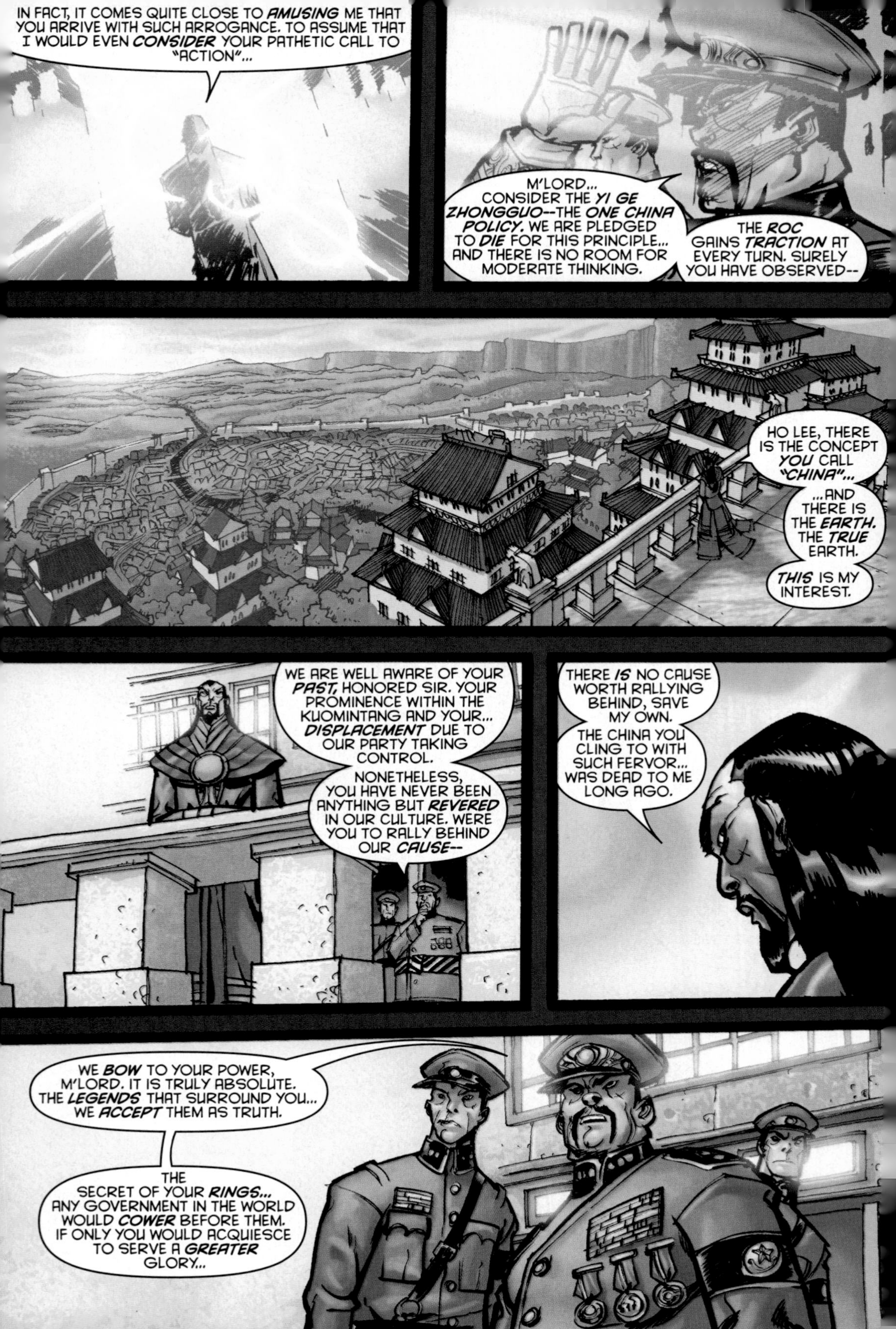

IN FACT, IT COMES QUITE CLOSE TO AMUSING ME THAT YOU ARRIVE WITH SUCH ARROGANCE. TO ASSUME THAT I WOULD EVEN CONSIDER YOUR PATHETIC CALL TO "ACTION"...
M'LORD... CONSIDER THE YI GE ZHONGGUO--THE ONE CHINA POLICY. WE ARE PLEDGED TO DIE FOR THIS PRINCIPLE... AND THERE IS NO ROOM FOR MODERATE THINKING.
THE ROC GAINS TRACTION AT EVERY TURN. SURELY YOU HAVE OBSERVED--
HO LEE, THERE IS THE CONCEPT YOU CALL "CHINA"...
...AND THERE IS THE EARTH. THE TRUE EARTH.
THIS IS MY INTEREST.
WE ARE WELL AWARE OF YOUR PAST, HONORED SIR. YOUR PROMINENCE WITHIN THE KUOMINTANG AND YOUR... DISPLACEMENT DUE TO OUR PARTY TAKING CONTROL.
NONETHELESS, YOU HAVE NEVER BEEN ANYTHING BUT REVERED IN OUR CULTURE. WERE YOU TO RALLY BEHIND OUR CAUSE--
THERE IS NO CAUSE WORTH RALLYING BEHIND, SAVE MY OWN.
THE CHINA YOU CLING TO WITH SUCH FERVOR... WAS DEAD TO ME LONG AGO.
WE BOW TO YOUR POWER, M'LORD. IT IS TRULY ABSOLUTE. THE LEGENDS THAT SURROUND YOU... WE ACCEPT THEM AS TRUTH.
THE SECRET OF YOUR RINGS... ANY GOVERNMENT IN THE WORLD WOULD COWER BEFORE THEM. IF ONLY YOU WOULD ACQUIESCE TO SERVE A GREATER GLORY...

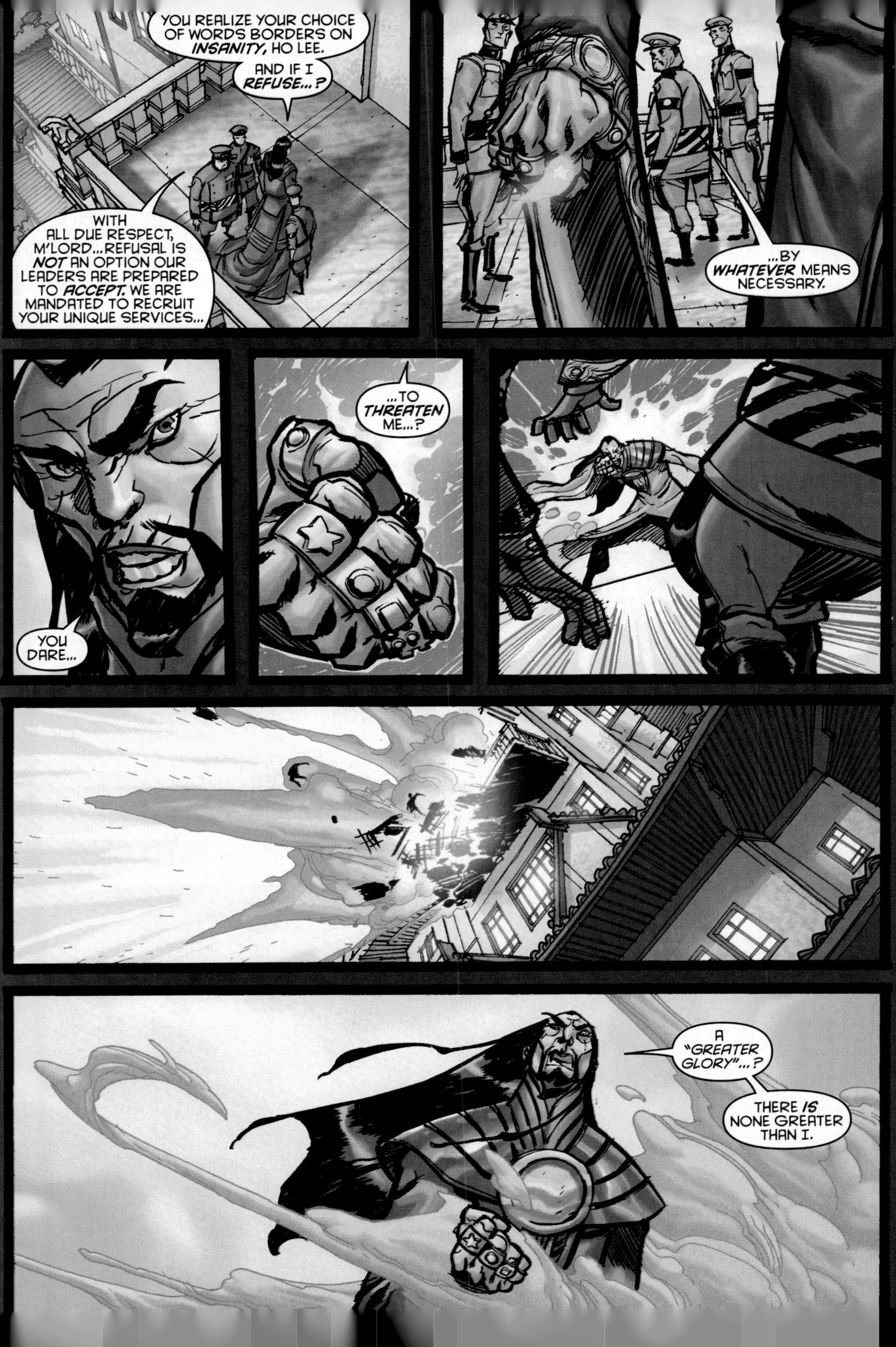
YOU REALIZE YOUR CHOICE OF WORDS BORDERS ON *INSANITY,* HO LEE.
AND IF I *REFUSE...?*
WITH ALL DUE RESPECT, M'LORD...REFUSAL IS *NOT* AN OPTION OUR LEADERS ARE PREPARED TO *ACCEPT.* WE ARE MANDATED TO RECRUIT YOUR UNIQUE SERVICES...
...BY *WHATEVER* MEANS NECESSARY.
YOU DARE...
...TO *THREATEN* ME...?
A "GREATER GLORY"...?
THERE *IS* NONE GREATER THAN I.

APPROACHING DROP ZONE--

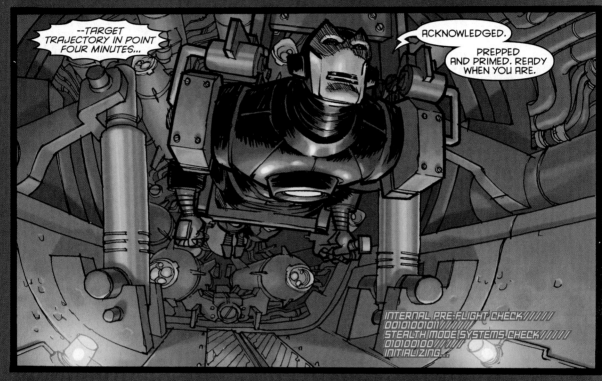

--TARGET TRAJECTORY IN POINT FOUR MINUTES...

ACKNOWLEDGED.

PREPPED AND PRIMED. READY WHEN YOU ARE.

INTERNAL PRE-FLIGHT CHECK//////
0010100101//////
STEALTH MODE SYSTEMS CHECK//////
010100100
INITIALIZING...

STRANGE ORDNANCE THIS TIME OUT, EH, PAULIE...?

TO SAY THE LEAST. BUT OURS IS NOT TO REASON WHY. HOLD ON A SECOND...

BOMB BAY, CONN. WE'RE ON TARGET. READY TO DISENGAGE--

--ON YOUR ORDER.

GO.

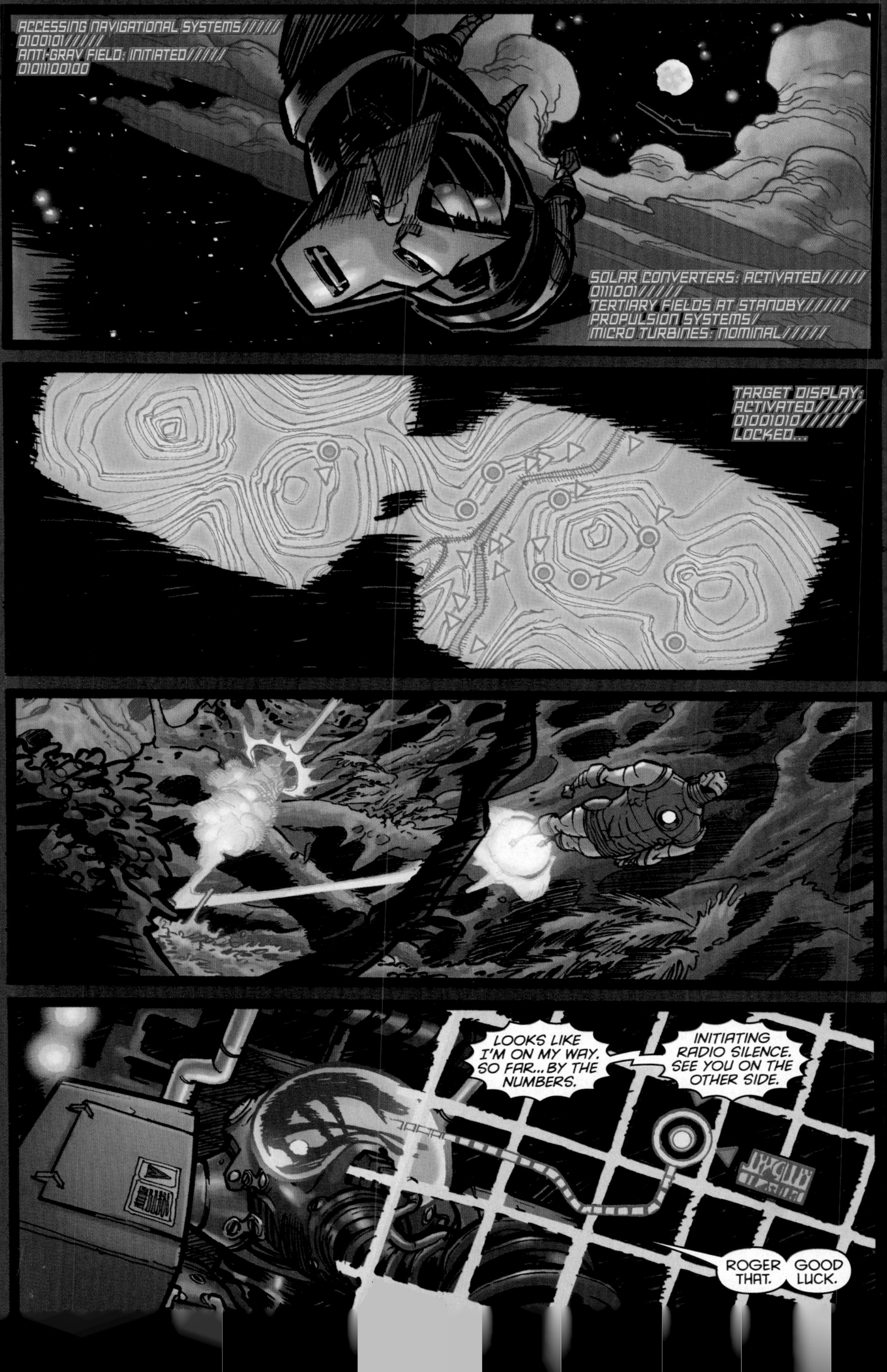
ACCESSING NAVIGATIONAL SYSTEMS//////
0100101//////
ANTI-GRAV FIELD: INITIATED//////
0101100100
SOLAR CONVERTERS: ACTIVATED//////
0111001//////
TERTIARY FIELDS AT STANDBY//////
PROPULSION SYSTEMS/
MICRO TURBINES: NOMINAL//////
TARGET DISPLAY: ACTIVATED//////
01001010//////
LOCKED...
LOOKS LIKE I'M ON MY WAY. SO FAR...BY THE NUMBERS.
INITIATING RADIO SILENCE. SEE YOU ON THE OTHER SIDE.
ROGER THAT.
GOOD LUCK.

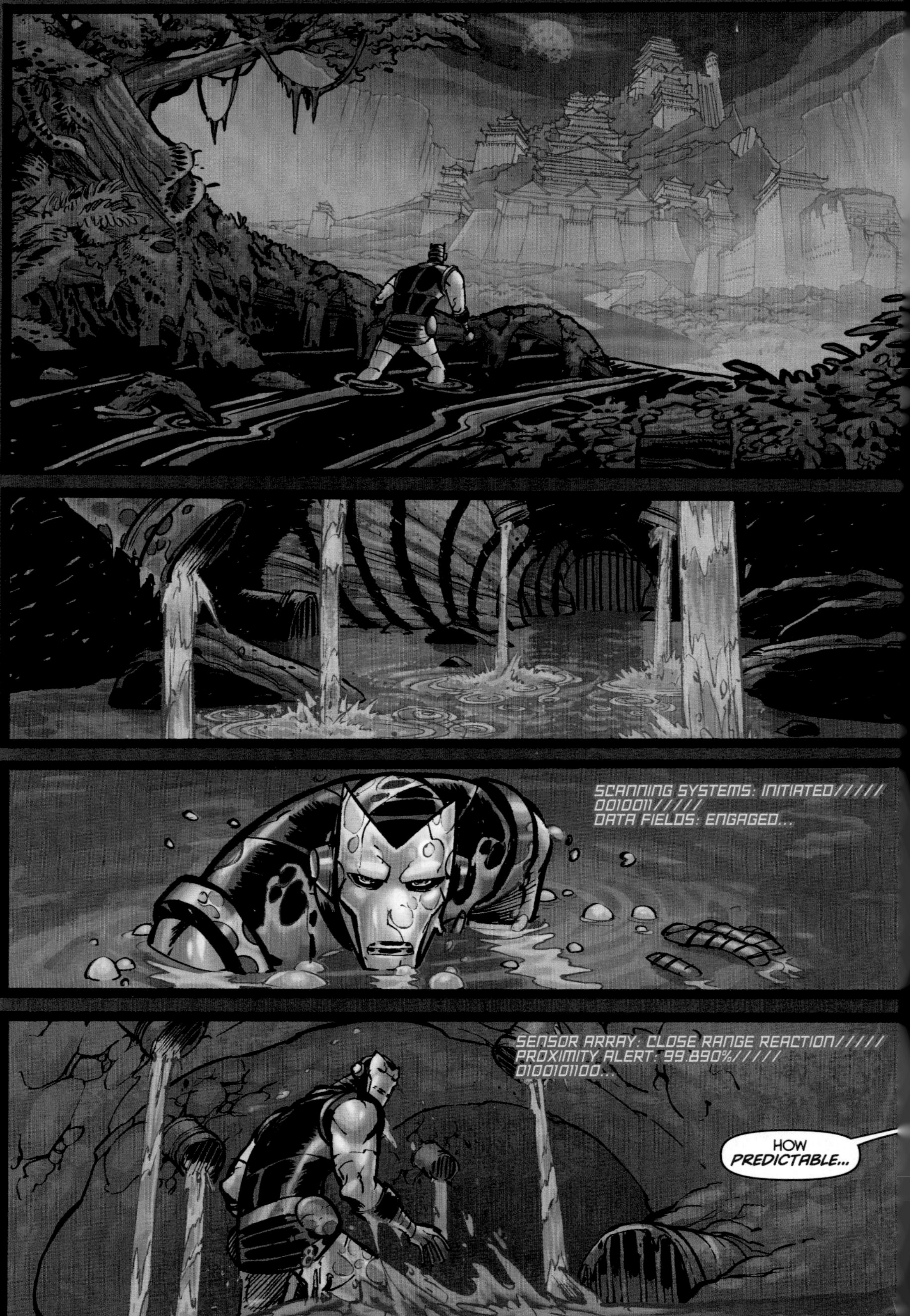
SCANNING SYSTEMS: INITIATED/////
0010011//////
DATA FIELDS: ENGAGED...
SENSOR ARRAY: CLOSE RANGE REACTION/////
PROXIMITY ALERT: 99.890%/////
0100101100...
HOW PREDICTABLE...

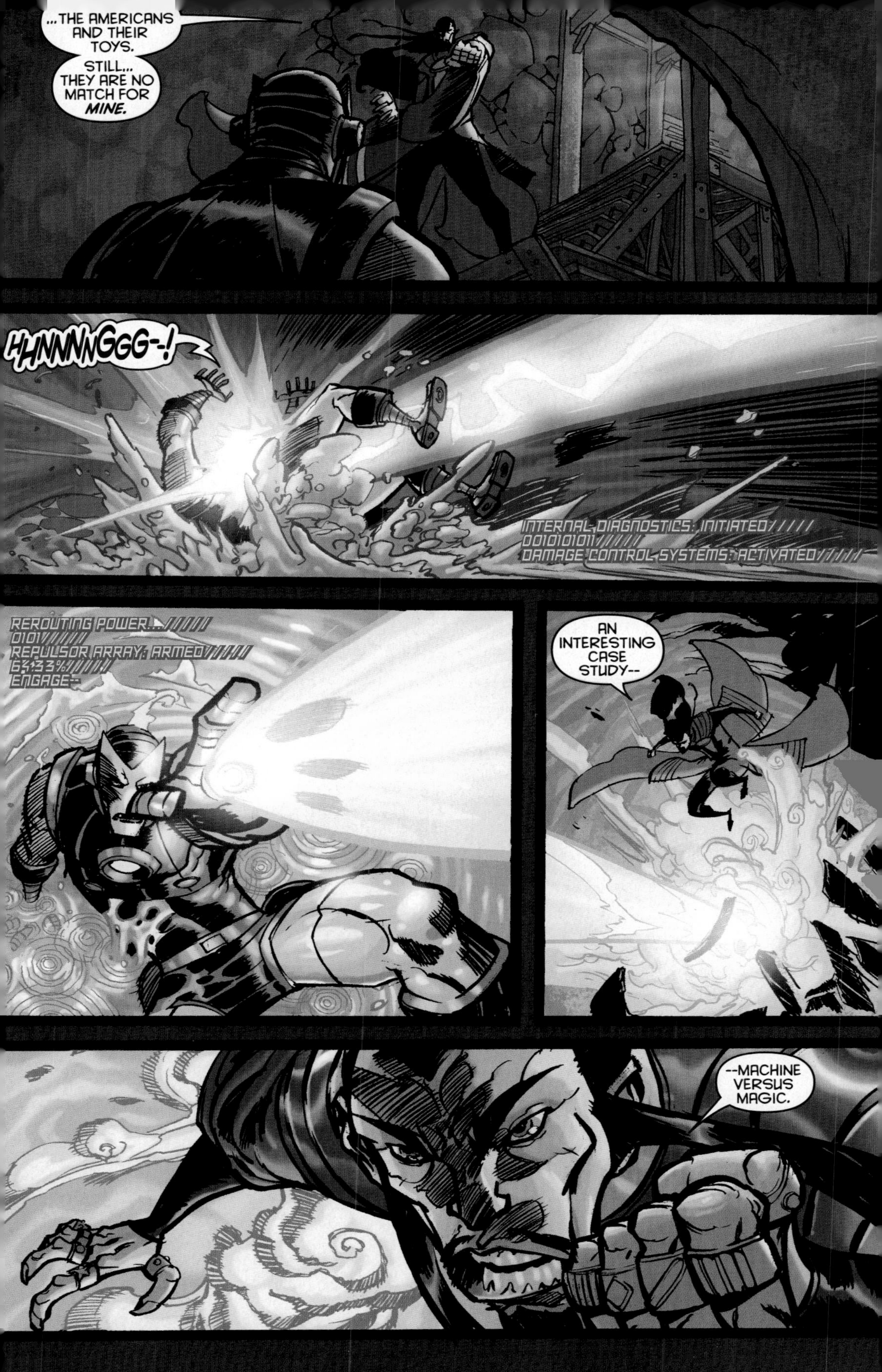
...THE AMERICANS AND THEIR TOYS.
STILL... THEY ARE NO MATCH FOR *MINE.*
HHNNNNGGG--!
INTERNAL DIAGNOSTICS: INITIATED//////
0010101011//////
DAMAGE CONTROL SYSTEMS: ACTIVATED//////
REROUTING POWER...//////
0101//////
REPULSOR ARRAY: ARMED//////
64.33%//////
ENGAGE--
AN INTERESTING CASE STUDY--
--MACHINE VERSUS MAGIC.

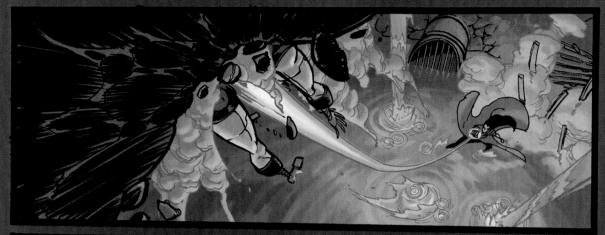

IMPACT BEAM AT SUCH CLOSE RANGE...TRULY DEVASTATING. WE SHALL *HOLD* THIS ONE FOR THE TIME BEING...

...ONE MUST BECOME *KNOWLEDGEABLE* ABOUT ONE'S ENEMIES TO FULLY *DOMINATE* THEM.

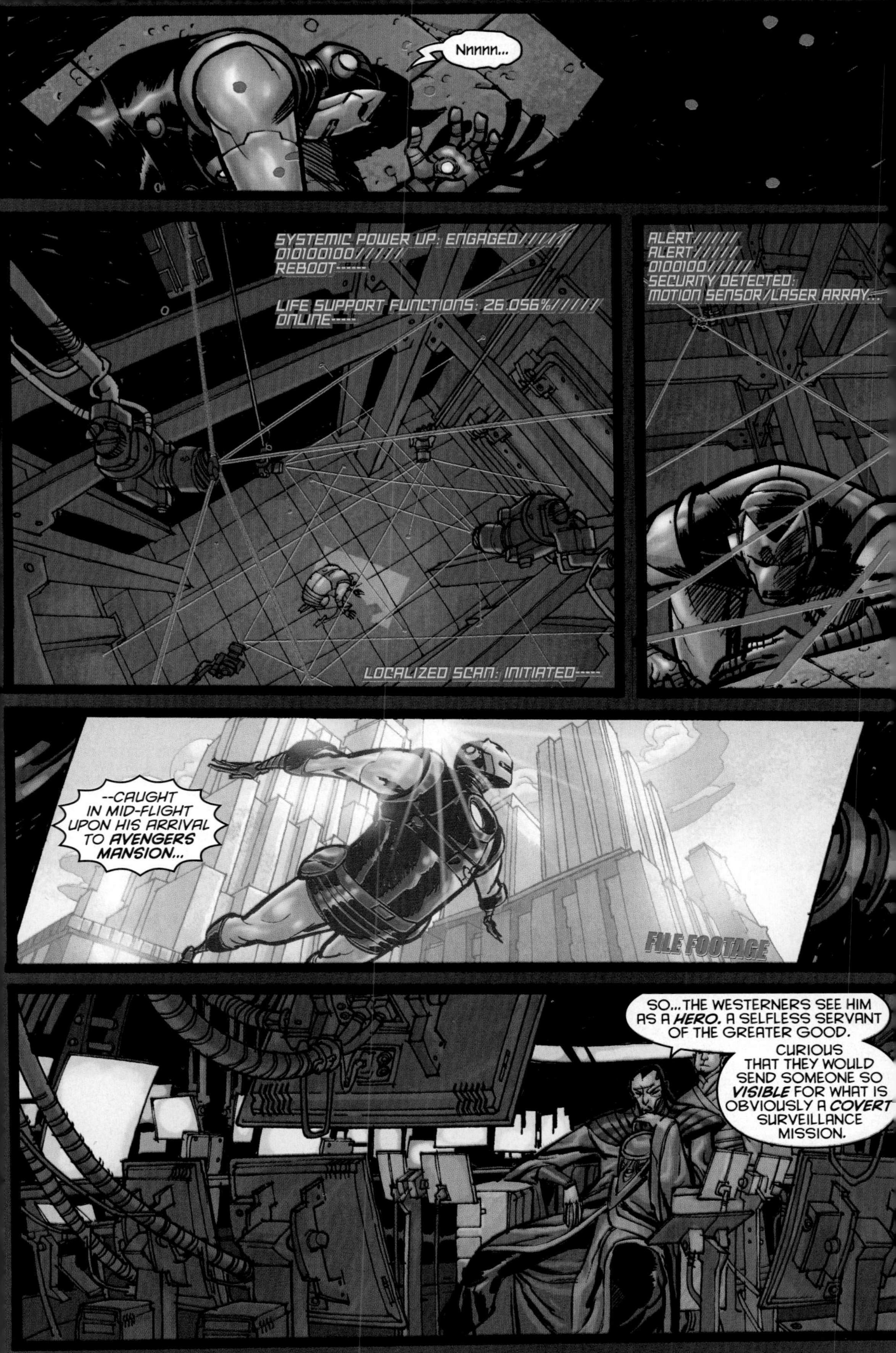

Nnnnn...
SYSTEMIC POWER UP: ENGAGED//////
010100100//////
REBOOT------
LIFE SUPPORT FUNCTIONS: 26.056%//////
ONLINE-----
LOCALIZED SCAN: INITIATED-----
ALERT//////
ALERT//////
0100100//////
SECURITY DETECTED:
MOTION SENSOR/LASER ARRAY...
--CAUGHT IN MID-FLIGHT UPON HIS ARRIVAL TO AVENGERS MANSION...
FILE FOOTAGE
SO...THE WESTERNERS SEE HIM AS A HERO. A SELFLESS SERVANT OF THE GREATER GOOD.
CURIOUS THAT THEY WOULD SEND SOMEONE SO VISIBLE FOR WHAT IS OBVIOUSLY A COVERT SURVEILLANCE MISSION.

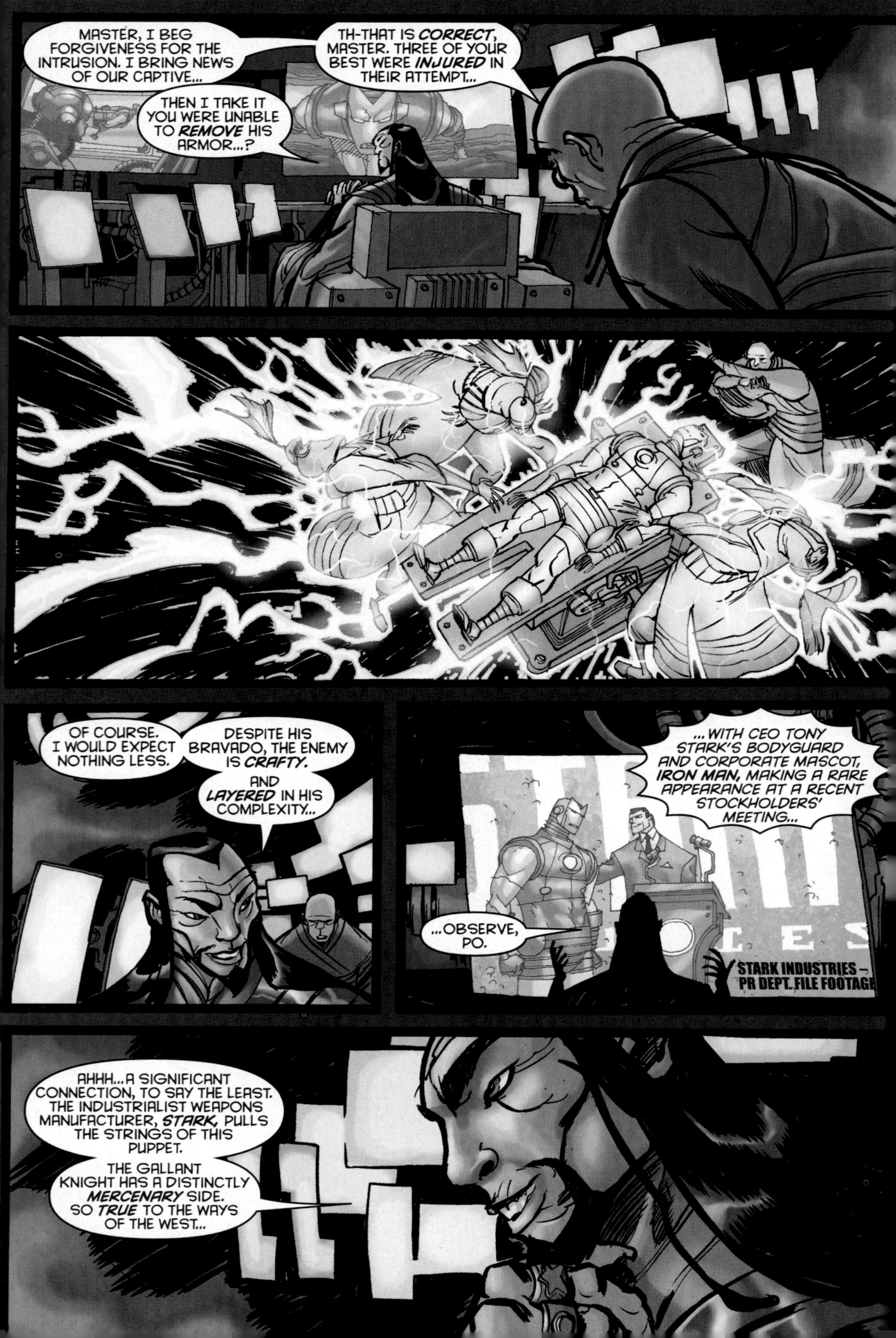
MASTER, I BEG FORGIVENESS FOR THE INTRUSION. I BRING NEWS OF OUR CAPTIVE...
THEN I TAKE IT YOU WERE UNABLE TO REMOVE HIS ARMOR...?
TH-THAT IS CORRECT, MASTER. THREE OF YOUR BEST WERE INJURED IN THEIR ATTEMPT...
OF COURSE. I WOULD EXPECT NOTHING LESS.
DESPITE HIS BRAVADO, THE ENEMY IS CRAFTY.
AND LAYERED IN HIS COMPLEXITY...
...WITH CEO TONY STARK'S BODYGUARD AND CORPORATE MASCOT, IRON MAN, MAKING A RARE APPEARANCE AT A RECENT STOCKHOLDERS' MEETING...
...OBSERVE, PO.
STARK INDUSTRIES — PR DEPT. FILE FOOTAGE
AHHH...A SIGNIFICANT CONNECTION, TO SAY THE LEAST. THE INDUSTRIALIST WEAPONS MANUFACTURER, STARK, PULLS THE STRINGS OF THIS PUPPET.
THE GALLANT KNIGHT HAS A DISTINCTLY MERCENARY SIDE. SO TRUE TO THE WAYS OF THE WEST...

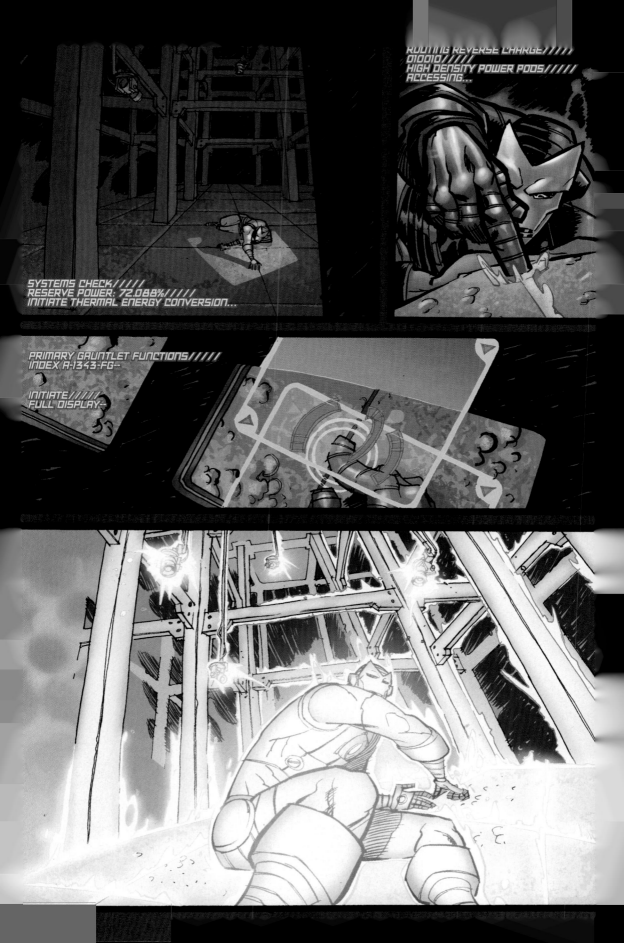

ROUTING REVERSE CHARGE//////
010010//////
HIGH DENSITY POWER PODS//////
ACCESSING...

SYSTEMS CHECK//////
RESERVE POWER: 72.088%//////
INITIATE THERMAL ENERGY CONVERSION...

PRIMARY GAUNTLET FUNCTIONS//////
INDEX A-1343-FG--

INITIATE//////
FULL DISPLAY--

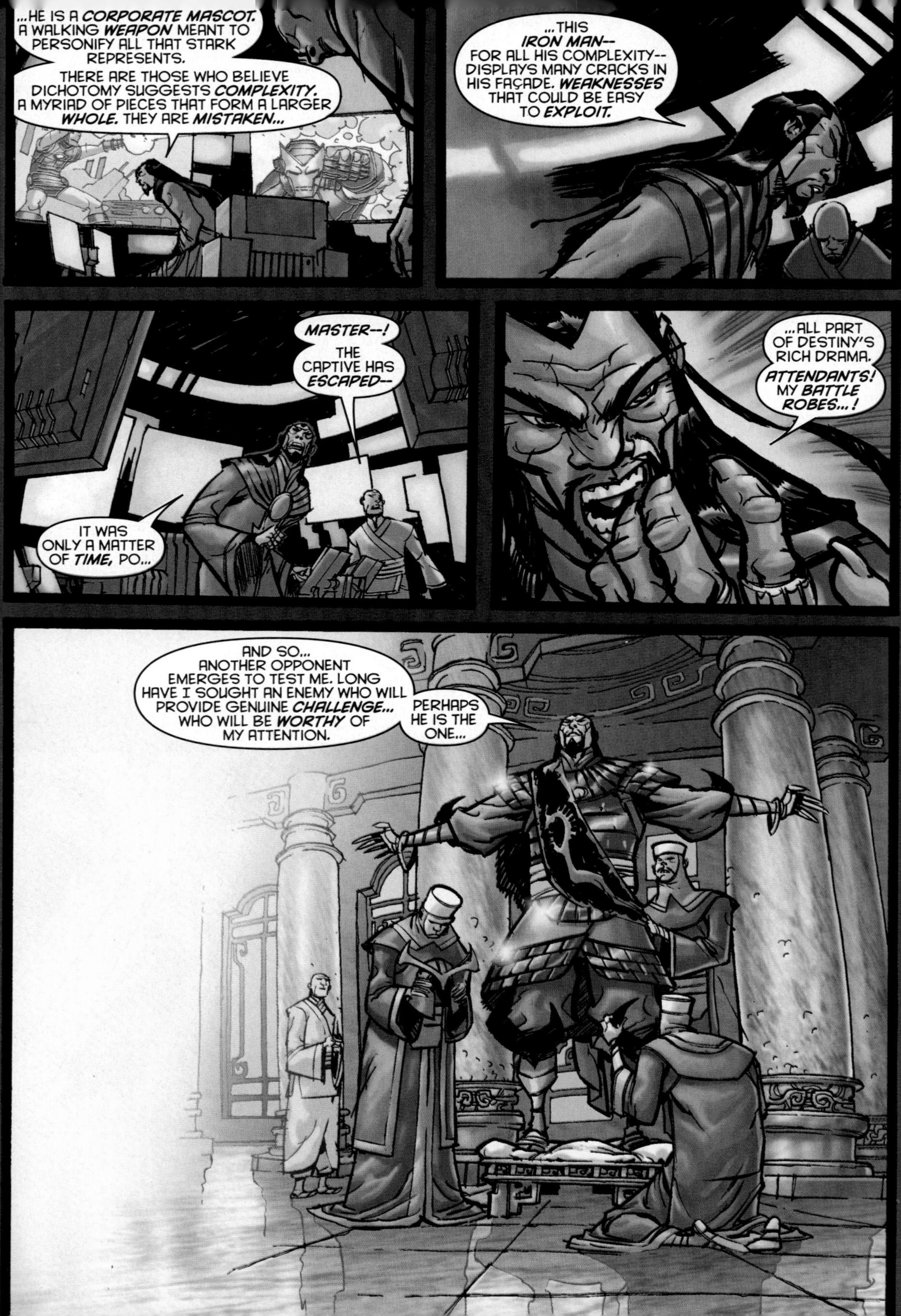
...HE IS A CORPORATE MASCOT. A WALKING WEAPON MEANT TO PERSONIFY ALL THAT STARK REPRESENTS.
THERE ARE THOSE WHO BELIEVE DICHOTOMY SUGGESTS COMPLEXITY. A MYRIAD OF PIECES THAT FORM A LARGER WHOLE. THEY ARE MISTAKEN...
...THIS IRON MAN-- FOR ALL HIS COMPLEXITY-- DISPLAYS MANY CRACKS IN HIS FAÇADE. WEAKNESSES THAT COULD BE EASY TO EXPLOIT.
MASTER--!
THE CAPTIVE HAS ESCAPED--
IT WAS ONLY A MATTER OF TIME, PO...
...ALL PART OF DESTINY'S RICH DRAMA.
ATTENDANTS! MY BATTLE ROBES...!
AND SO... ANOTHER OPPONENT EMERGES TO TEST ME. LONG HAVE I SOUGHT AN ENEMY WHO WILL PROVIDE GENUINE CHALLENGE... WHO WILL BE WORTHY OF MY ATTENTION.
PERHAPS HE IS THE ONE...

CRYOGENIC SUPPLY: 82.665%//////
INITIATE LLOCLAIZED TRACKING SYSTEMS//////
01001001--

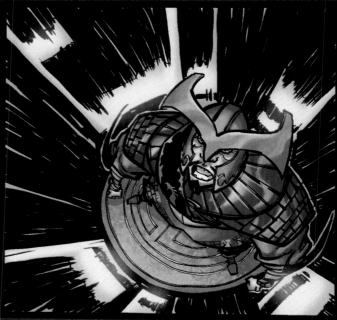

SEARCH FOR: TRACE MAGNO-GRAVITIC PARTICLES//////
WIDE SPECTRUM SWEEP--

ENERGY SIGNATURE CONFIRMED//////
PROXIMITY ALERT//////
PREP DEFENSE SYSTEMS--

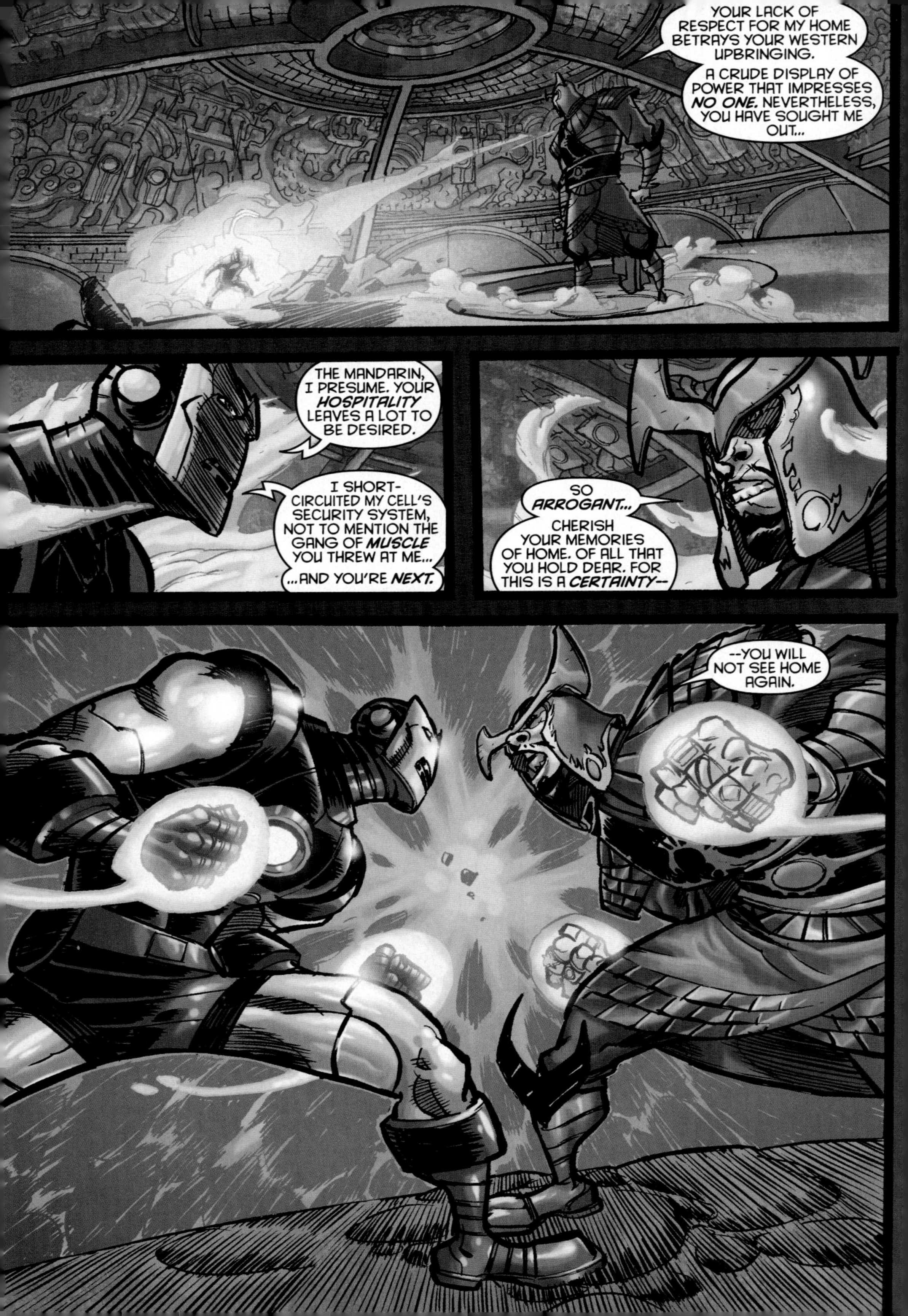
YOUR LACK OF RESPECT FOR MY HOME BETRAYS YOUR WESTERN UPBRINGING.
A CRUDE DISPLAY OF POWER THAT IMPRESSES **NO ONE.** NEVERTHELESS, YOU HAVE SOUGHT ME OUT...
THE MANDARIN, I PRESUME. YOUR ***HOSPITALITY*** LEAVES A LOT TO BE DESIRED.
I SHORT-CIRCUITED MY CELL'S SECURITY SYSTEM, NOT TO MENTION THE GANG OF ***MUSCLE*** YOU THREW AT ME...
...AND YOU'RE ***NEXT.***
SO ***ARROGANT...***
CHERISH YOUR MEMORIES OF HOME. OF ALL THAT YOU HOLD DEAR. FOR THIS IS A ***CERTAINTY***--
--YOU WILL NOT SEE HOME AGAIN.

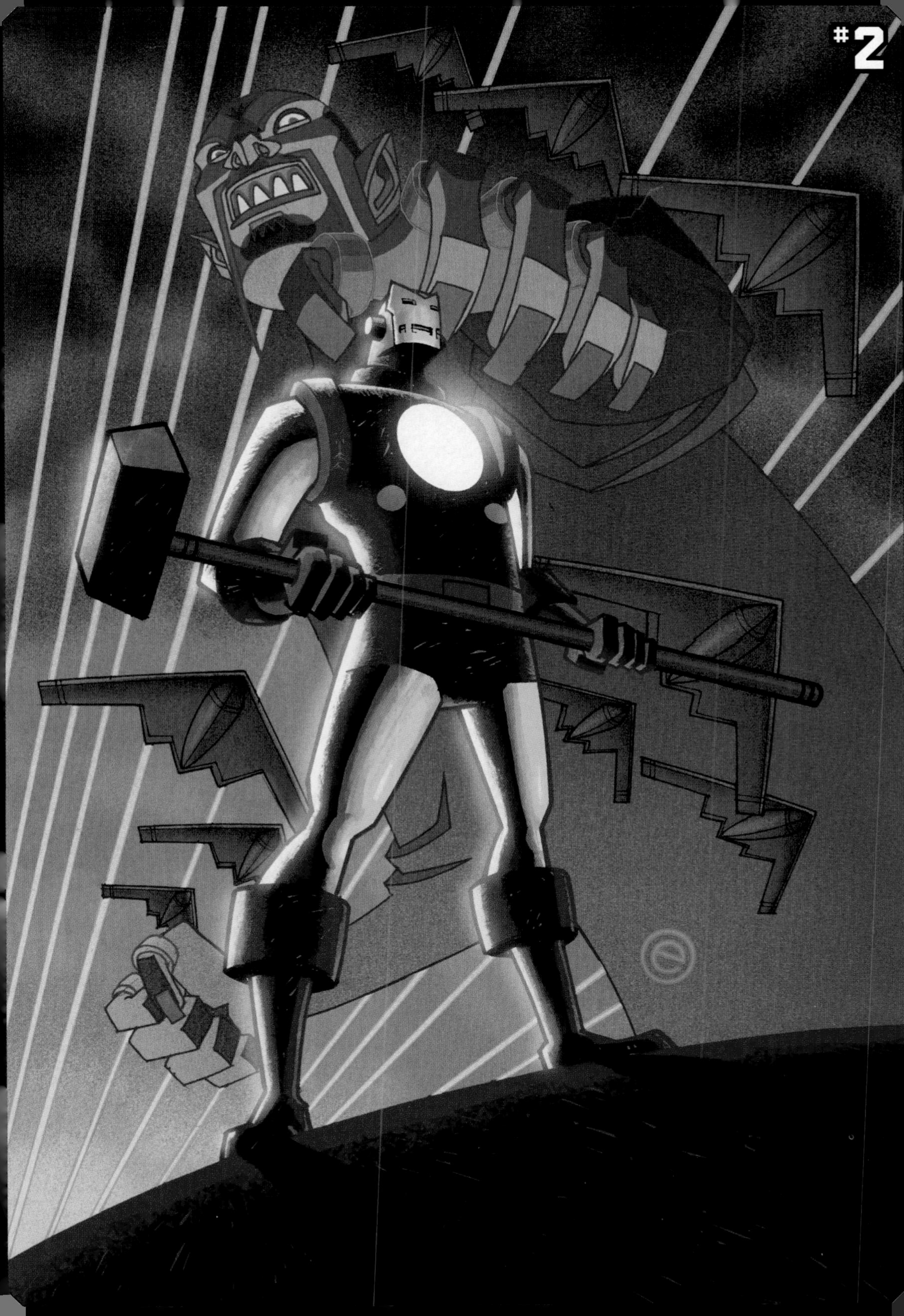
#2

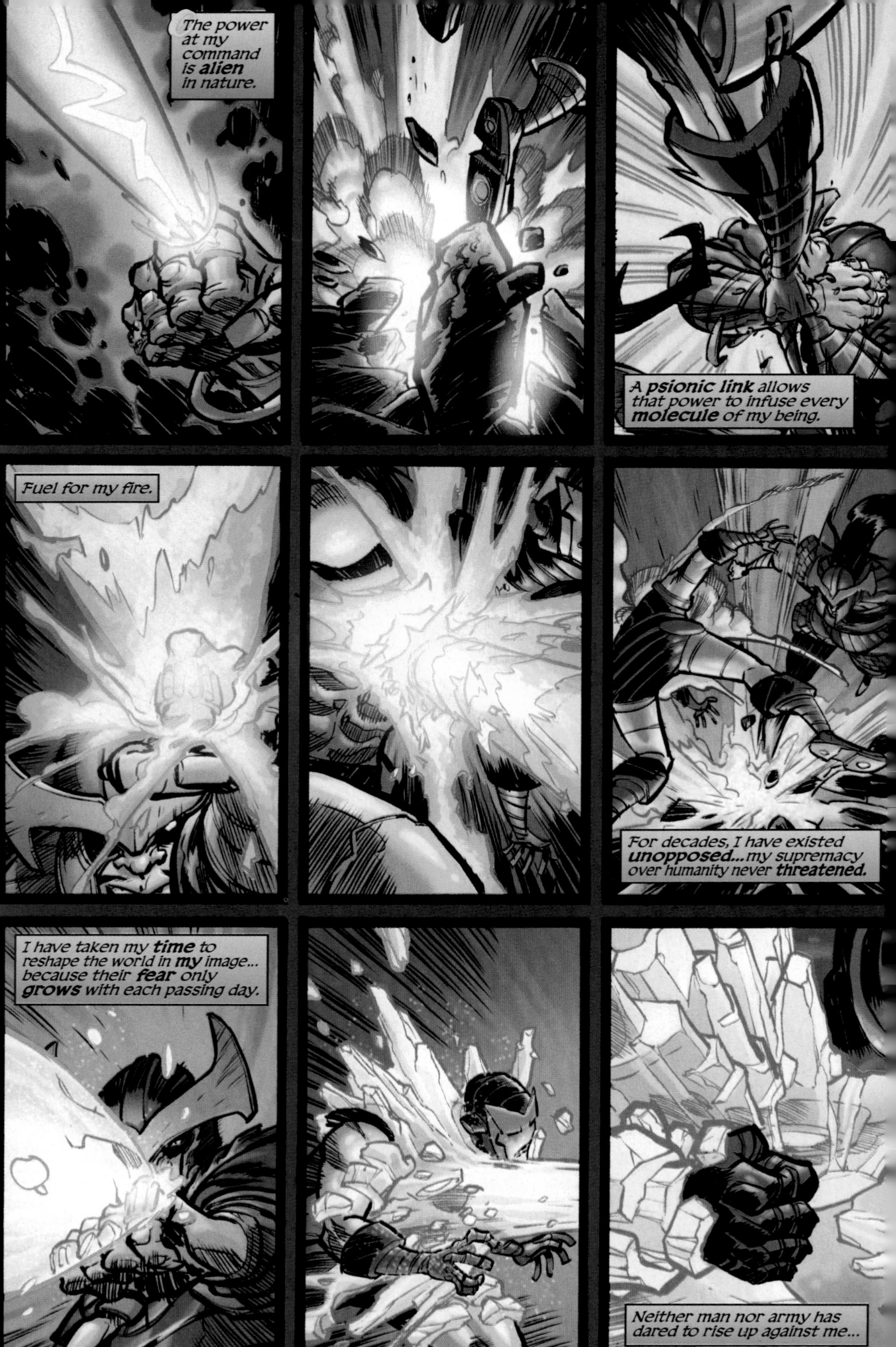
The power at my command is **alien** in nature.
A **psionic link** allows that power to infuse every **molecule** of my being.
Fuel for my fire.
For decades, I have existed **unopposed...** my supremacy over humanity never **threatened.**
I have taken my **time** to reshape the world in **my** image... because their **fear** only **grows** with each passing day.
Neither man nor army has dared to rise up against me...

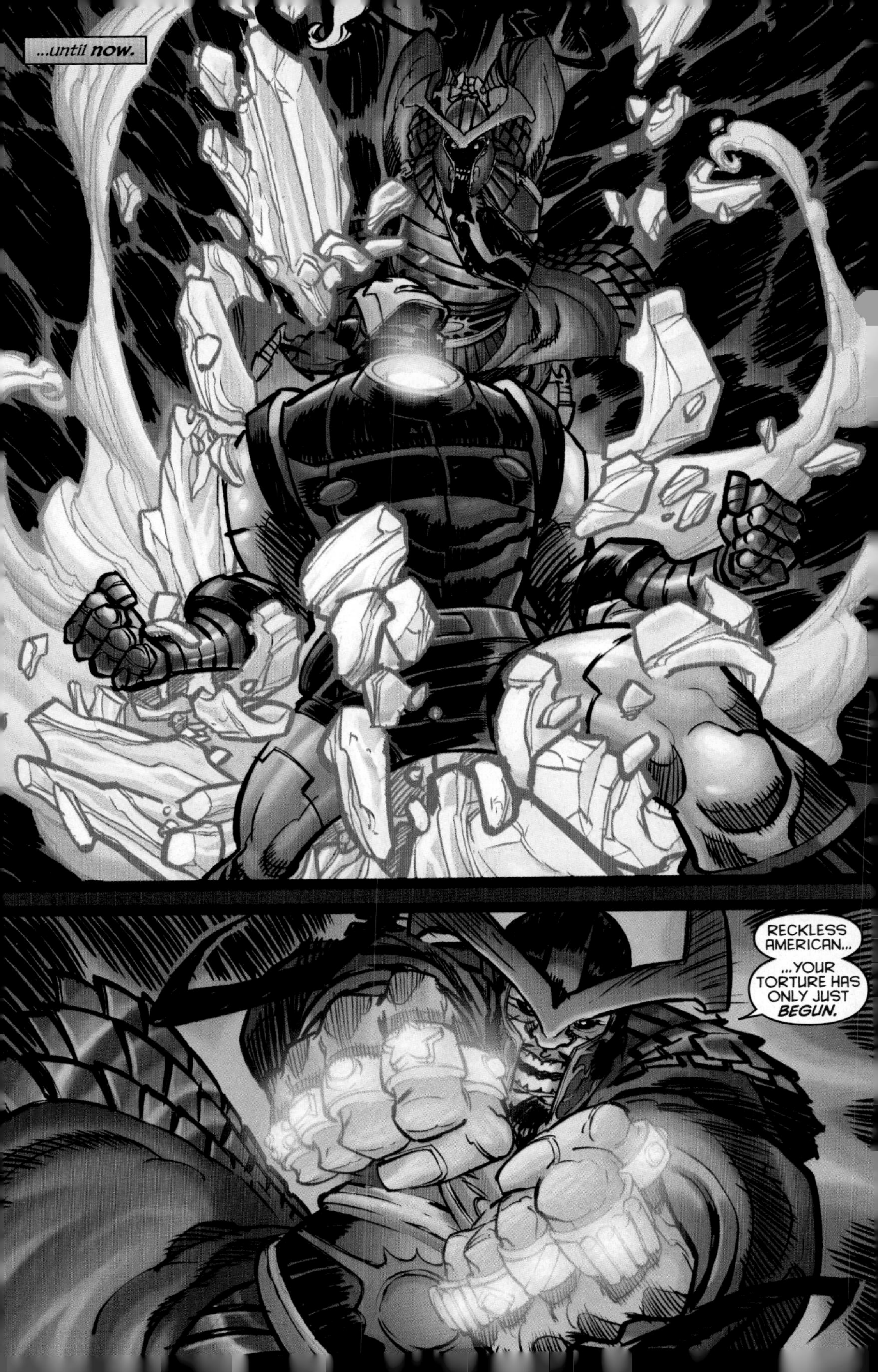
...until now.
RECKLESS AMERICAN...
...YOUR TORTURE HAS ONLY JUST BEGUN.

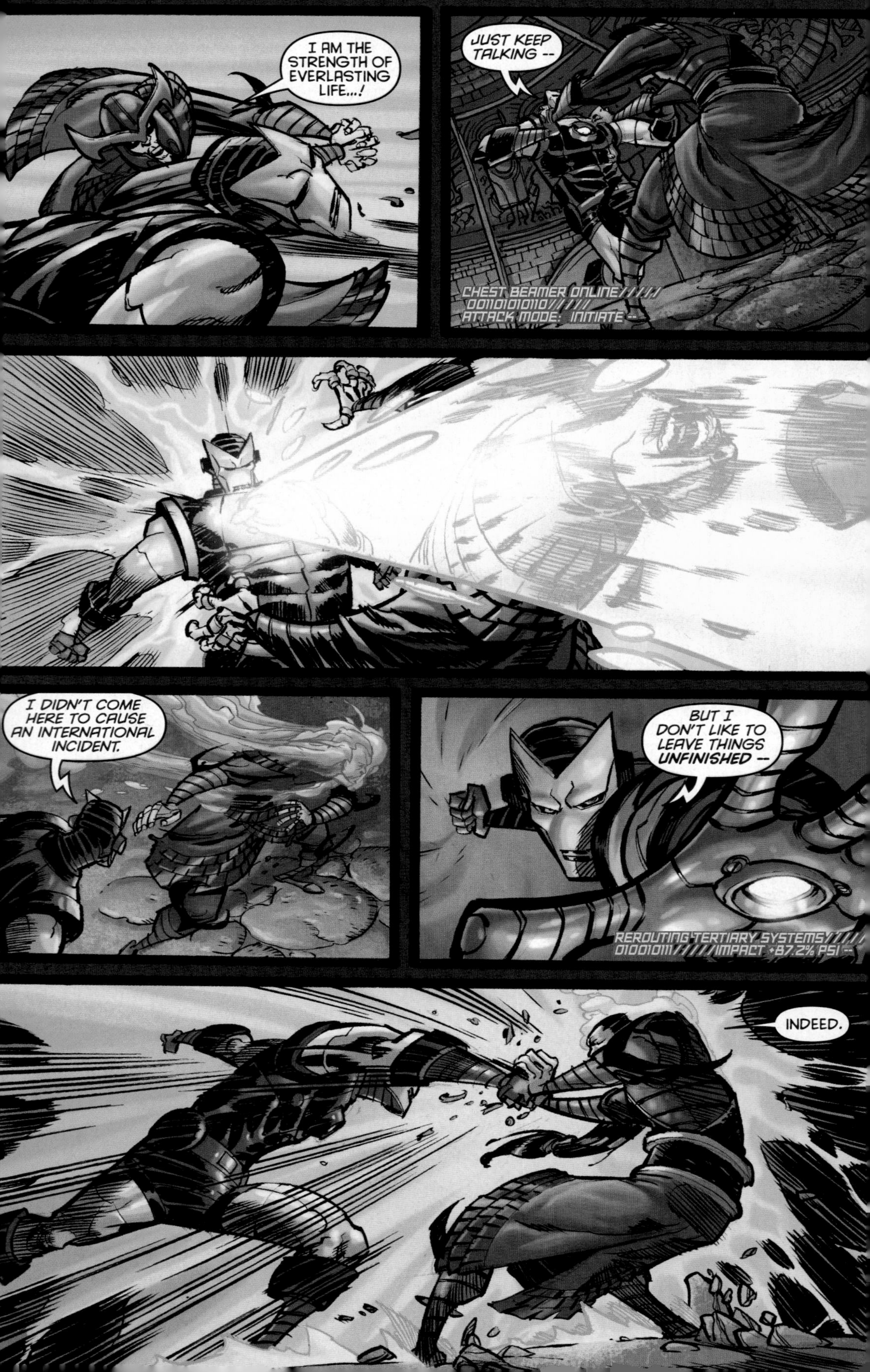
I AM THE STRENGTH OF EVERLASTING LIFE...!
JUST KEEP TALKING --
CHEST BEAMER ONLINE//////
001101010110//////
ATTACK MODE: INITIATE --
I DIDN'T COME HERE TO CAUSE AN INTERNATIONAL INCIDENT.
BUT I DON'T LIKE TO LEAVE THINGS UNFINISHED --
REROUTING TERTIARY SYSTEMS//////
010010111//////IMPACT +87.2% PSI --
INDEED.

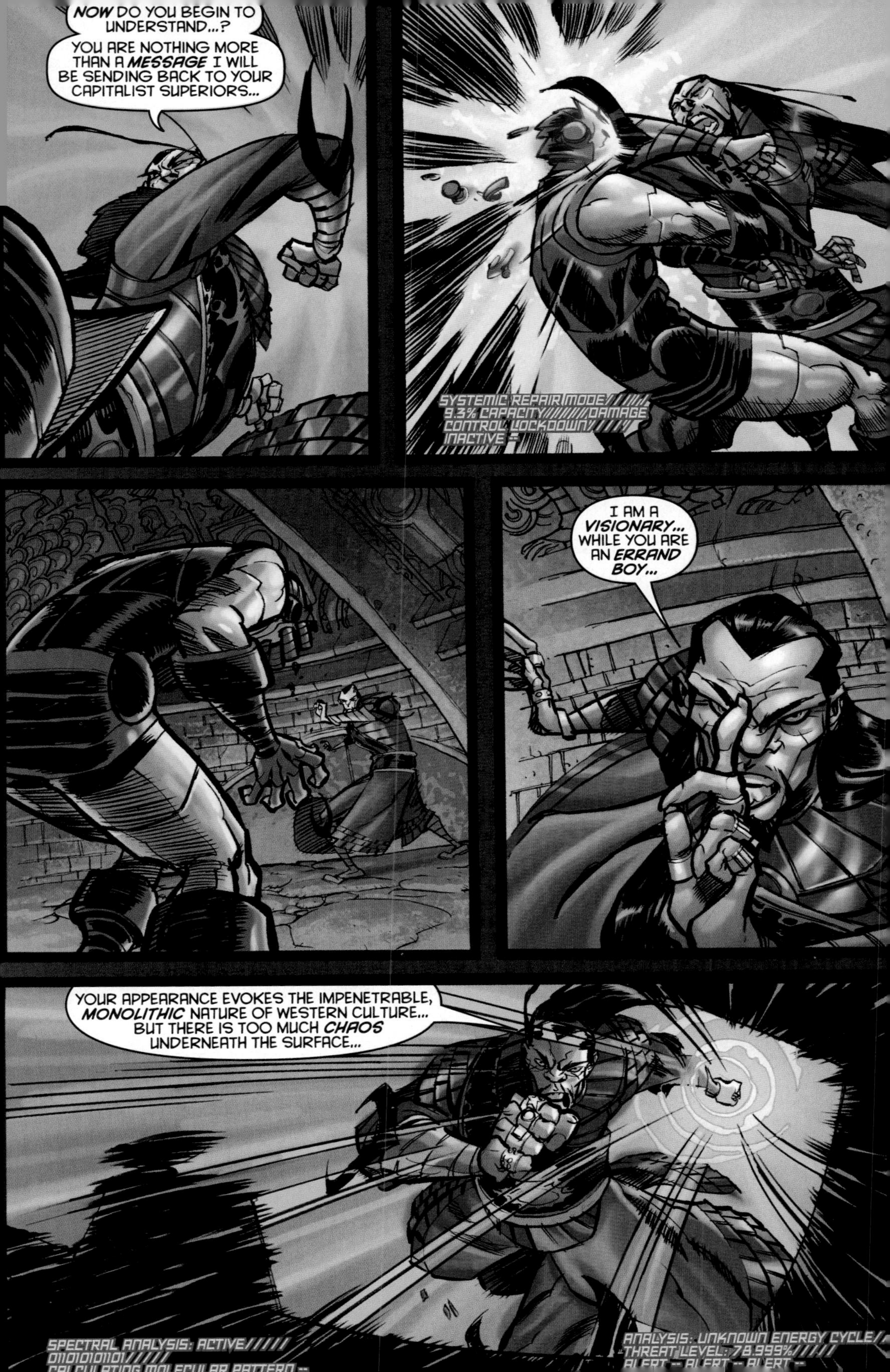
NOW DO YOU BEGIN TO UNDERSTAND...?
YOU ARE NOTHING MORE THAN A MESSAGE I WILL BE SENDING BACK TO YOUR CAPITALIST SUPERIORS...
SYSTEMIC REPAIR MODE/////// 9.3% CAPACITY//////////DAMAGE CONTROL LOCKDOWN////// INACTIVE --
I AM A VISIONARY... WHILE YOU ARE AN ERRAND BOY...
YOUR APPEARANCE EVOKES THE IMPENETRABLE, MONOLITHIC NATURE OF WESTERN CULTURE... BUT THERE IS TOO MUCH CHAOS UNDERNEATH THE SURFACE...
SPECTRAL ANALYSIS: ACTIVE////// 01101010101101////// CALCULATING MOLECULAR PATTERN --
ANALYSIS: UNKNOWN ENERGY CYCLE// THREAT LEVEL: 78.999%////// ALERT -- ALERT -- ALERT --

WHAT DID THEY *TELL* YOU ABOUT ME... THAT I HAVE *UPSET* THE BALANCE? THAT I DO NOT FIT INTO THEIR PLANS OF *GLOBALIZATION?*

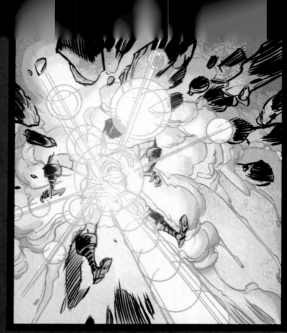

THEY *UNDERESTIMATE* ME.

0110101011//////PROPULSION SYSTEMS: ACTIVATE FULL—

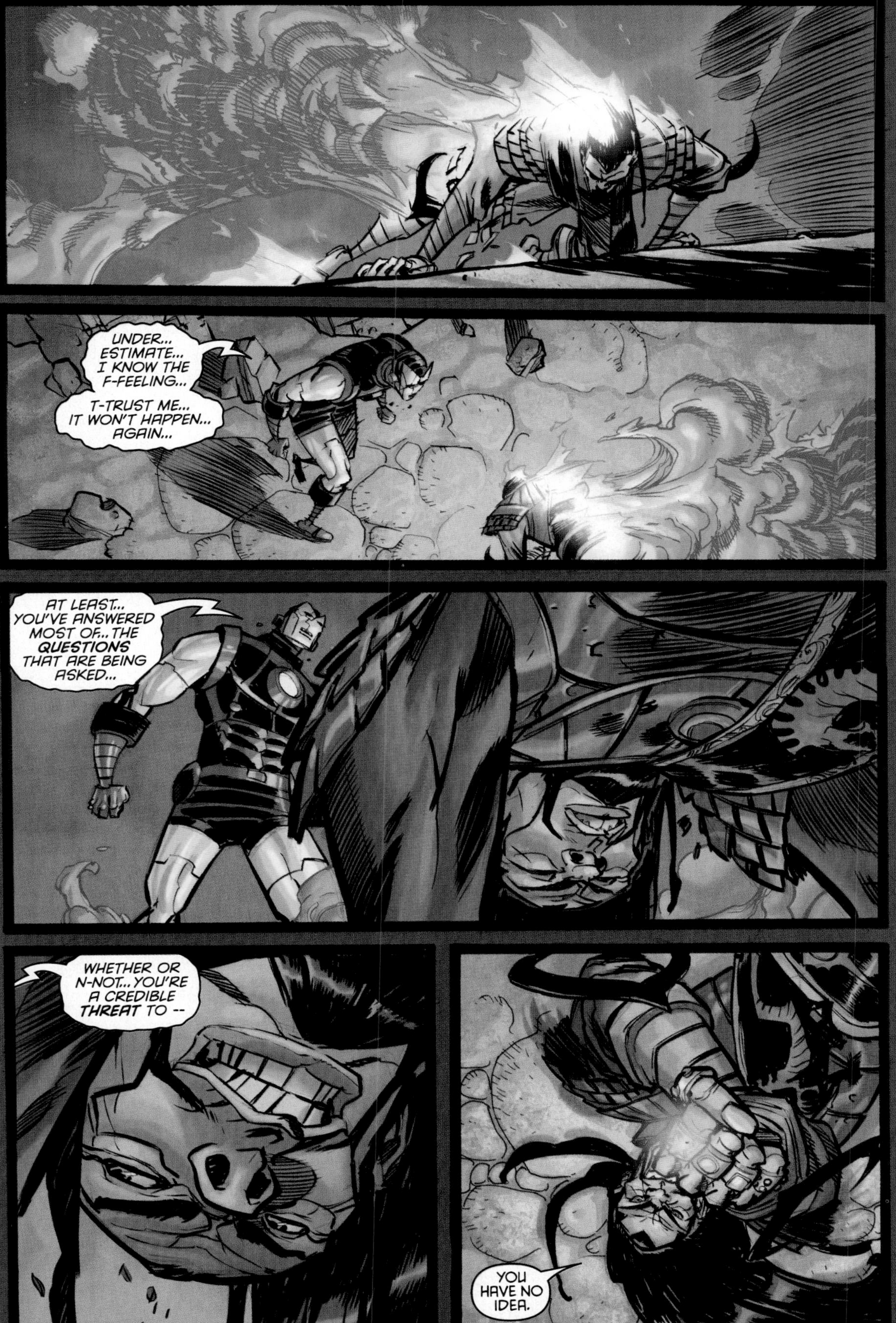
UNDER... ESTIMATE... I KNOW THE F-FEELING...
T-TRUST ME... IT WON'T HAPPEN... AGAIN...
AT LEAST... YOU'VE ANSWERED MOST OF... THE QUESTIONS THAT ARE BEING ASKED...
WHETHER OR N-NOT... YOU'RE A CREDIBLE THREAT TO --
YOU HAVE NO IDEA.

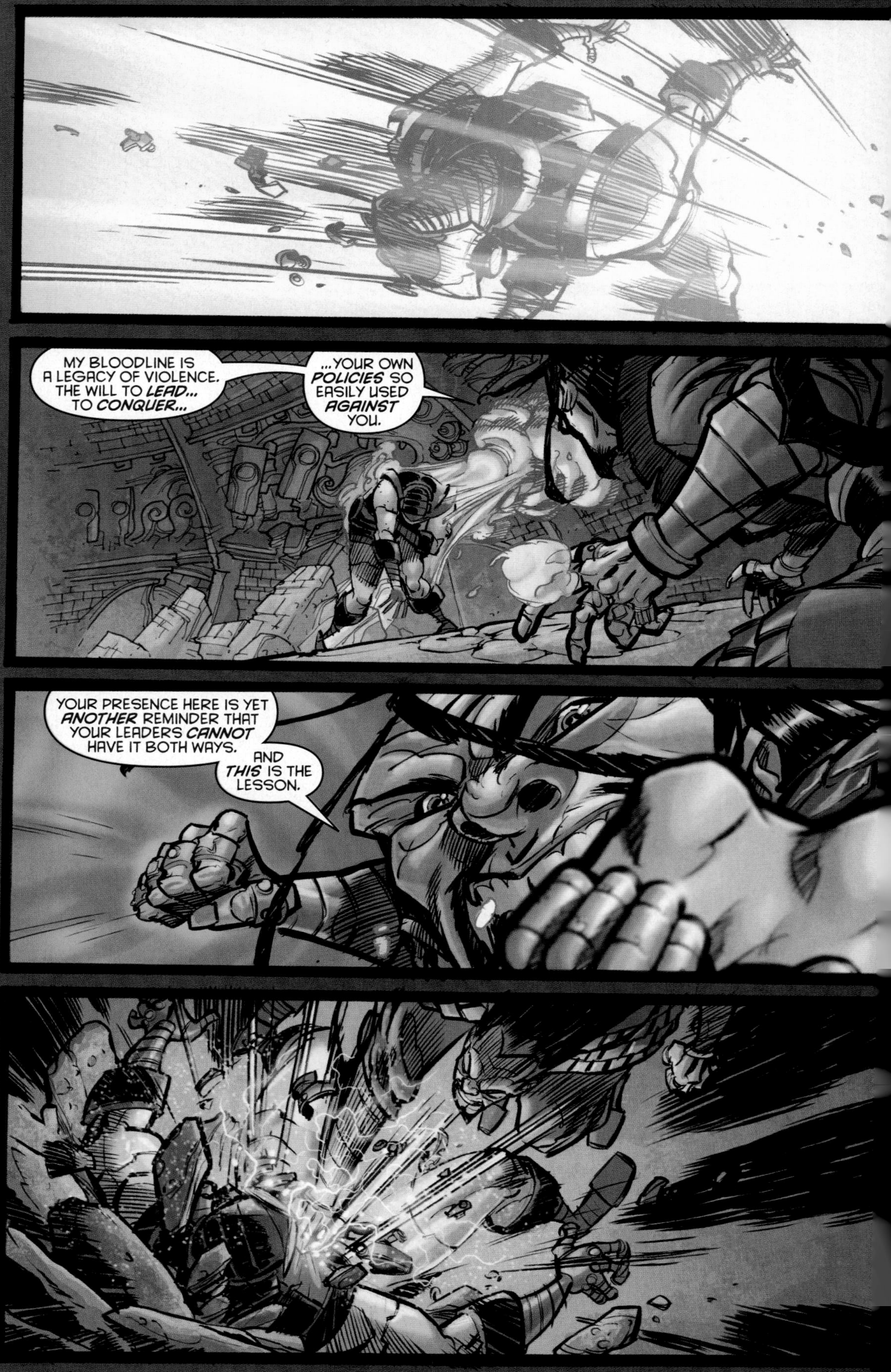
MY BLOODLINE IS A LEGACY OF VIOLENCE. THE WILL TO LEAD... TO CONQUER...
...YOUR OWN POLICIES SO EASILY USED AGAINST YOU.
YOUR PRESENCE HERE IS YET ANOTHER REMINDER THAT YOUR LEADERS CANNOT HAVE IT BOTH WAYS.
AND THIS IS THE LESSON.

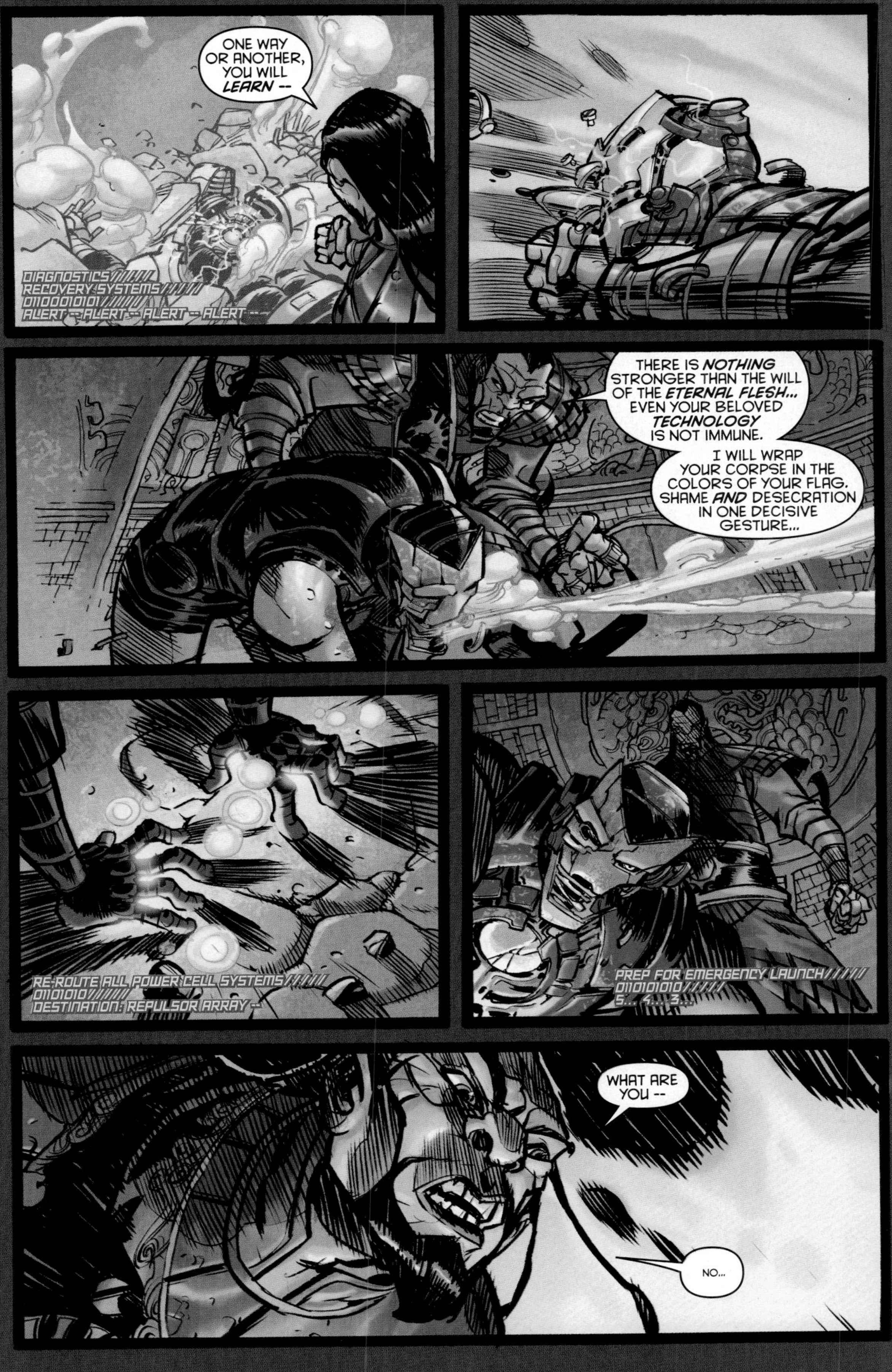

ONE WAY OR ANOTHER, YOU WILL LEARN --
DIAGNOSTICS//////
RECOVERY SYSTEMS//////
01100010101///////
ALERT -- ALERT -- ALERT -- ALERT --
THERE IS NOTHING STRONGER THAN THE WILL OF THE ETERNAL FLESH... EVEN YOUR BELOVED TECHNOLOGY IS NOT IMMUNE.
I WILL WRAP YOUR CORPSE IN THE COLORS OF YOUR FLAG. SHAME AND DESECRATION IN ONE DECISIVE GESTURE...
RE-ROUTE ALL POWER CELL SYSTEMS///////
01101010///////
DESTINATION: REPULSOR ARRAY --
PREP FOR EMERGENCY LAUNCH///////
0110101010//////
5... 4... 3...
WHAT ARE YOU --
NO...

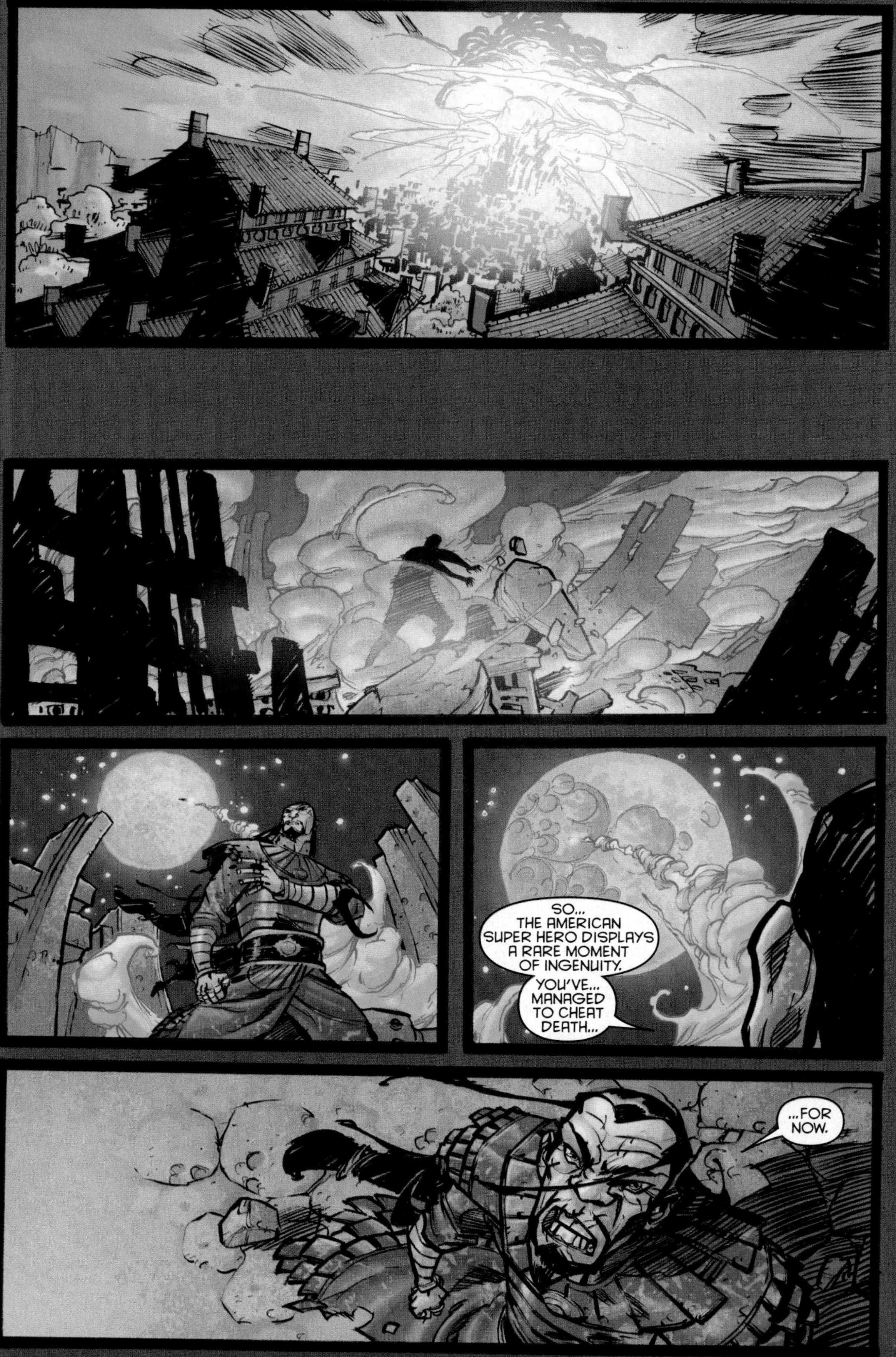
SO... THE AMERICAN SUPER HERO DISPLAYS A RARE MOMENT OF INGENUITY.
YOU'VE... MANAGED TO CHEAT DEATH...
...FOR NOW.

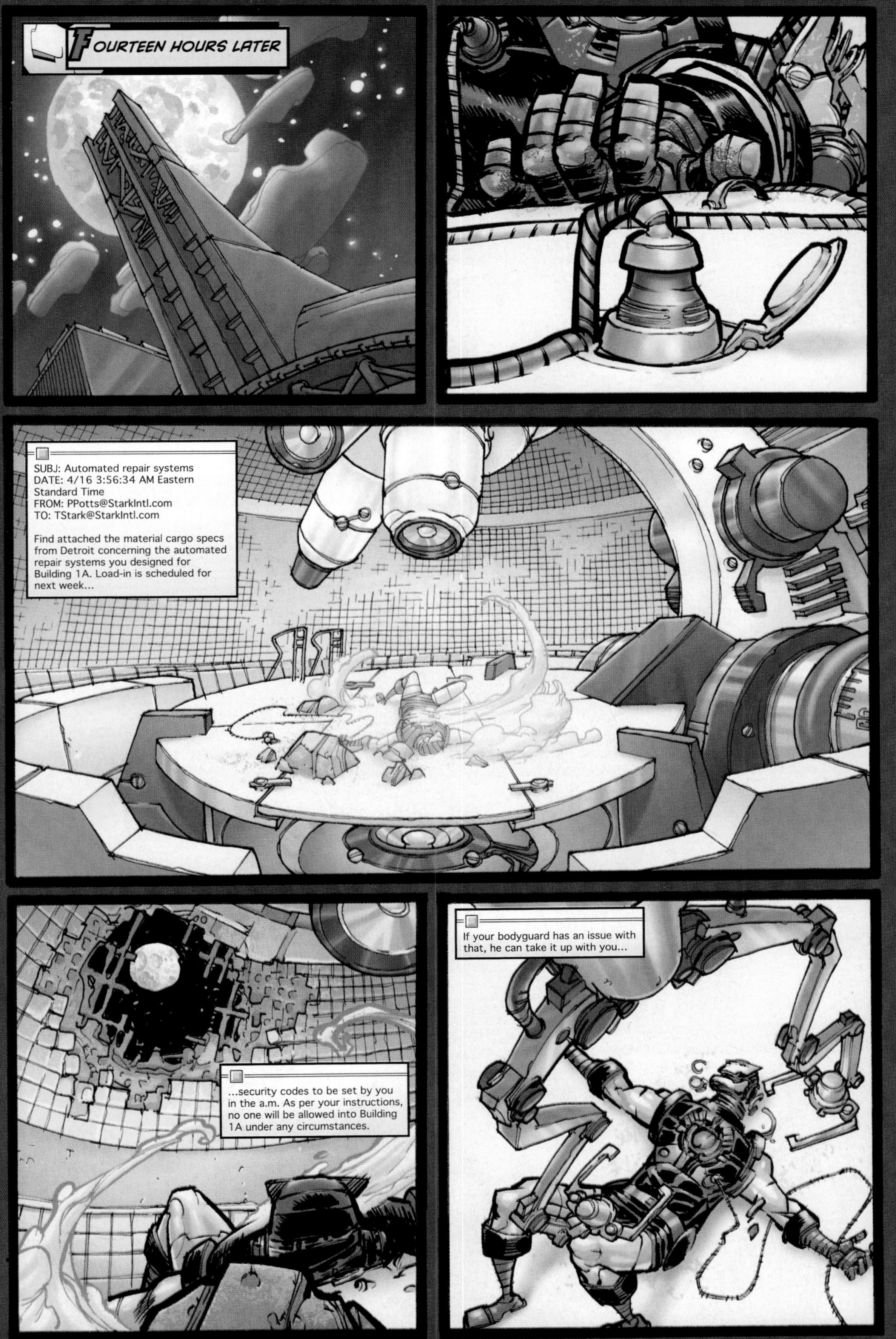
FOURTEEN HOURS LATER
SUBJ: Automated repair systems
DATE: 4/16 3:56:34 AM Eastern Standard Time
FROM: PPotts@StarkIntl.com
TO: TStark@StarkIntl.com
Find attached the material cargo specs from Detroit concerning the automated repair systems you designed for Building 1A. Load-in is scheduled for next week...
...security codes to be set by you in the a.m. As per your instructions, no one will be allowed into Building 1A under any circumstances.
If your bodyguard has an issue with that, he can take it up with you...

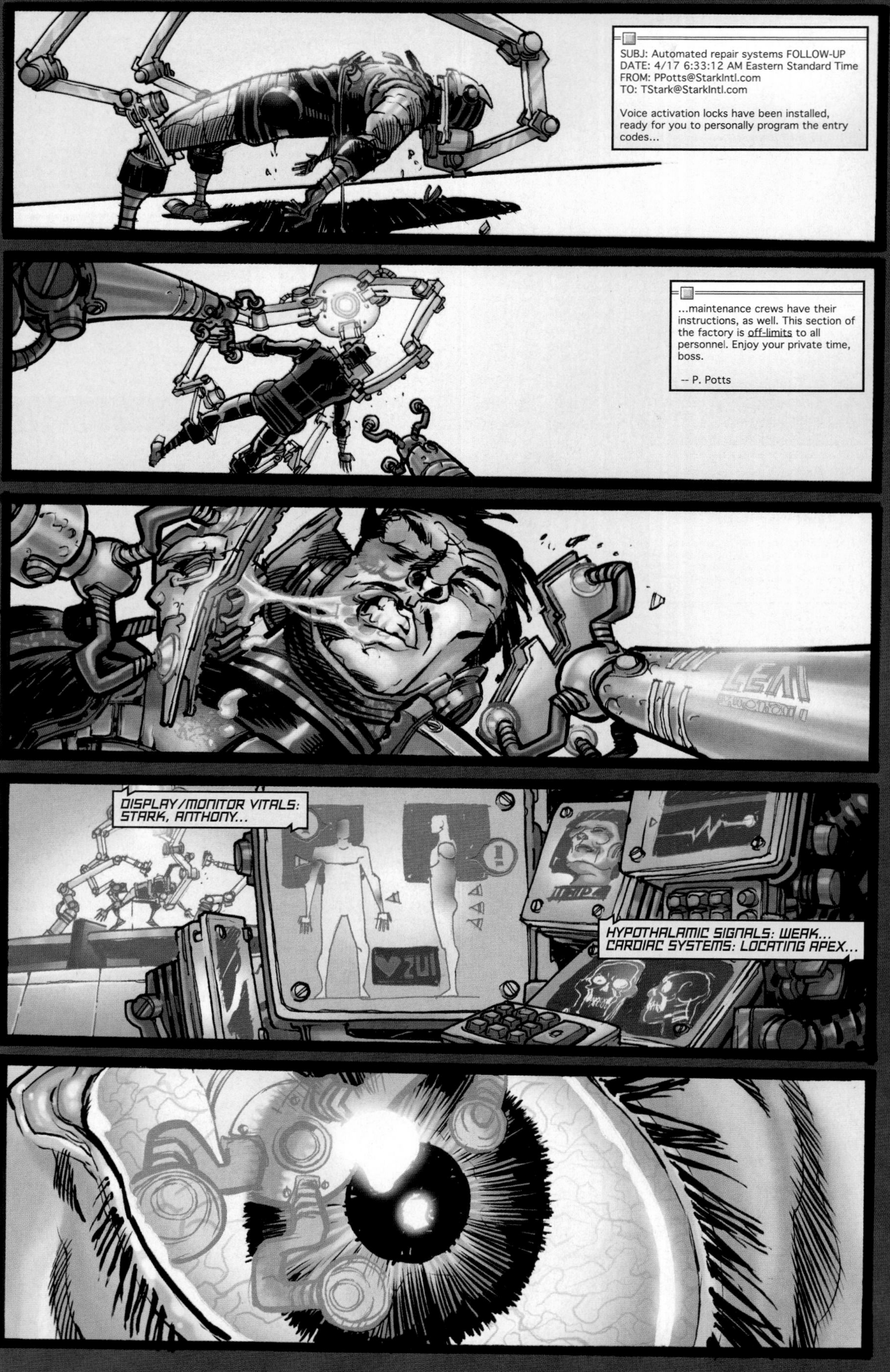
SUBJ: Automated repair systems FOLLOW-UP
DATE: 4/17 6:33:12 AM Eastern Standard Time
FROM: PPotts@StarkIntl.com
TO: TStark@StarkIntl.com
Voice activation locks have been installed, ready for you to personally program the entry codes...
...maintenance crews have their instructions, as well. This section of the factory is off-limits to all personnel. Enjoy your private time, boss.
-- P. Potts
DISPLAY/MONITOR VITALS: STARK, ANTHONY...
HYPOTHALAMIC SIGNALS: WEAK... CARDIAC SYSTEMS: LOCATING APEX...

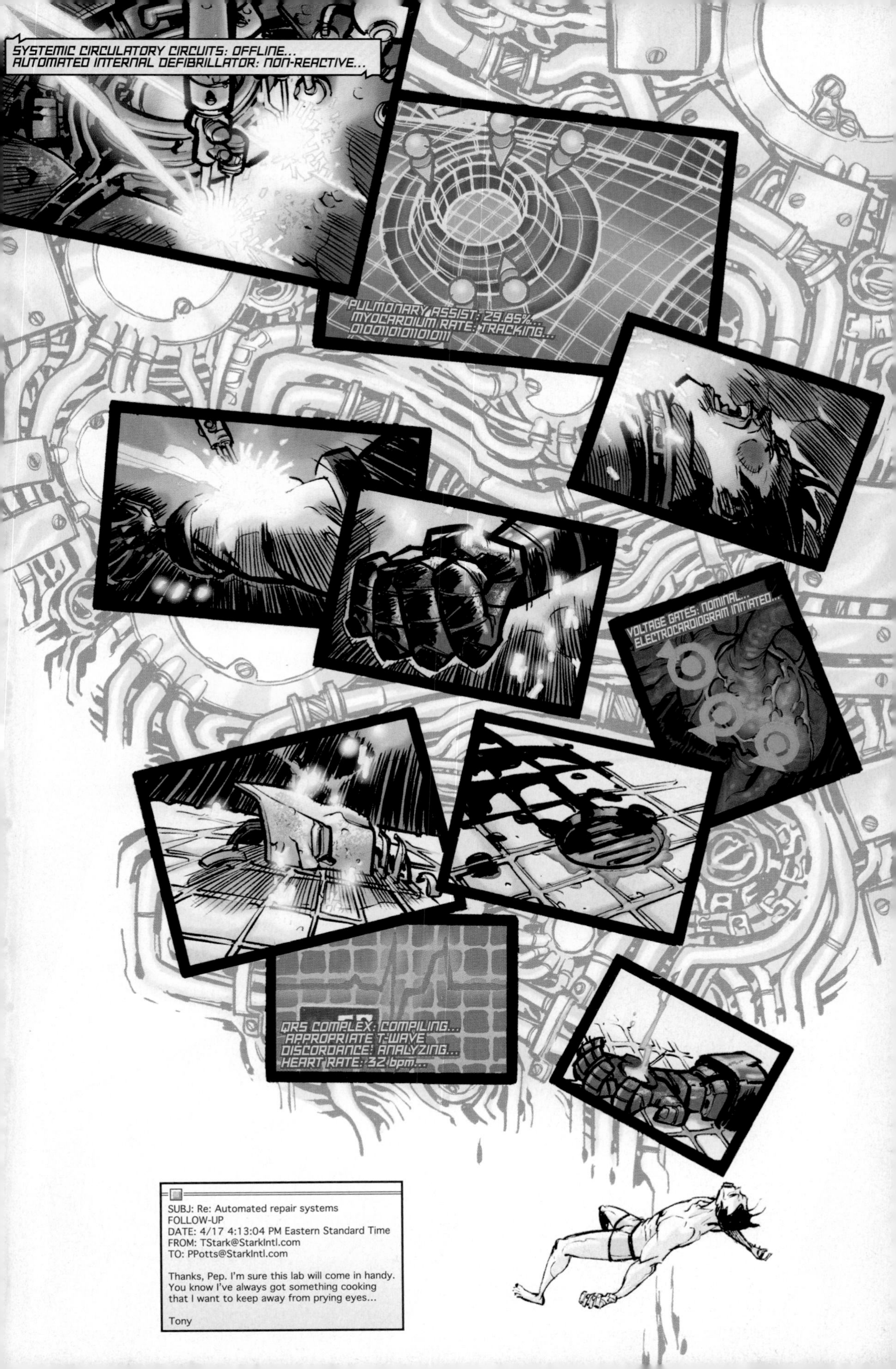
SYSTEMIC CIRCULATORY CIRCUITS: OFFLINE...
AUTOMATED INTERNAL DEFIBRILLATOR: NON-REACTIVE...
PULMONARY ASSIST: 29.85%...
MYOCARDIUM RATE: TRACKING...
0100110101101010111
VOLTAGE GATES: NOMINAL...
ELECTROCARDIOGRAM INITIATED...
QRS COMPLEX: COMPILING...
APPROPRIATE T-WAVE
DISCORDANCE: ANALYZING...
HEART RATE: 32 bpm...
SUBJ: Re: Automated repair systems
FOLLOW-UP
DATE: 4/17 4:13:04 PM Eastern Standard Time
FROM: TStark@StarkIntl.com
TO: PPotts@StarkIntl.com
Thanks, Pep. I'm sure this lab will come in handy. You know I've always got something cooking that I want to keep away from prying eyes...
Tony

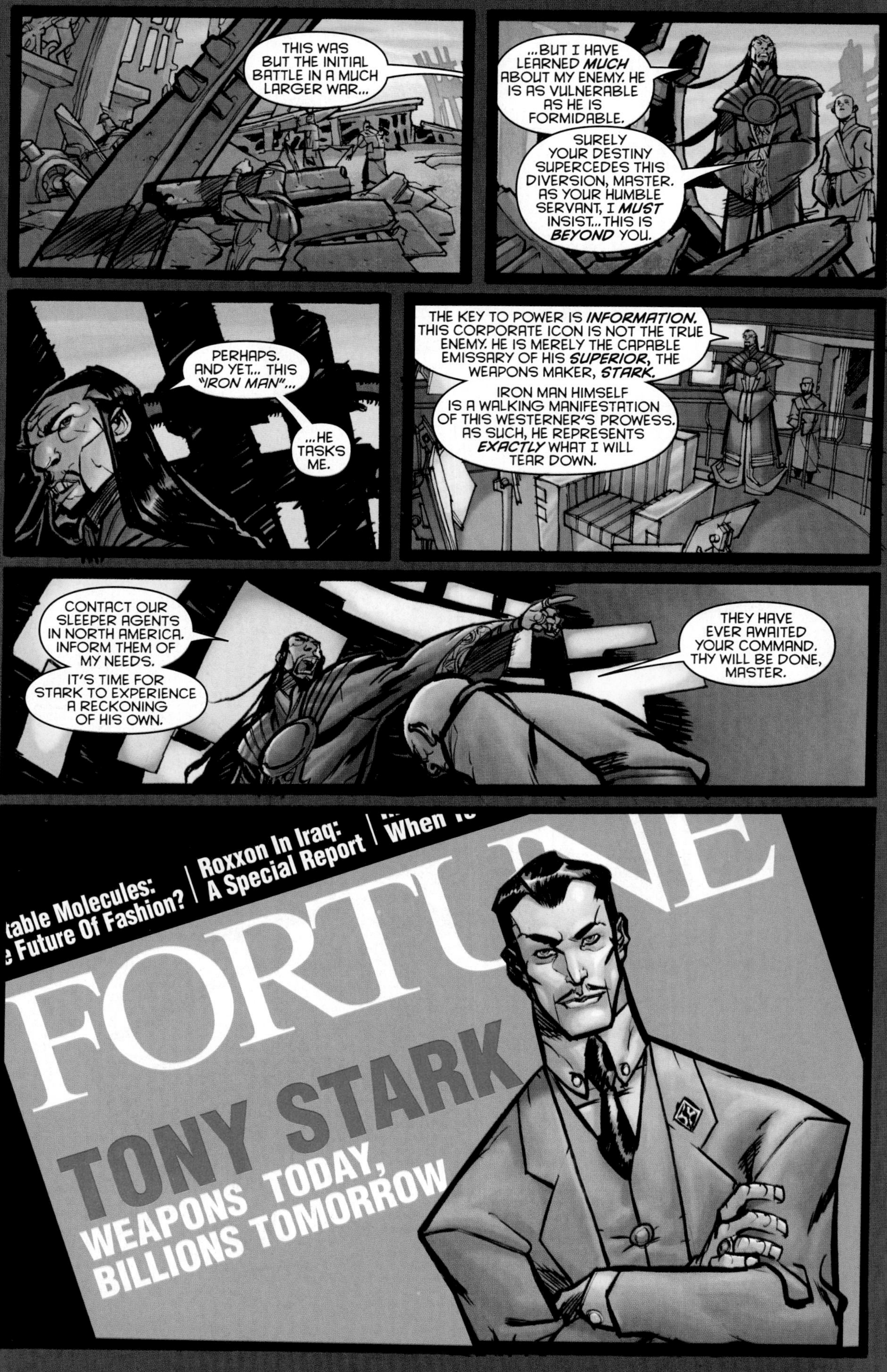
THIS WAS BUT THE INITIAL BATTLE IN A MUCH LARGER WAR...
...BUT I HAVE LEARNED *MUCH* ABOUT MY ENEMY. HE IS AS VULNERABLE AS HE IS FORMIDABLE.
SURELY YOUR DESTINY SUPERCEDES THIS DIVERSION, MASTER. AS YOUR HUMBLE SERVANT, I *MUST* INSIST... THIS IS *BEYOND* YOU.
PERHAPS. AND YET... THIS *"IRON MAN"*...
...HE TASKS ME.
THE KEY TO POWER IS *INFORMATION.* THIS CORPORATE ICON IS NOT THE TRUE ENEMY. HE IS MERELY THE CAPABLE EMISSARY OF HIS *SUPERIOR*, THE WEAPONS MAKER, *STARK.*
IRON MAN HIMSELF IS A WALKING MANIFESTATION OF THIS WESTERNER'S PROWESS. AS SUCH, HE REPRESENTS *EXACTLY* WHAT I WILL TEAR DOWN.
CONTACT OUR SLEEPER AGENTS IN NORTH AMERICA. INFORM THEM OF MY NEEDS.
IT'S TIME FOR STARK TO EXPERIENCE A RECKONING OF HIS OWN.
THEY HAVE EVER AWAITED YOUR COMMAND. THY WILL BE DONE, MASTER.
table Molecules:
e Future Of Fashion?
Roxxon In Iraq:
A Special Report
When
FORTUNE
TONY STARK
WEAPONS TODAY,
BILLIONS TOMORROW

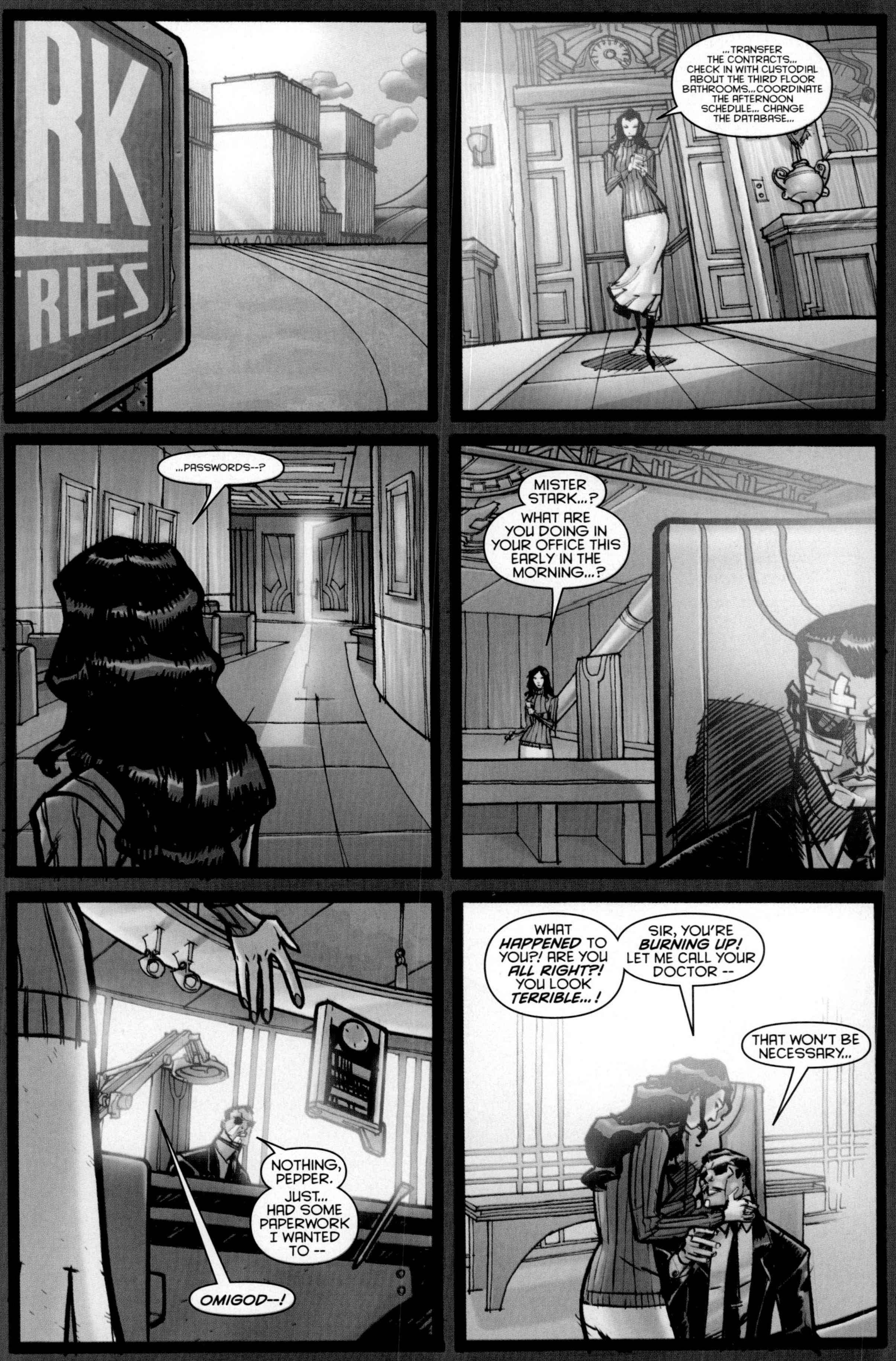
RK
TRIES
...TRANSFER THE CONTRACTS... CHECK IN WITH CUSTODIAL ABOUT THE THIRD FLOOR BATHROOMS... COORDINATE THE AFTERNOON SCHEDULE... CHANGE THE DATABASE...
...PASSWORDS--?
MISTER STARK...? WHAT ARE YOU DOING IN YOUR OFFICE THIS EARLY IN THE MORNING...?
NOTHING, PEPPER. JUST... HAD SOME PAPERWORK I WANTED TO --
OMIGOD--!
WHAT HAPPENED TO YOU?! ARE YOU ALL RIGHT?! YOU LOOK TERRIBLE...!
SIR, YOU'RE BURNING UP! LET ME CALL YOUR DOCTOR --
THAT WON'T BE NECESSARY...

JUST A LITTLE TROUBLE IN THE LAB, THAT'S ALL...YOU KNOW HOW *VOLATILE* CHEMICAL BONDING PROCESSES CAN BE. AND ME WITHOUT MY SAFETY GOGGLES...

LOOK, PEPPER, DO ME A FAVOR... SHUT THE DOOR ON YOUR WAY OUT.

GO ON. I'M FINE.

...LOVE FOR SALE... APPETIZING YOUNG LOVE FOR SALE...

WHAT'S UP, SEXY? NOTHING LIKE A NEW DAY T'PUT A LITTLE *SPRING* IN YER STEP. THE BOSS IN THERE...?

SORT OF HAPPY.

GREENWICH VILLAGE

THE WORLD YOU KNOW WILL NOT REMAIN...

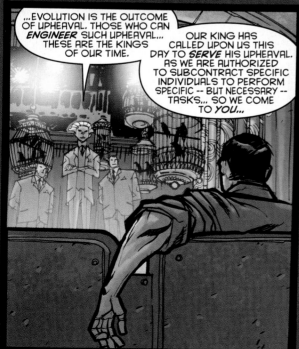

...EVOLUTION IS THE OUTCOME OF UPHEAVAL. THOSE WHO CAN *ENGINEER* SUCH UPHEAVAL... THESE ARE THE KINGS OF OUR TIME.

OUR KING HAS CALLED UPON US THIS DAY TO *SERVE* HIS UPHEAVAL. AS WE ARE AUTHORIZED TO SUBCONTRACT SPECIFIC INDIVIDUALS TO PERFORM SPECIFIC -- BUT NECESSARY -- TASKS... SO WE COME TO *YOU*...

...*EBENEZER LAUGHTON.* ARE *YOU* PREPARED TO *EVOLVE*...?

PRETTY GOOD ENGLISH YOU SPEAK THERE, MR. MIYAGI. BUT I THINK YOU'VE GOT THE WRONG GUY.

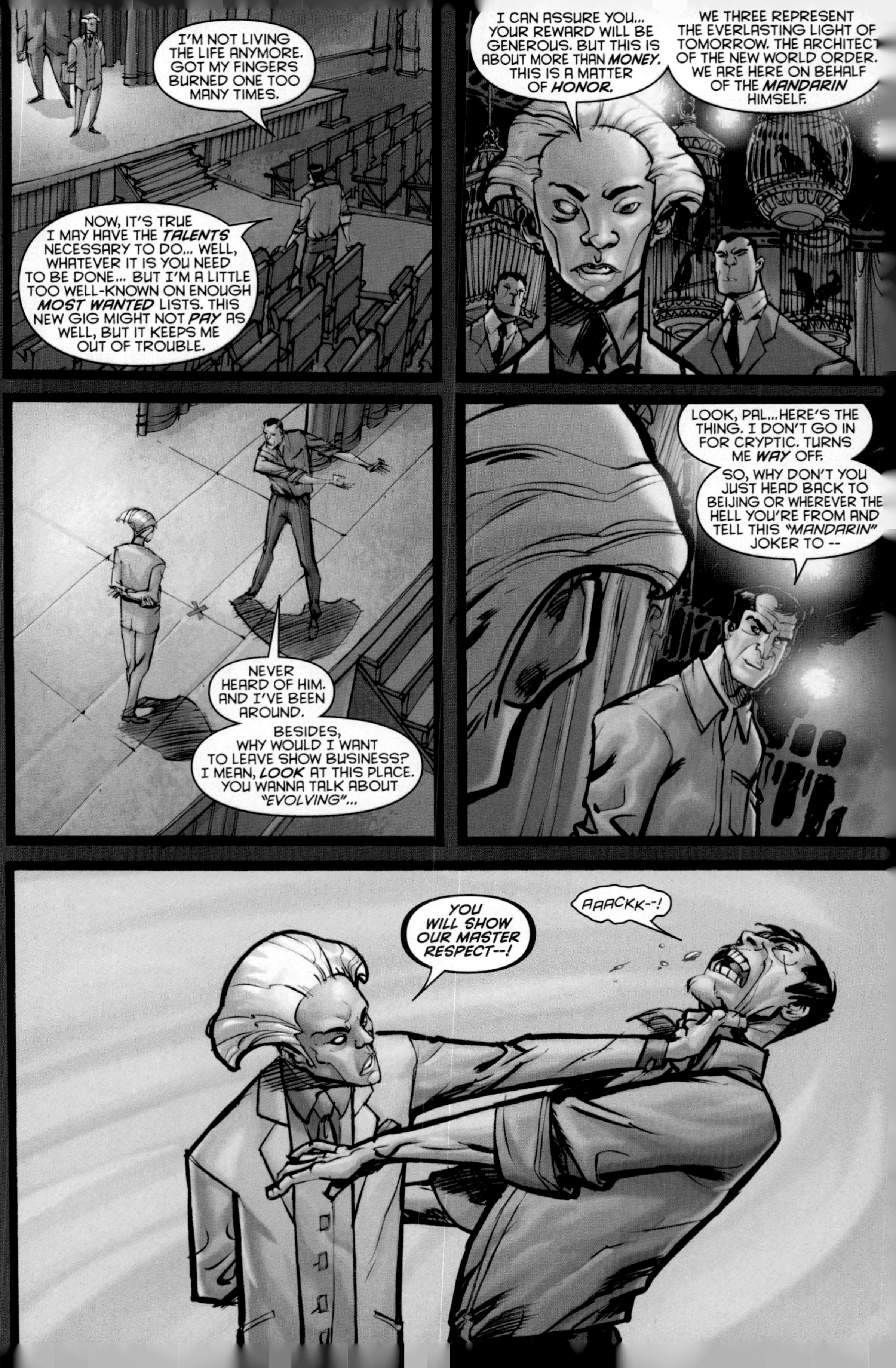

I'M NOT LIVING THE LIFE ANYMORE. GOT MY FINGERS BURNED ONE TOO MANY TIMES.
NOW, IT'S TRUE I MAY HAVE THE TALENTS NECESSARY TO DO... WELL, WHATEVER IT IS YOU NEED TO BE DONE... BUT I'M A LITTLE TOO WELL-KNOWN ON ENOUGH MOST WANTED LISTS. THIS NEW GIG MIGHT NOT PAY AS WELL, BUT IT KEEPS ME OUT OF TROUBLE.
I CAN ASSURE YOU... YOUR REWARD WILL BE GENEROUS. BUT THIS IS ABOUT MORE THAN MONEY. THIS IS A MATTER OF HONOR.
WE THREE REPRESENT THE EVERLASTING LIGHT OF TOMORROW. THE ARCHITECT OF THE NEW WORLD ORDER. WE ARE HERE ON BEHALF OF THE MANDARIN HIMSELF.
NEVER HEARD OF HIM. AND I'VE BEEN AROUND.
BESIDES, WHY WOULD I WANT TO LEAVE SHOW BUSINESS? I MEAN, LOOK AT THIS PLACE. YOU WANNA TALK ABOUT "EVOLVING"...
LOOK, PAL...HERE'S THE THING. I DON'T GO IN FOR CRYPTIC. TURNS ME WAY OFF.
SO, WHY DON'T YOU JUST HEAD BACK TO BEIJING OR WHEREVER THE HELL YOU'RE FROM AND TELL THIS "MANDARIN" JOKER TO --
YOU WILL SHOW OUR MASTER RESPECT--!
AAACKK--!

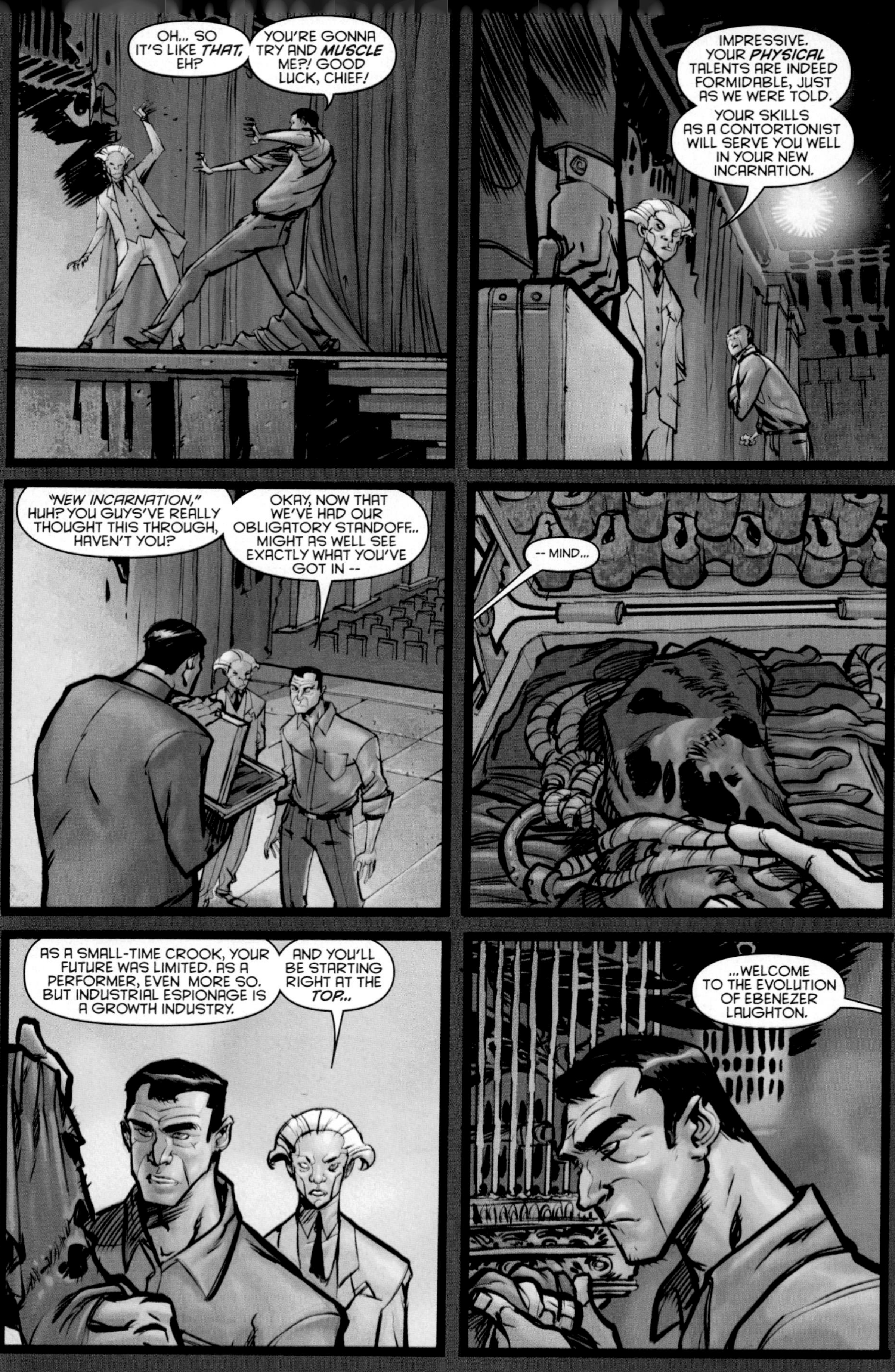
OH... SO IT'S LIKE *THAT,* EH?
YOU'RE GONNA TRY AND *MUSCLE* ME?! GOOD LUCK, CHIEF!
IMPRESSIVE. YOUR *PHYSICAL* TALENTS ARE INDEED FORMIDABLE, JUST AS WE WERE TOLD.
YOUR SKILLS AS A CONTORTIONIST WILL SERVE YOU WELL IN YOUR NEW INCARNATION.
"NEW INCARNATION," HUH? YOU GUYS'VE REALLY THOUGHT THIS THROUGH, HAVEN'T YOU?
OKAY, NOW THAT WE'VE HAD OUR OBLIGATORY STANDOFF... MIGHT AS WELL SEE EXACTLY WHAT YOU'VE GOT IN --
-- MIND...
AS A SMALL-TIME CROOK, YOUR FUTURE WAS LIMITED. AS A PERFORMER, EVEN MORE SO. BUT INDUSTRIAL ESPIONAGE IS A GROWTH INDUSTRY.
AND YOU'LL BE STARTING RIGHT AT THE *TOP...*
...WELCOME TO THE EVOLUTION OF EBENEZER LAUGHTON.

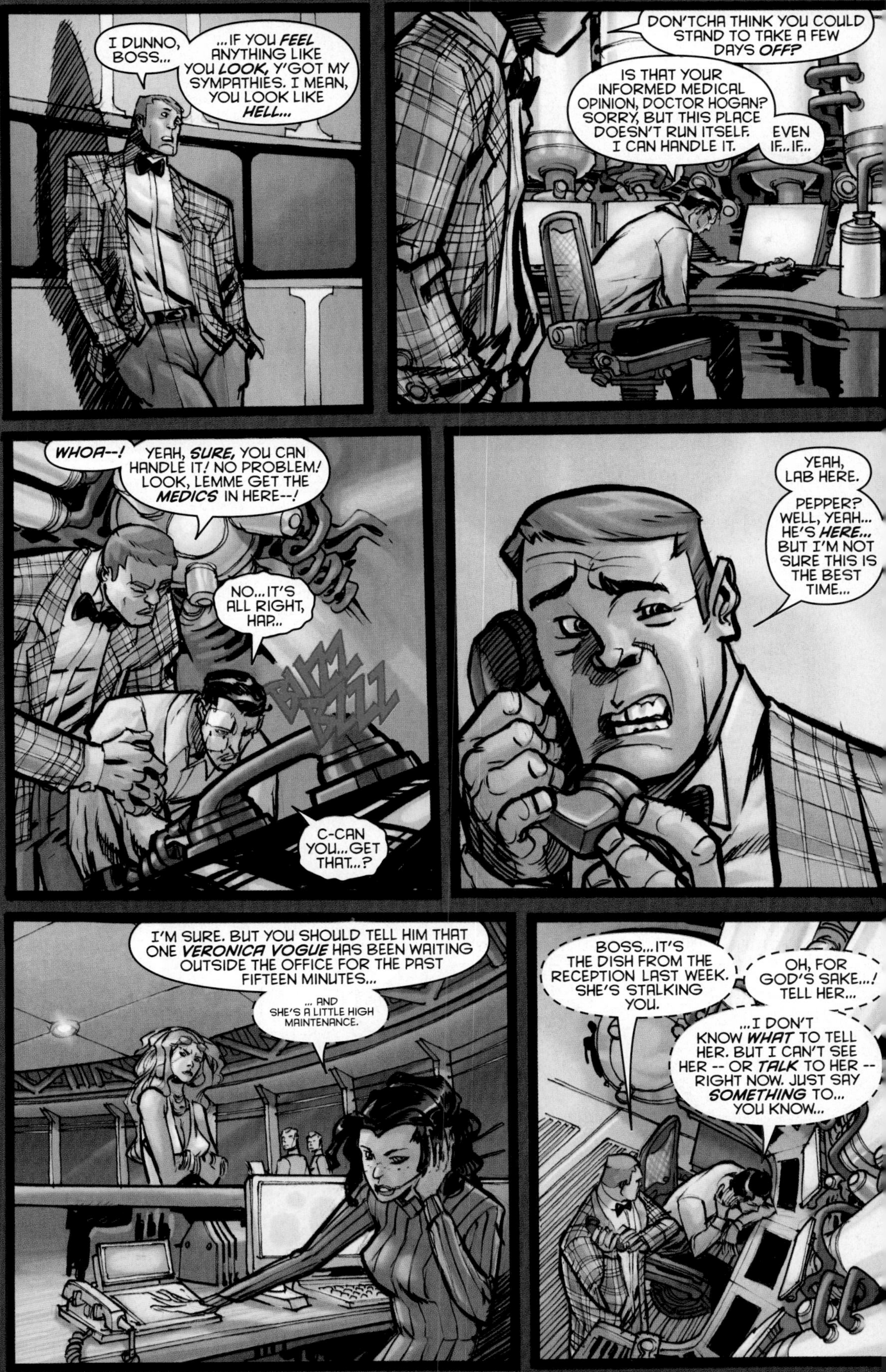
I DUNNO, BOSS...
...IF YOU FEEL ANYTHING LIKE YOU LOOK, Y'GOT MY SYMPATHIES. I MEAN, YOU LOOK LIKE HELL...
DON'TCHA THINK YOU COULD STAND TO TAKE A FEW DAYS OFF?
IS THAT YOUR INFORMED MEDICAL OPINION, DOCTOR HOGAN? SORRY, BUT THIS PLACE DOESN'T RUN ITSELF. I CAN HANDLE IT.
EVEN IF...IF...
WHOA--!
YEAH, SURE, YOU CAN HANDLE IT! NO PROBLEM! LOOK, LEMME GET THE MEDICS IN HERE--!
NO...IT'S ALL RIGHT, HAP...
C-CAN YOU...GET THAT...?
YEAH, LAB HERE.
PEPPER? WELL, YEAH... HE'S HERE... BUT I'M NOT SURE THIS IS THE BEST TIME...
I'M SURE. BUT YOU SHOULD TELL HIM THAT ONE VERONICA VOGUE HAS BEEN WAITING OUTSIDE THE OFFICE FOR THE PAST FIFTEEN MINUTES...
... AND SHE'S A LITTLE HIGH MAINTENANCE.
BOSS...IT'S THE DISH FROM THE RECEPTION LAST WEEK. SHE'S STALKING YOU.
OH, FOR GOD'S SAKE...! TELL HER...
...I DON'T KNOW WHAT TO TELL HER. BUT I CAN'T SEE HER -- OR TALK TO HER -- RIGHT NOW. JUST SAY SOMETHING TO... YOU KNOW...

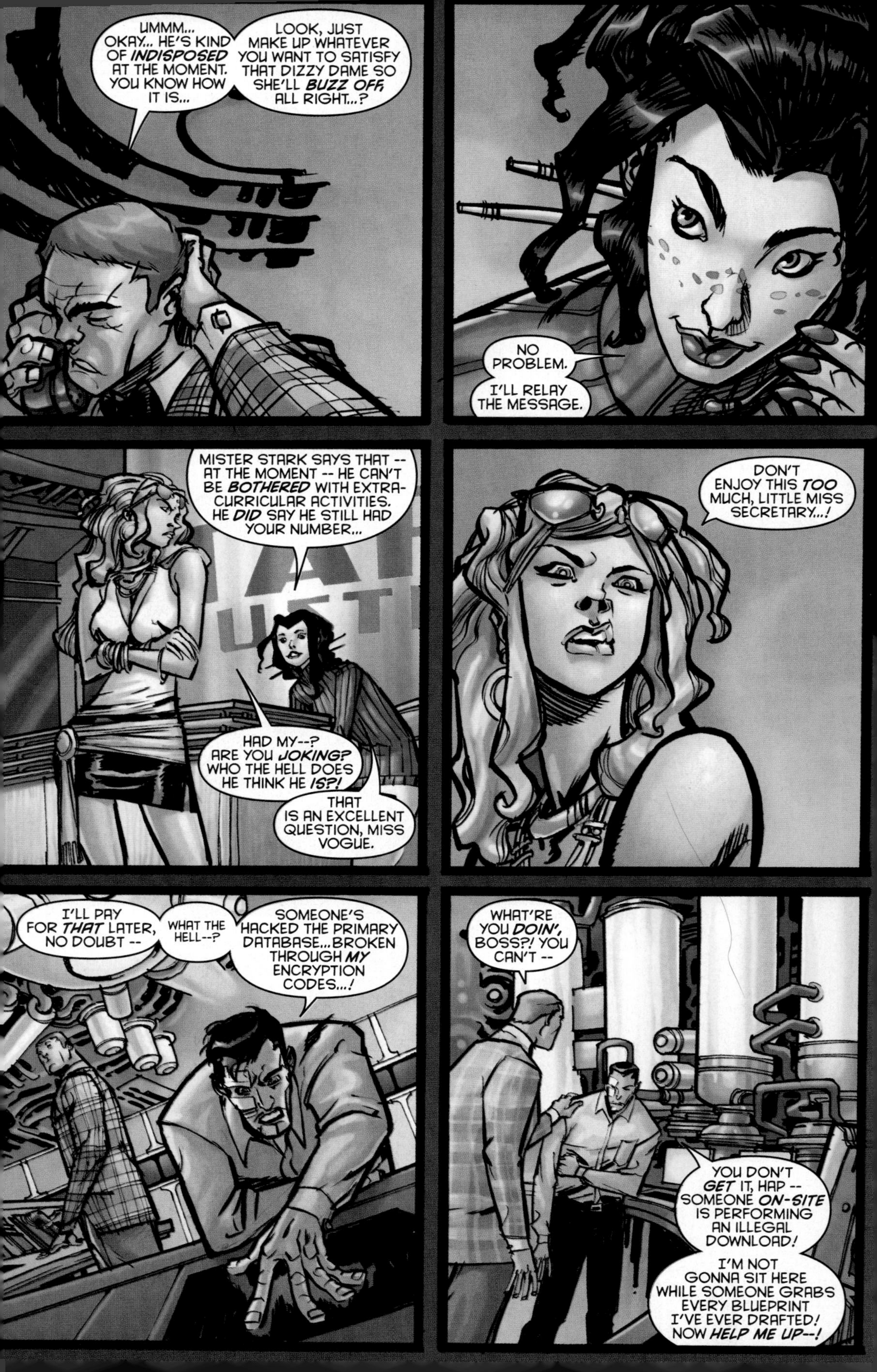
UMMM... OKAY... HE'S KIND OF INDISPOSED AT THE MOMENT. YOU KNOW HOW IT IS...
LOOK, JUST MAKE UP WHATEVER YOU WANT TO SATISFY THAT DIZZY DAME SO SHE'LL BUZZ OFF, ALL RIGHT...?
NO PROBLEM.
I'LL RELAY THE MESSAGE.
MISTER STARK SAYS THAT -- AT THE MOMENT -- HE CAN'T BE BOTHERED WITH EXTRA-CURRICULAR ACTIVITIES. HE DID SAY HE STILL HAD YOUR NUMBER...
HAD MY--? ARE YOU JOKING? WHO THE HELL DOES HE THINK HE IS?!
THAT IS AN EXCELLENT QUESTION, MISS VOGUE.
DON'T ENJOY THIS TOO MUCH, LITTLE MISS SECRETARY...!
I'LL PAY FOR THAT LATER, NO DOUBT --
WHAT THE HELL--?
SOMEONE'S HACKED THE PRIMARY DATABASE...BROKEN THROUGH MY ENCRYPTION CODES...!
WHAT'RE YOU DOIN', BOSS?! YOU CAN'T --
YOU DON'T GET IT, HAP -- SOMEONE ON-SITE IS PERFORMING AN ILLEGAL DOWNLOAD!
I'M NOT GONNA SIT HERE WHILE SOMEONE GRABS EVERY BLUEPRINT I'VE EVER DRAFTED! NOW HELP ME UP--!

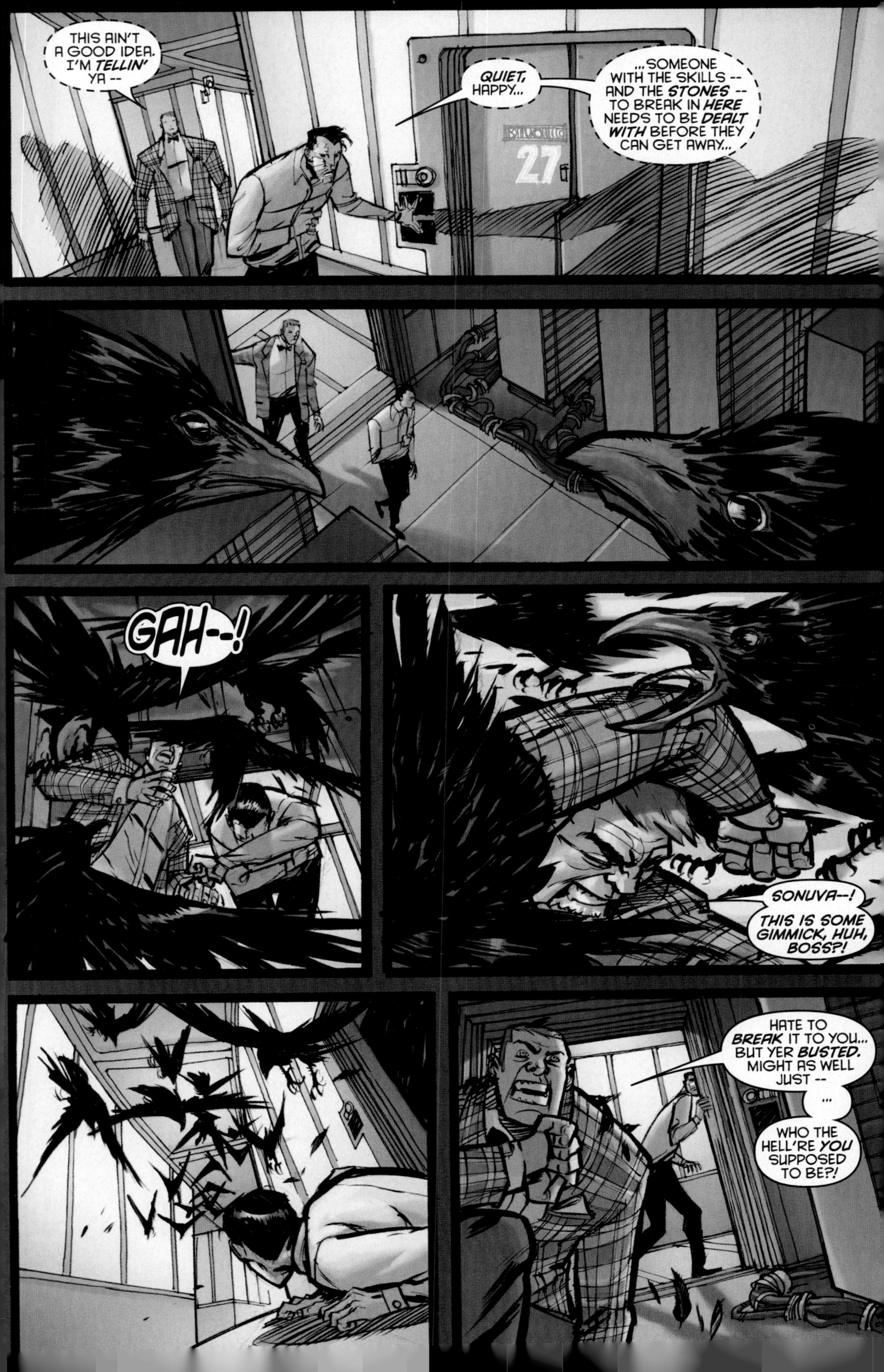
THIS AIN'T A GOOD IDEA. I'M TELLIN' YA --
QUIET, HAPPY...
...SOMEONE WITH THE SKILLS -- AND THE STONES -- TO BREAK IN HERE NEEDS TO BE DEALT WITH BEFORE THEY CAN GET AWAY...
27
GAH--!
SONUVA--!
THIS IS SOME GIMMICK, HUH, BOSS?!
HATE TO BREAK IT TO YOU... BUT YER BUSTED. MIGHT AS WELL JUST --
...
WHO THE HELL'RE YOU SUPPOSED TO BE?!

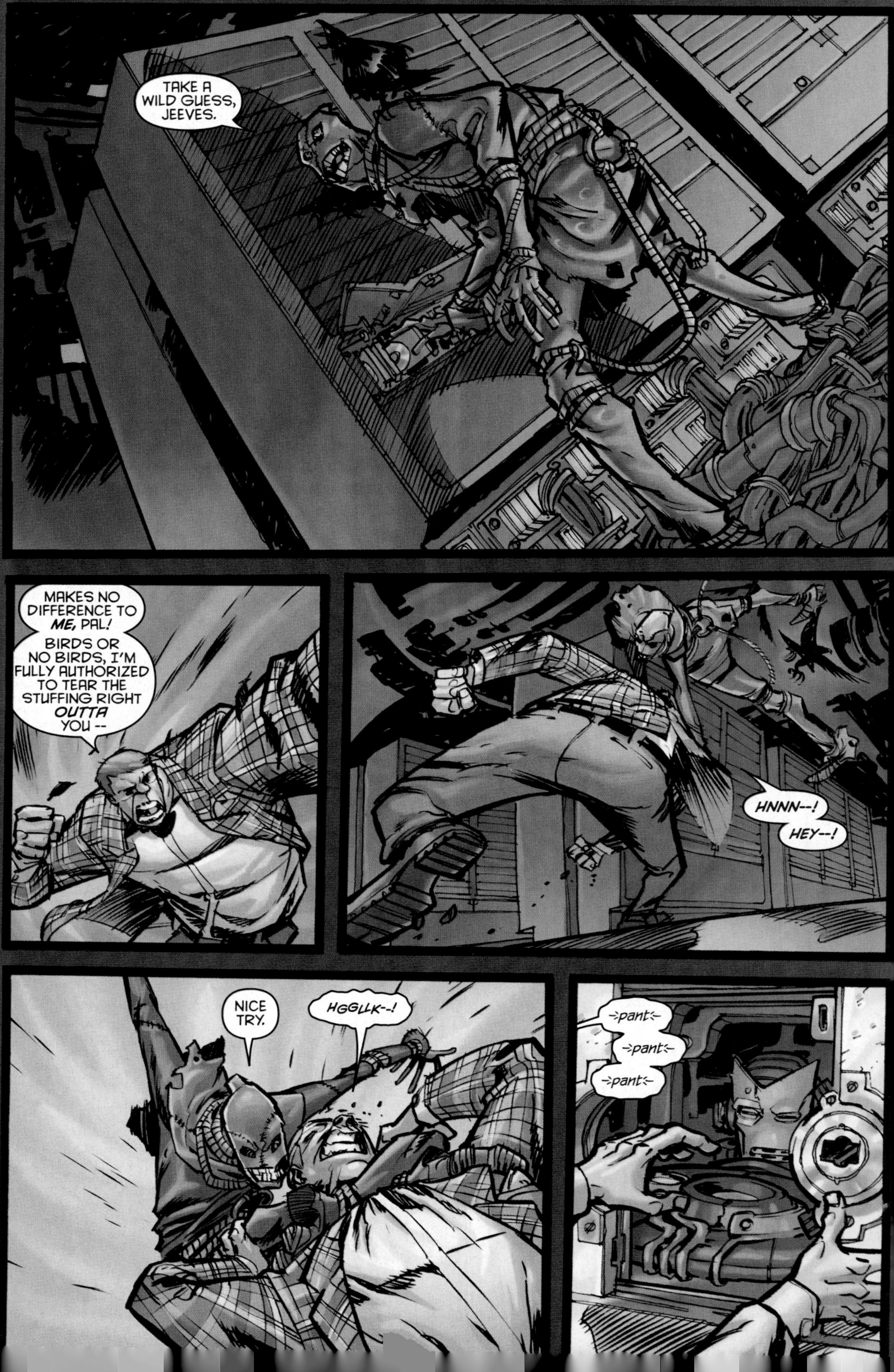
TAKE A WILD GUESS, JEEVES.
MAKES NO DIFFERENCE TO ME, PAL!
BIRDS OR NO BIRDS, I'M FULLY AUTHORIZED TO TEAR THE STUFFING RIGHT OUTTA YOU --
HNNN--!
HEY--!
NICE TRY.
HGGLLK--!
pant
pant
pant

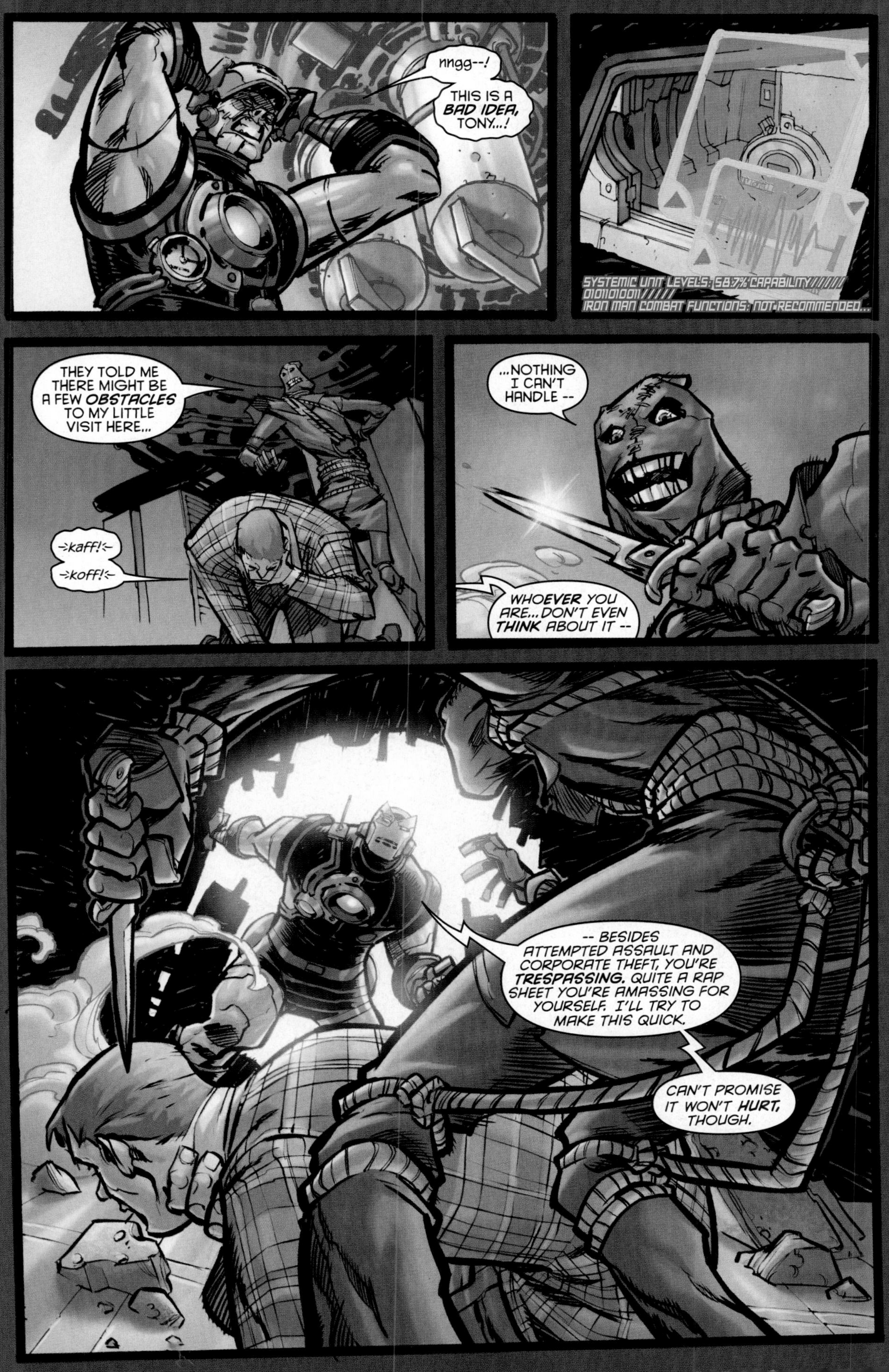
nngg--!
THIS IS A BAD IDEA, TONY...!
SYSTEMIC UNIT LEVELS: 58.7% CAPABILITY//////
0101101001//////
IRON MAN COMBAT FUNCTIONS: NOT RECOMMENDED...
THEY TOLD ME THERE MIGHT BE A FEW OBSTACLES TO MY LITTLE VISIT HERE...
-kaff!-
-koff!-
...NOTHING I CAN'T HANDLE --
WHOEVER YOU ARE...DON'T EVEN THINK ABOUT IT --
-- BESIDES ATTEMPTED ASSAULT AND CORPORATE THEFT, YOU'RE TRESPASSING. QUITE A RAP SHEET YOU'RE AMASSING FOR YOURSELF. I'LL TRY TO MAKE THIS QUICK.
CAN'T PROMISE IT WON'T HURT, THOUGH.

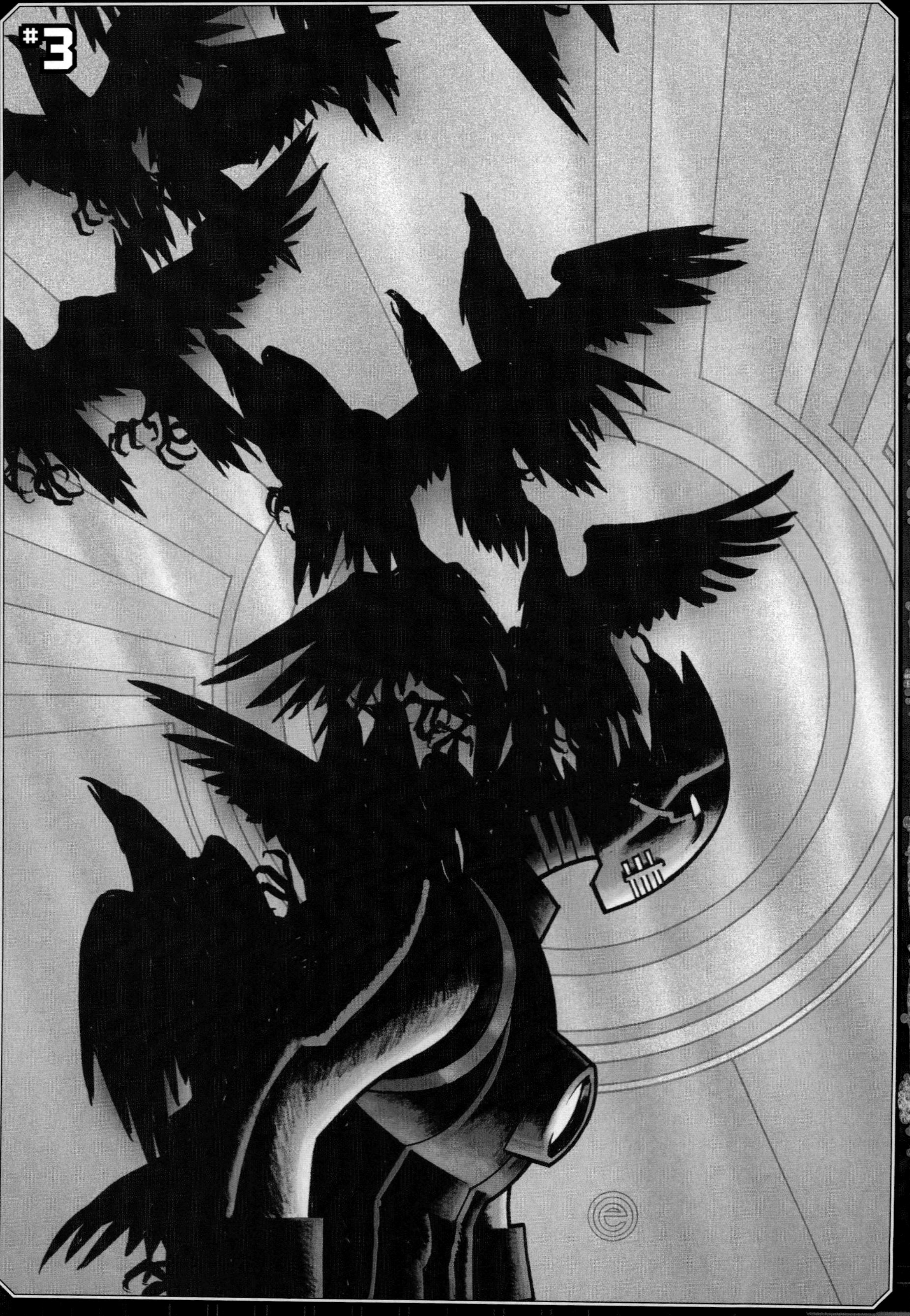
#3

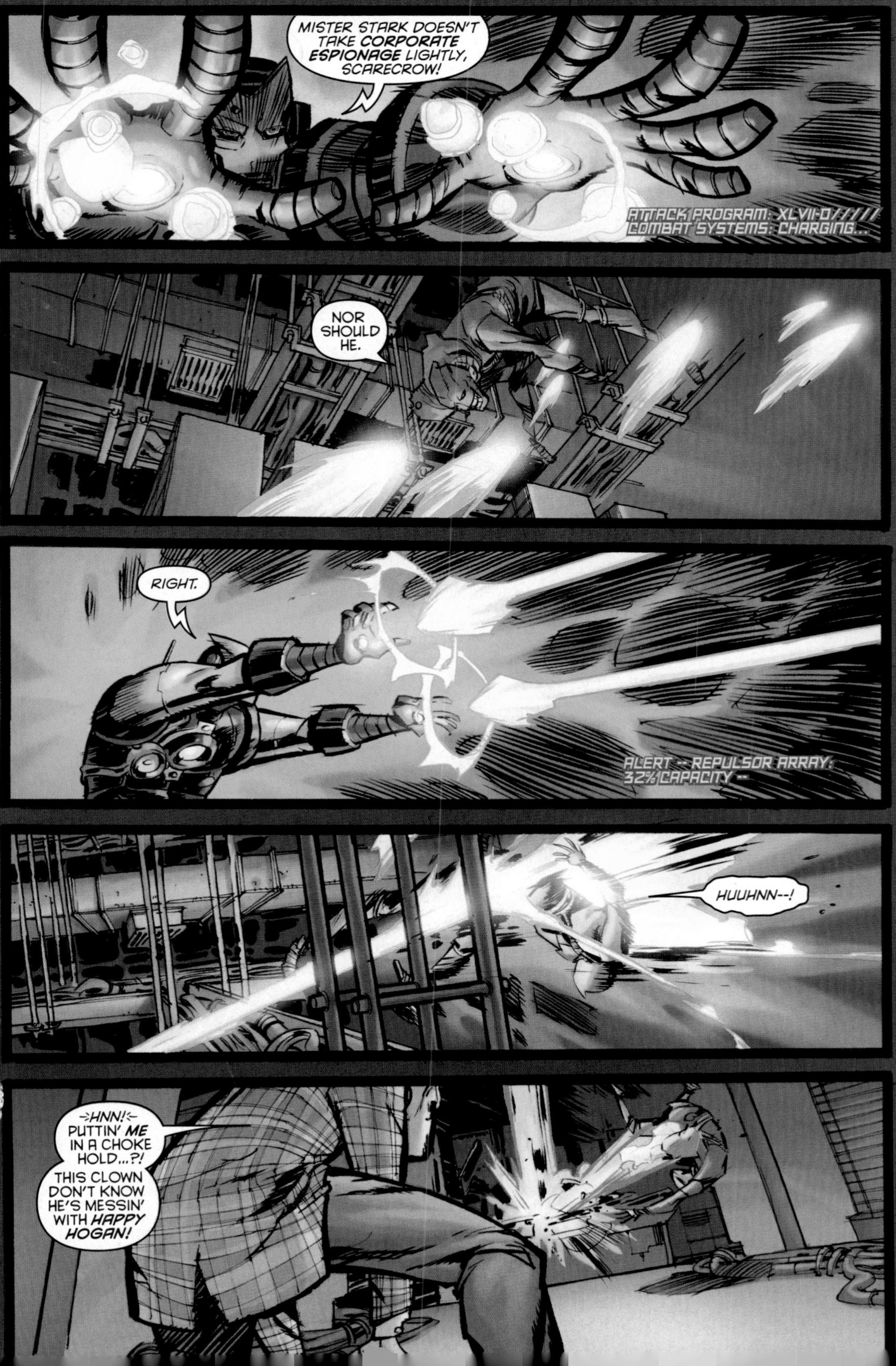
MISTER STARK DOESN'T TAKE CORPORATE ESPIONAGE LIGHTLY, SCARECROW!
ATTACK PROGRAM: XLVII-D//////
COMBAT SYSTEMS: CHARGING...
NOR SHOULD HE.
RIGHT.
ALERT -- REPULSOR ARRAY: 32% CAPACITY --
HUUHNN--!
-HNN!- PUTTIN' ME IN A CHOKE HOLD...?! THIS CLOWN DON'T KNOW HE'S MESSIN' WITH HAPPY HOGAN!

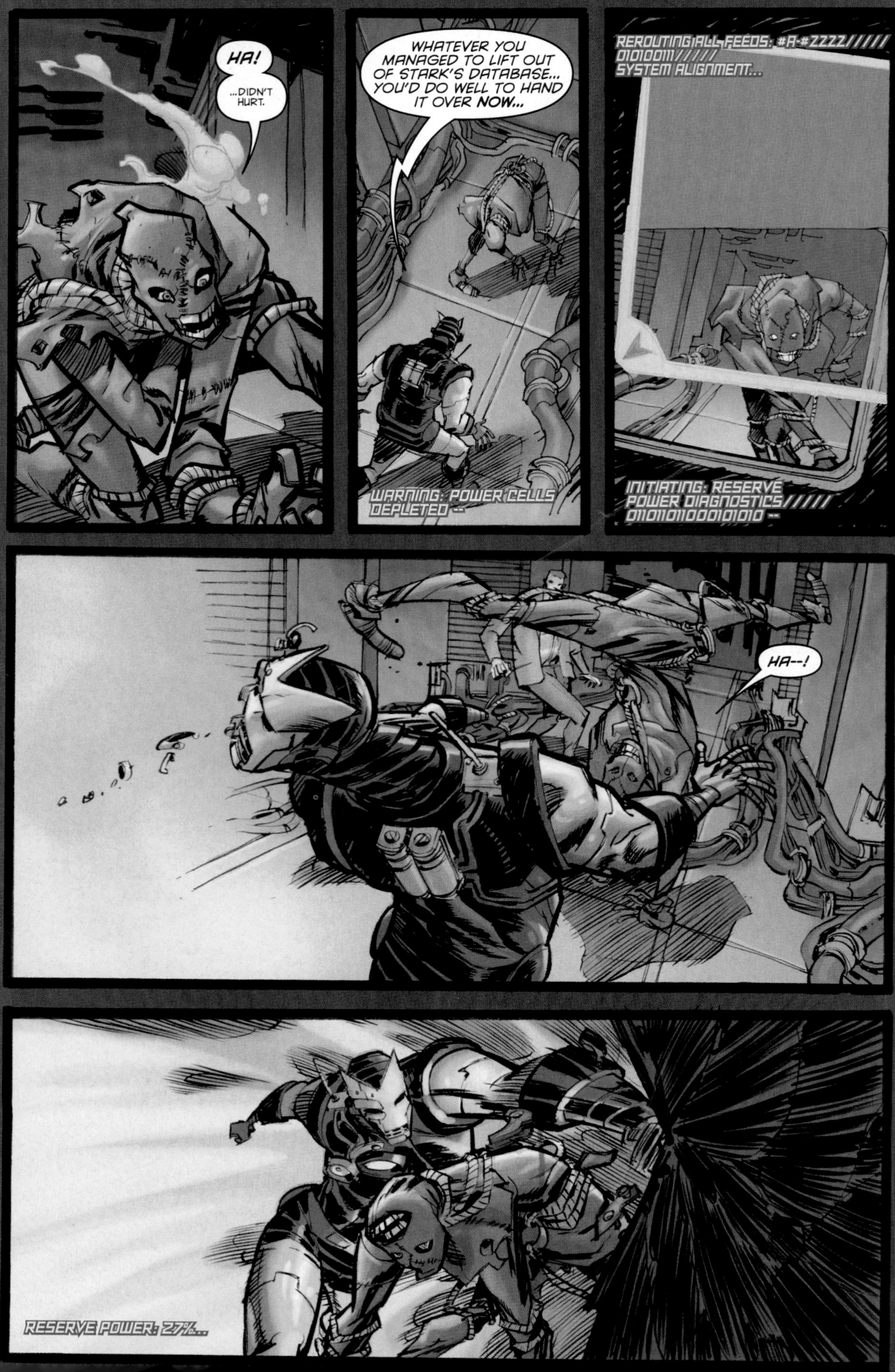
HA!
...DIDN'T HURT.
WHATEVER YOU MANAGED TO LIFT OUT OF STARK'S DATABASE... YOU'D DO WELL TO HAND IT OVER NOW...
WARNING: POWER CELLS DEPLETED --
REROUTING ALL FEEDS: #A-#ZZZZ////// 010100111////// SYSTEM ALIGNMENT...
INITIATING: RESERVE POWER DIAGNOSTICS////// 0110110110001010101010 --
HA--!
RESERVE POWER: 27%...

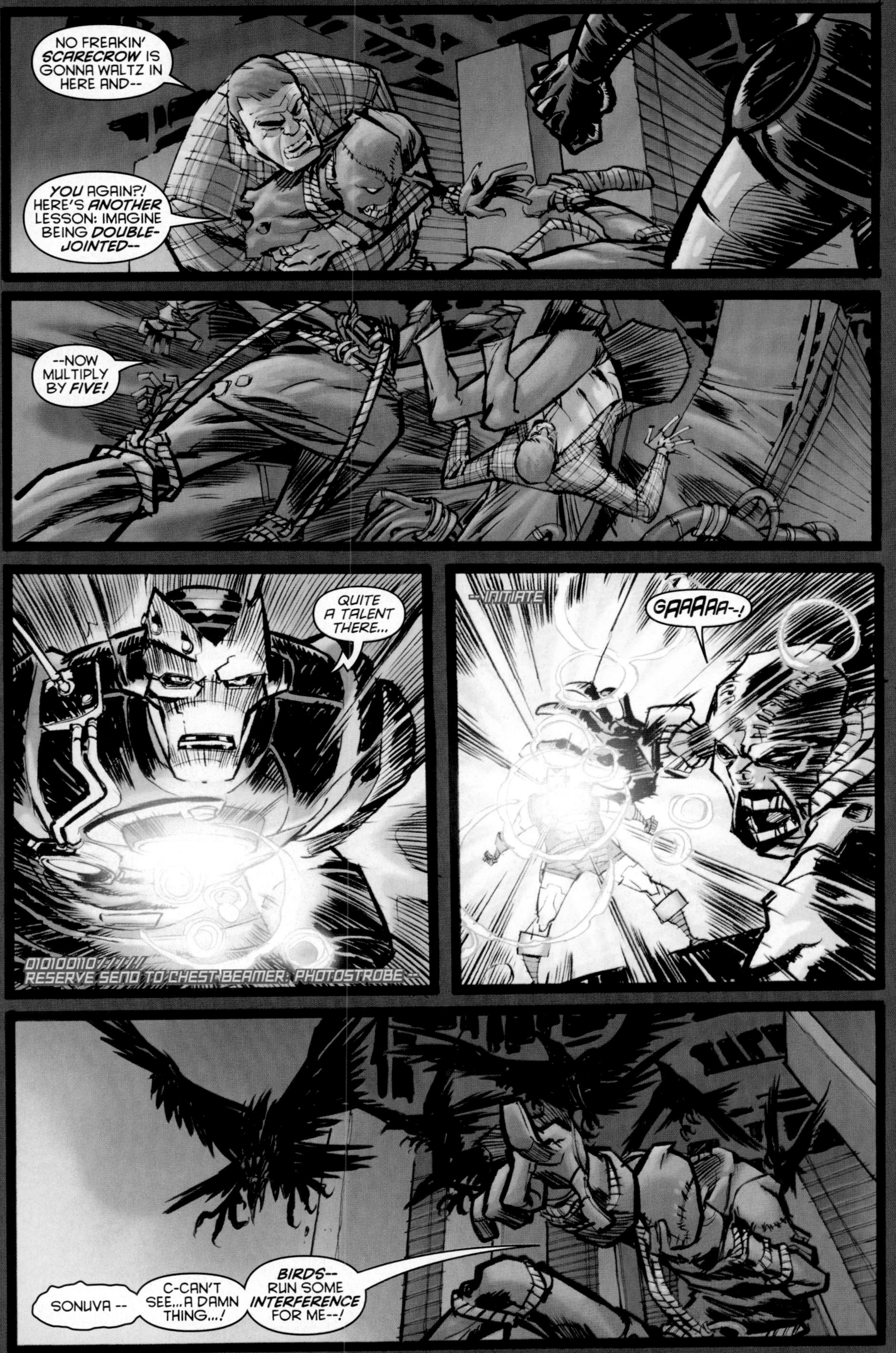
NO FREAKIN' SCARECROW IS GONNA WALTZ IN HERE AND--
YOU AGAIN?! HERE'S ANOTHER LESSON: IMAGINE BEING DOUBLE-JOINTED--
--NOW MULTIPLY BY FIVE!
QUITE A TALENT THERE...
0101001101////
RESERVE SEND TO CHEST BEAMER: PHOTOSTROBE --
--INITIATE
GAAAAA--!
SONUVA --
C-CAN'T SEE...A DAMN THING...!
BIRDS-- RUN SOME INTERFERENCE FOR ME--!

PROXIMITY ALERT: MULTIPLE TARGETS/////
SURFACE SENSOR OVERLOAD --

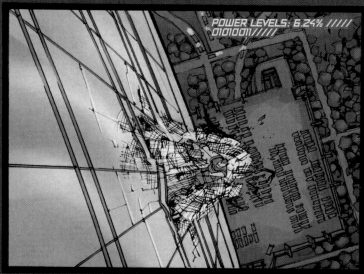

POWER LEVELS: 6.24% /////
^0101001/////

DAMMIT--!

PROPULSION SYSTEMS: OFFLINE --

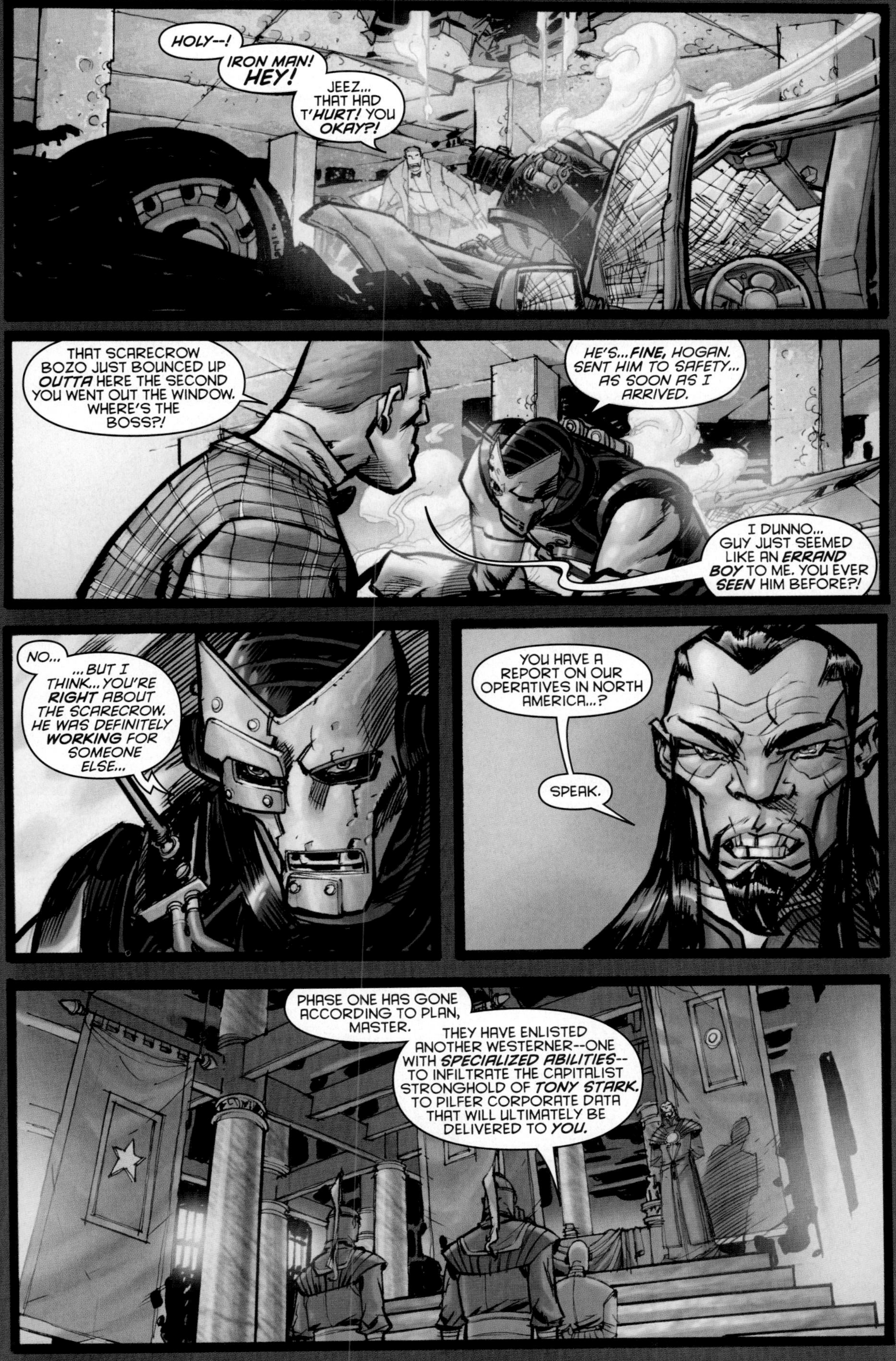
HOLY--!
IRON MAN! HEY!
JEEZ... THAT HAD T'HURT! YOU OKAY?!
THAT SCARECROW BOZO JUST BOUNCED UP OUTTA HERE THE SECOND YOU WENT OUT THE WINDOW. WHERE'S THE BOSS?!
HE'S...FINE, HOGAN. SENT HIM TO SAFETY... AS SOON AS I ARRIVED.
I DUNNO... GUY JUST SEEMED LIKE AN ERRAND BOY TO ME. YOU EVER SEEN HIM BEFORE?!
NO...
...BUT I THINK...YOU'RE RIGHT ABOUT THE SCARECROW. HE WAS DEFINITELY WORKING FOR SOMEONE ELSE...
YOU HAVE A REPORT ON OUR OPERATIVES IN NORTH AMERICA...?
SPEAK.
PHASE ONE HAS GONE ACCORDING TO PLAN, MASTER.
THEY HAVE ENLISTED ANOTHER WESTERNER--ONE WITH SPECIALIZED ABILITIES--TO INFILTRATE THE CAPITALIST STRONGHOLD OF TONY STARK. TO PILFER CORPORATE DATA THAT WILL ULTIMATELY BE DELIVERED TO YOU.

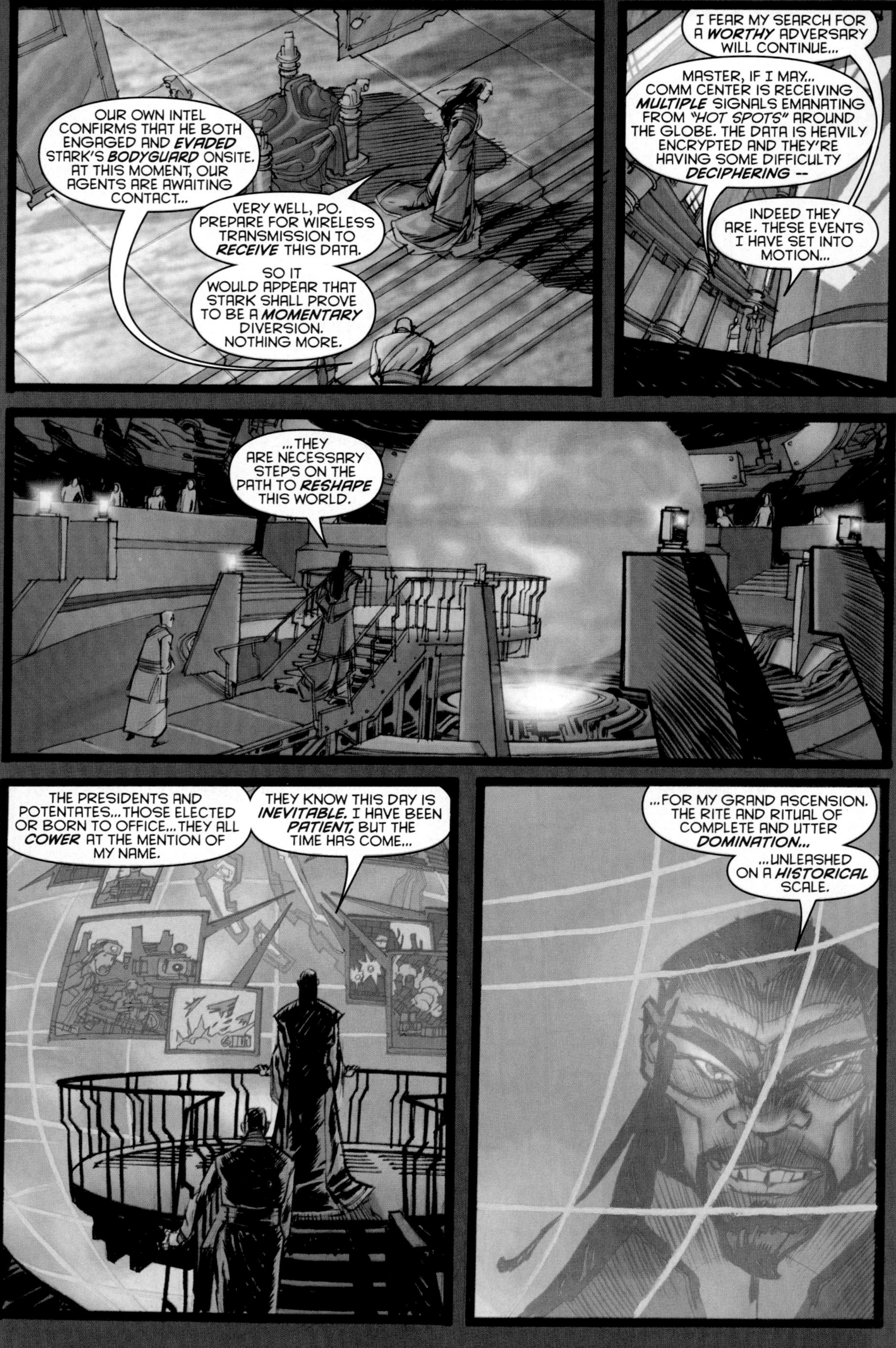
OUR OWN INTEL CONFIRMS THAT HE BOTH ENGAGED AND EVADED STARK'S BODYGUARD ONSITE. AT THIS MOMENT, OUR AGENTS ARE AWAITING CONTACT...
VERY WELL, PO. PREPARE FOR WIRELESS TRANSMISSION TO RECEIVE THIS DATA.
SO IT WOULD APPEAR THAT STARK SHALL PROVE TO BE A MOMENTARY DIVERSION. NOTHING MORE.
I FEAR MY SEARCH FOR A WORTHY ADVERSARY WILL CONTINUE...
MASTER, IF I MAY... COMM CENTER IS RECEIVING MULTIPLE SIGNALS EMANATING FROM "HOT SPOTS" AROUND THE GLOBE. THE DATA IS HEAVILY ENCRYPTED AND THEY'RE HAVING SOME DIFFICULTY DECIPHERING --
INDEED THEY ARE. THESE EVENTS I HAVE SET INTO MOTION...
...THEY ARE NECESSARY STEPS ON THE PATH TO RESHAPE THIS WORLD.
THE PRESIDENTS AND POTENTATES... THOSE ELECTED OR BORN TO OFFICE... THEY ALL COWER AT THE MENTION OF MY NAME.
THEY KNOW THIS DAY IS INEVITABLE. I HAVE BEEN PATIENT, BUT THE TIME HAS COME...
...FOR MY GRAND ASCENSION. THE RITE AND RITUAL OF COMPLETE AND UTTER DOMINATION...
...UNLEASHED ON A HISTORICAL SCALE.

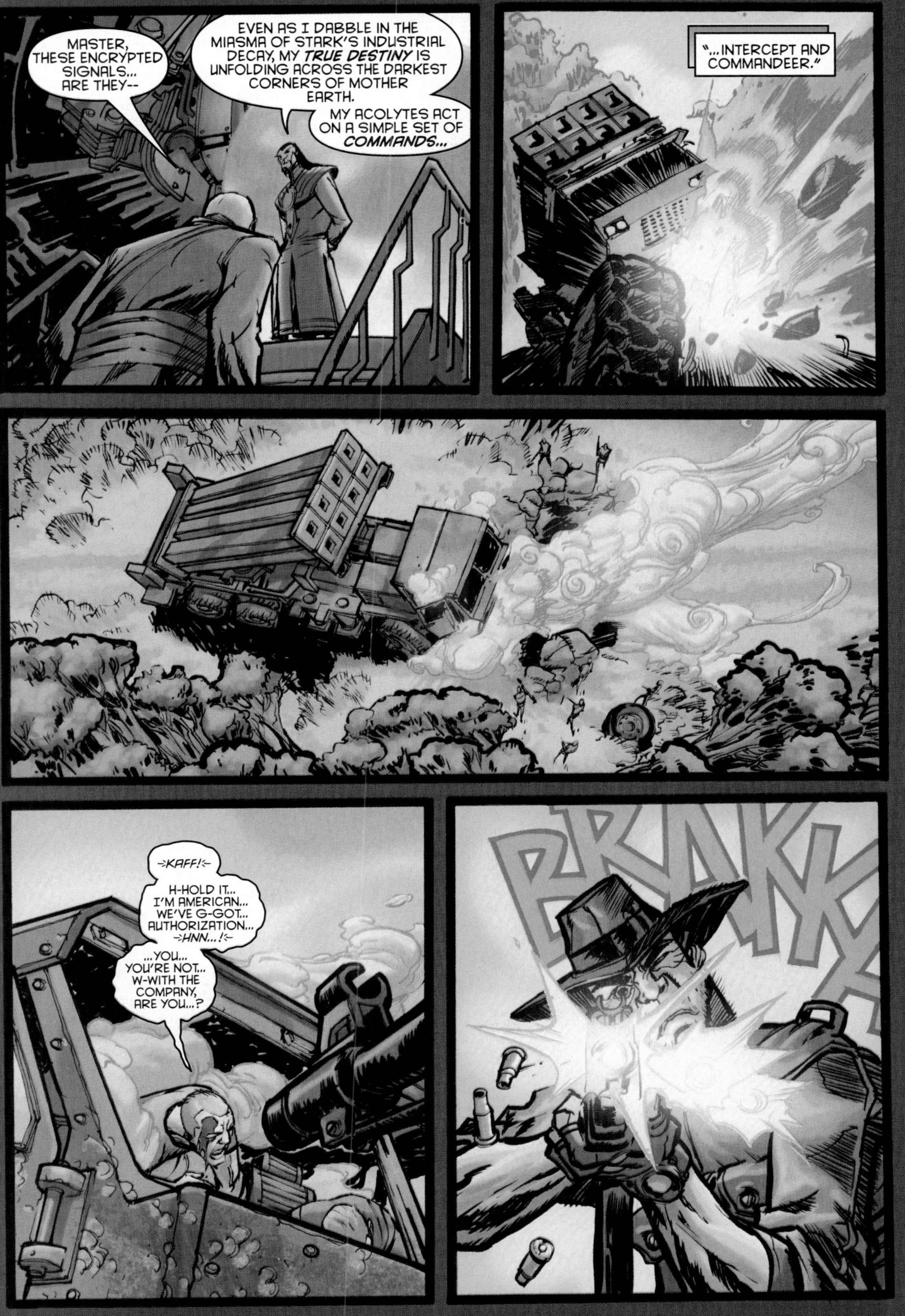
MASTER, THESE ENCRYPTED SIGNALS... ARE THEY--
EVEN AS I DABBLE IN THE MIASMA OF STARK'S INDUSTRIAL DECAY, MY *TRUE DESTINY* IS UNFOLDING ACROSS THE DARKEST CORNERS OF MOTHER EARTH.
MY ACOLYTES ACT ON A SIMPLE SET OF *COMMANDS...*
"...INTERCEPT AND COMMANDEER."
-KAFF!-
H-HOLD IT... I'M AMERICAN... WE'VE G-GOT... AUTHORIZATION... -HNN...!-
...YOU... YOU'RE NOT... W-WITH THE COMPANY, ARE YOU...?
BRAKK

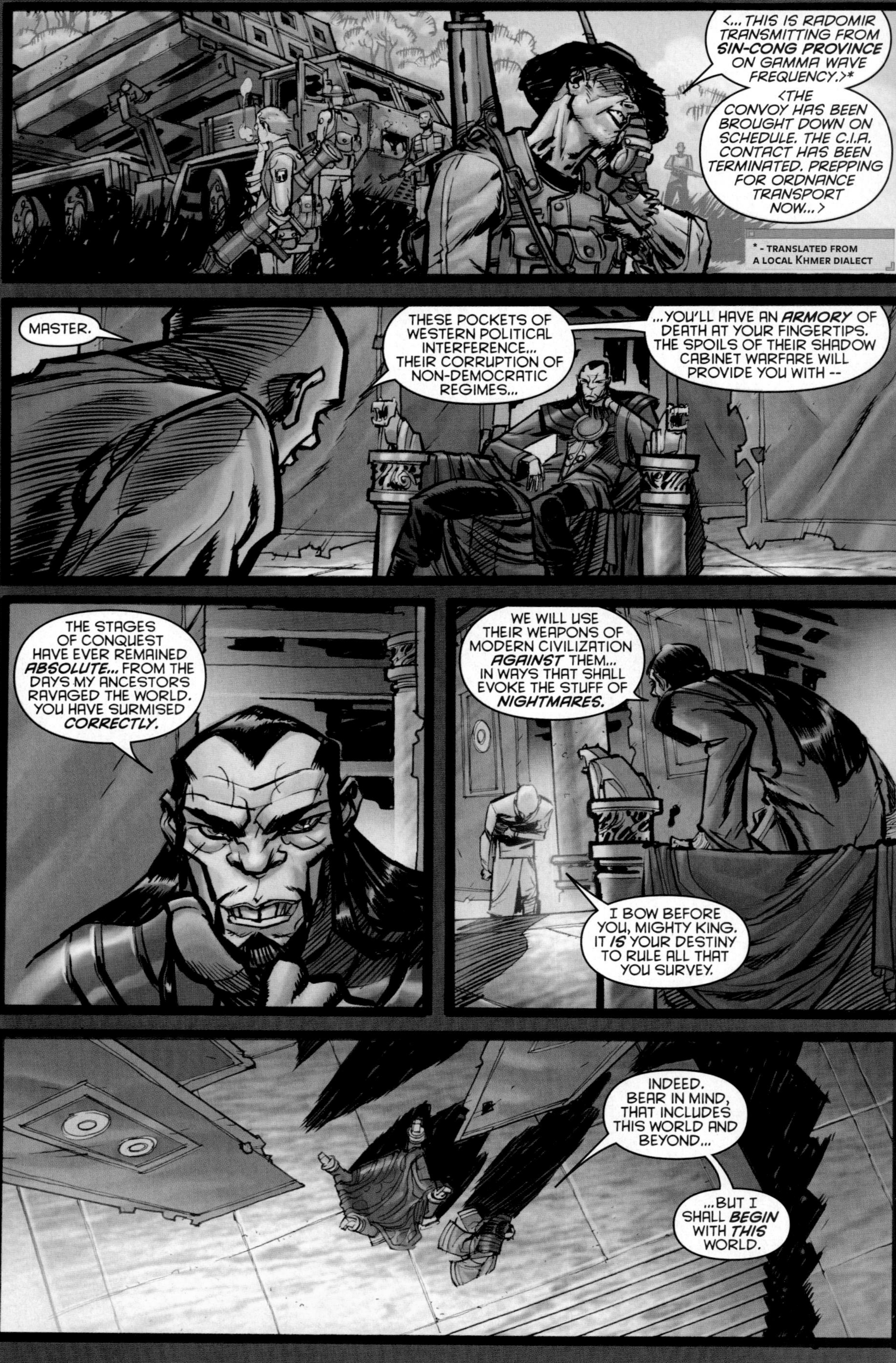
<...THIS IS RADOMIR TRANSMITTING FROM ***SIN-CONG PROVINCE*** ON GAMMA WAVE FREQUENCY.>*
<THE CONVOY HAS BEEN BROUGHT DOWN ON SCHEDULE. THE C.I.A. CONTACT HAS BEEN TERMINATED. PREPPING FOR ORDNANCE TRANSPORT NOW...>
* - TRANSLATED FROM A LOCAL KHMER DIALECT
MASTER.
THESE POCKETS OF WESTERN POLITICAL INTERFERENCE... THEIR CORRUPTION OF NON-DEMOCRATIC REGIMES...
...YOU'LL HAVE AN ***ARMORY*** OF DEATH AT YOUR FINGERTIPS. THE SPOILS OF THEIR SHADOW CABINET WARFARE WILL PROVIDE YOU WITH --
THE STAGES OF CONQUEST HAVE EVER REMAINED ***ABSOLUTE...*** FROM THE DAYS MY ANCESTORS RAVAGED THE WORLD. YOU HAVE SURMISED ***CORRECTLY.***
WE WILL USE THEIR WEAPONS OF MODERN CIVILIZATION ***AGAINST*** THEM... IN WAYS THAT SHALL EVOKE THE STUFF OF ***NIGHTMARES.***
I BOW BEFORE YOU, MIGHTY KING. IT ***IS*** YOUR DESTINY TO RULE ALL THAT YOU SURVEY.
INDEED. BEAR IN MIND, THAT INCLUDES THIS WORLD AND BEYOND...
...BUT I SHALL ***BEGIN*** WITH ***THIS*** WORLD.

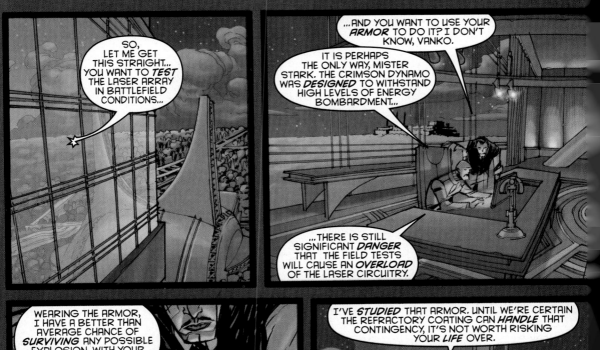

SO, LET ME GET THIS STRAIGHT... YOU WANT TO *TEST* THE LASER ARRAY IN BATTLEFIELD CONDITIONS...

...AND YOU WANT TO USE YOUR *ARMOR* TO DO IT? I DON'T KNOW, VANKO.

IT IS PERHAPS THE ONLY WAY, MISTER STARK. THE CRIMSON DYNAMO WAS *DESIGNED* TO WITHSTAND HIGH LEVELS OF ENERGY BOMBARDMENT...

...THERE IS STILL SIGNIFICANT *DANGER* THAT THE FIELD TESTS WILL CAUSE AN *OVERLOAD* OF THE LASER CIRCUITRY.

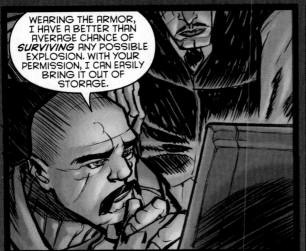

WEARING THE ARMOR, I HAVE A BETTER THAN AVERAGE CHANCE OF *SURVIVING* ANY POSSIBLE EXPLOSION. WITH YOUR PERMISSION, I CAN EASILY BRING IT OUT OF STORAGE.

I'VE *STUDIED* THAT ARMOR. UNTIL WE'RE CERTAIN THE REFRACTORY COATING CAN *HANDLE* THAT CONTINGENCY, IT'S NOT WORTH RISKING YOUR *LIFE* OVER.

NOT THAT I DON'T APPRECIATE YOUR *INITIATIVE.*

"YOU'VE COME A LONG WAY, MY FRIEND."

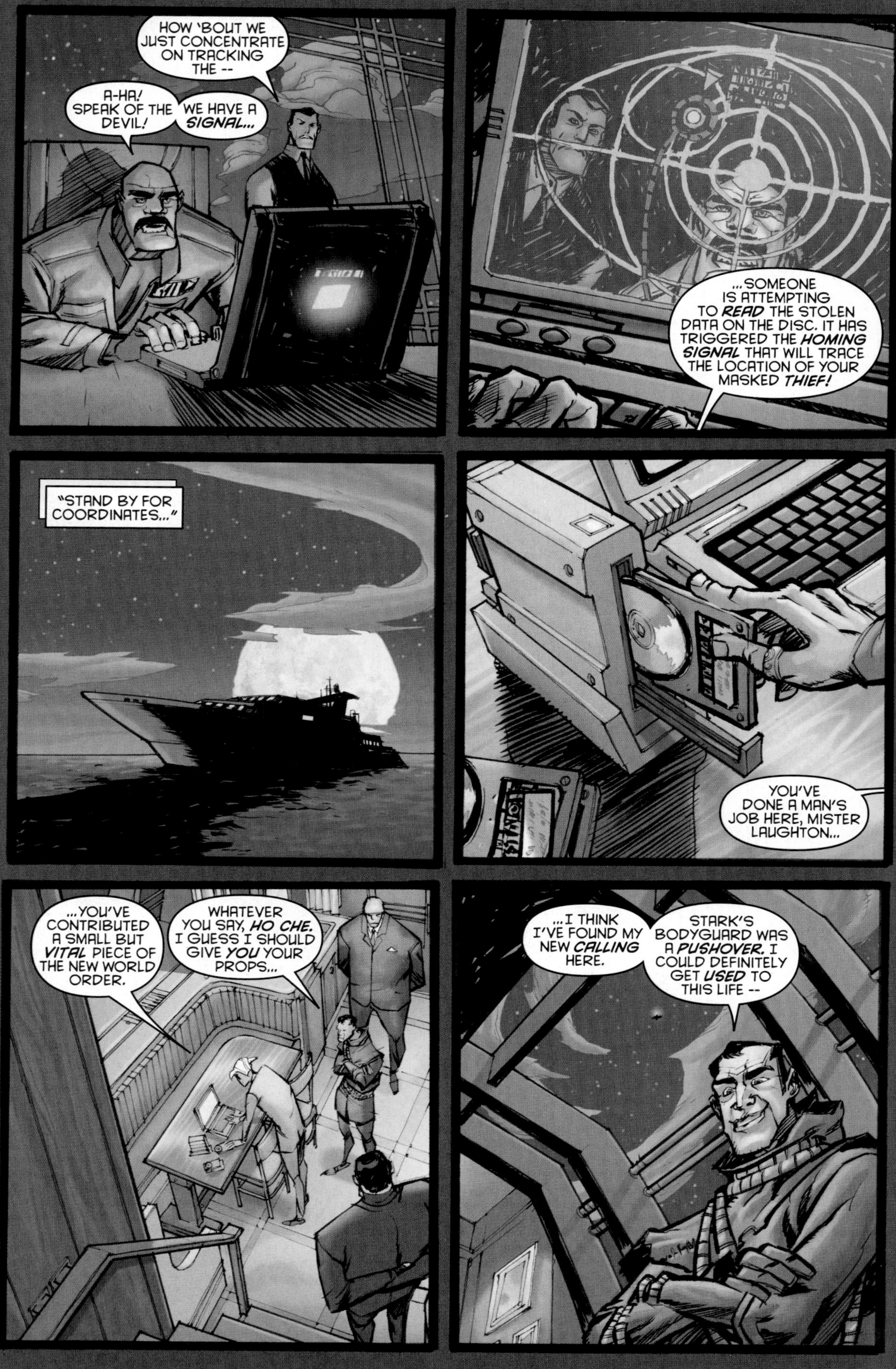
HOW 'BOUT WE JUST CONCENTRATE ON TRACKING THE --
A-HA! SPEAK OF THE DEVIL!
WE HAVE A SIGNAL...
...SOMEONE IS ATTEMPTING TO READ THE STOLEN DATA ON THE DISC. IT HAS TRIGGERED THE HOMING SIGNAL THAT WILL TRACE THE LOCATION OF YOUR MASKED THIEF!
"STAND BY FOR COORDINATES..."
YOU'VE DONE A MAN'S JOB HERE, MISTER LAUGHTON...
...YOU'VE CONTRIBUTED A SMALL BUT VITAL PIECE OF THE NEW WORLD ORDER.
WHATEVER YOU SAY, HO CHE. I GUESS I SHOULD GIVE YOU YOUR PROPS...
...I THINK I'VE FOUND MY NEW CALLING HERE.
STARK'S BODYGUARD WAS A PUSHOVER. I COULD DEFINITELY GET USED TO THIS LIFE --

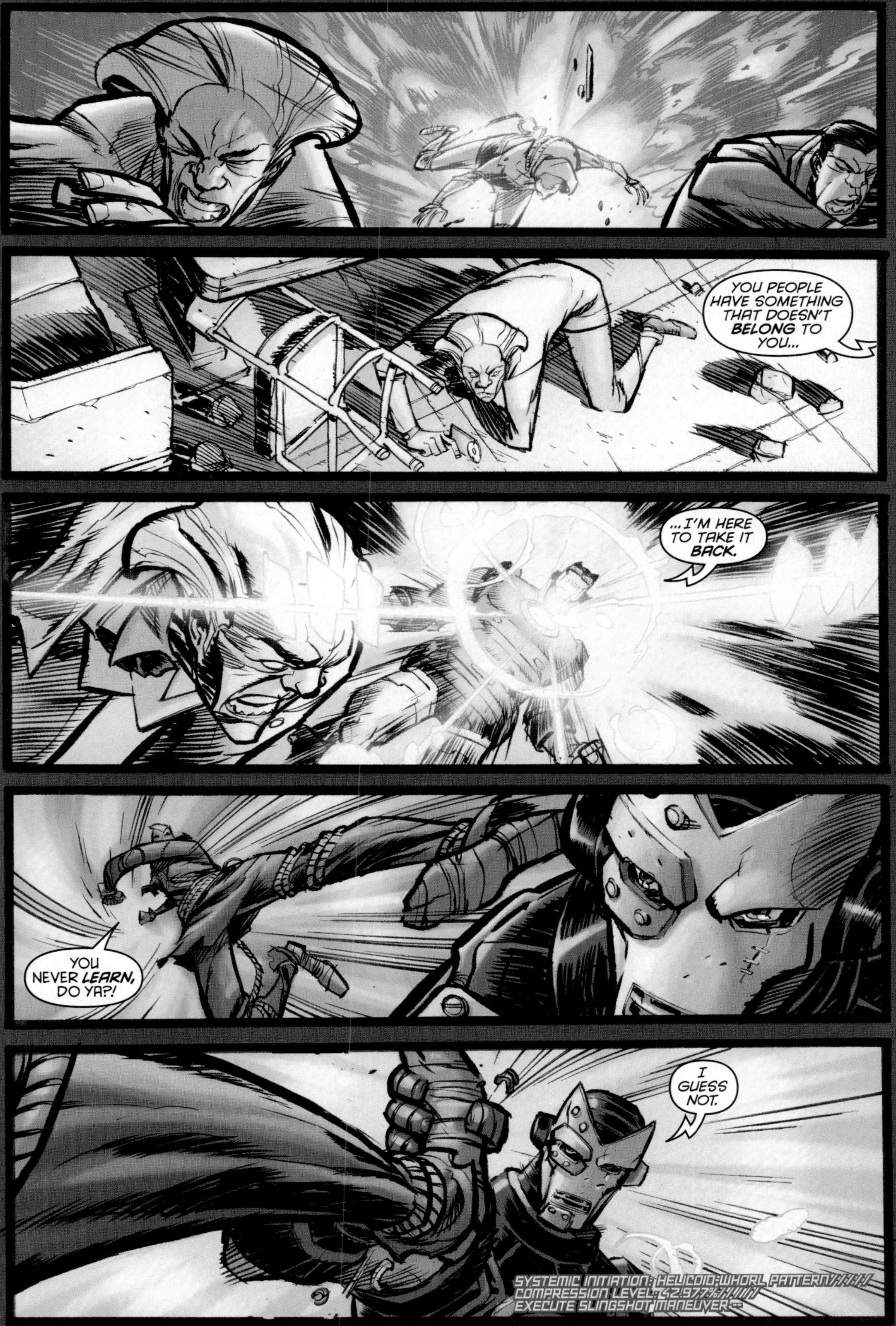
YOU PEOPLE HAVE SOMETHING THAT DOESN'T BELONG TO YOU...
...I'M HERE TO TAKE IT BACK.
YOU NEVER LEARN, DO YA?!
I GUESS NOT.
SYSTEMIC INITIATION: HELICOID:WHORL PATTERN//////
COMPRESSION LEVEL: 42.977%///////
EXECUTE SLINGSHOT MANEUVER --

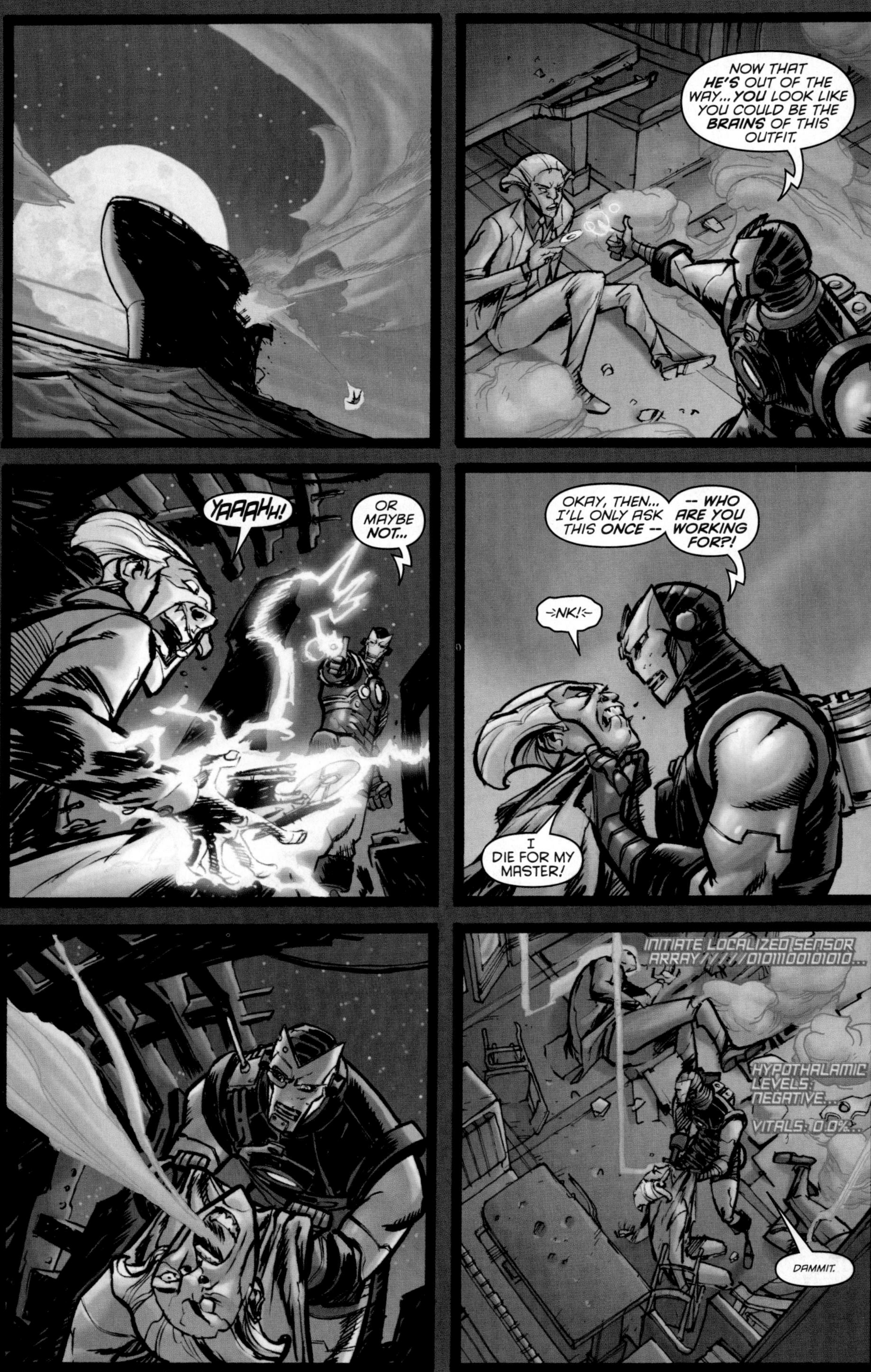

NOW THAT HE'S OUT OF THE WAY... YOU LOOK LIKE YOU COULD BE THE BRAINS OF THIS OUTFIT.
YAAAAH!
OR MAYBE NOT...
OKAY, THEN... I'LL ONLY ASK THIS ONCE --
-- WHO ARE YOU WORKING FOR?!
-NK!-
I DIE FOR MY MASTER!
INITIATE LOCALIZED SENSOR ARRAY//////010111001010101O...
HYPOTHALAMIC LEVELS: NEGATIVE...
VITALS: 0.0%...
DAMMIT.

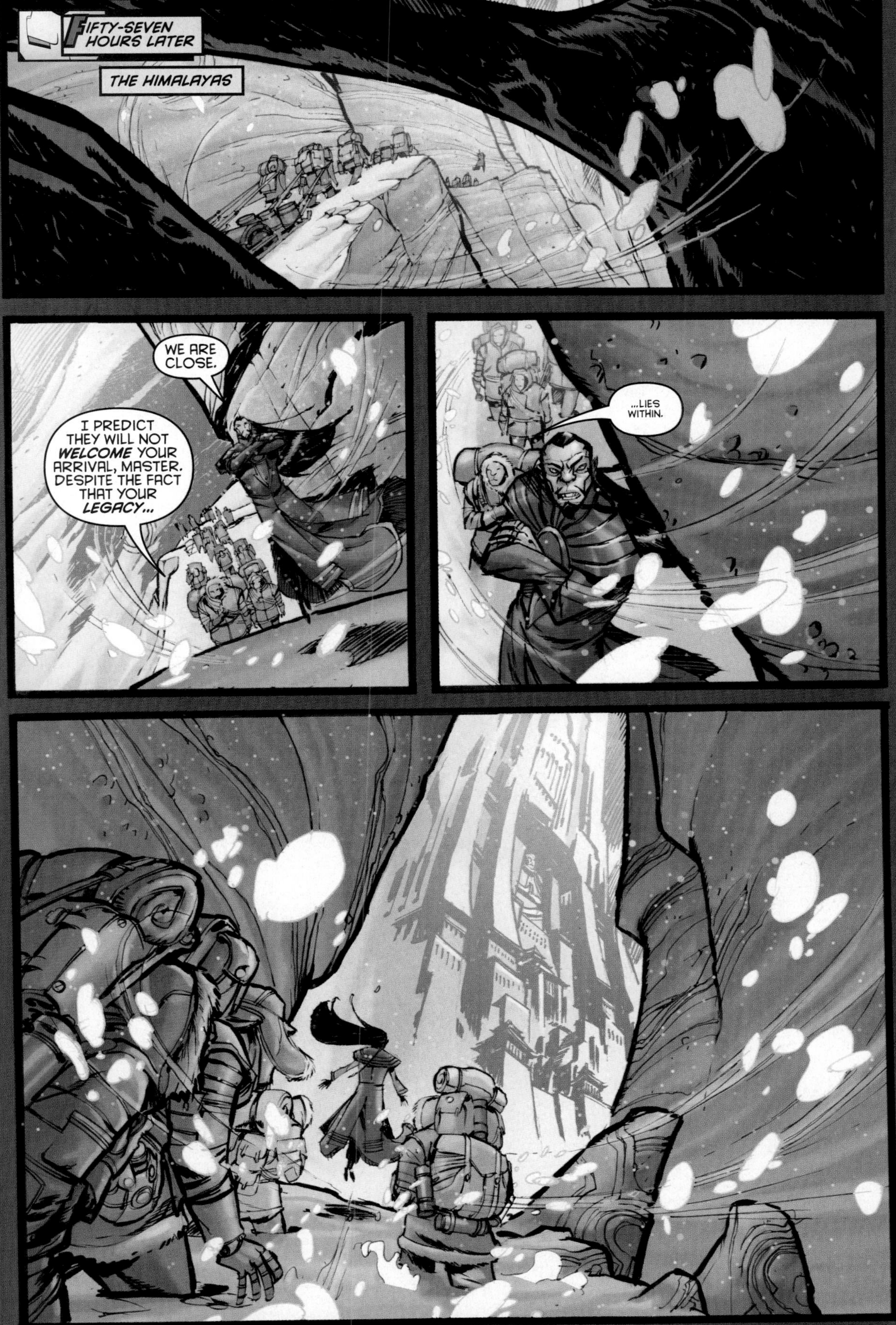
FIFTY-SEVEN HOURS LATER
THE HIMALAYAS
WE ARE CLOSE.
I PREDICT THEY WILL NOT WELCOME YOUR ARRIVAL, MASTER. DESPITE THE FACT THAT YOUR LEGACY...
...LIES WITHIN.

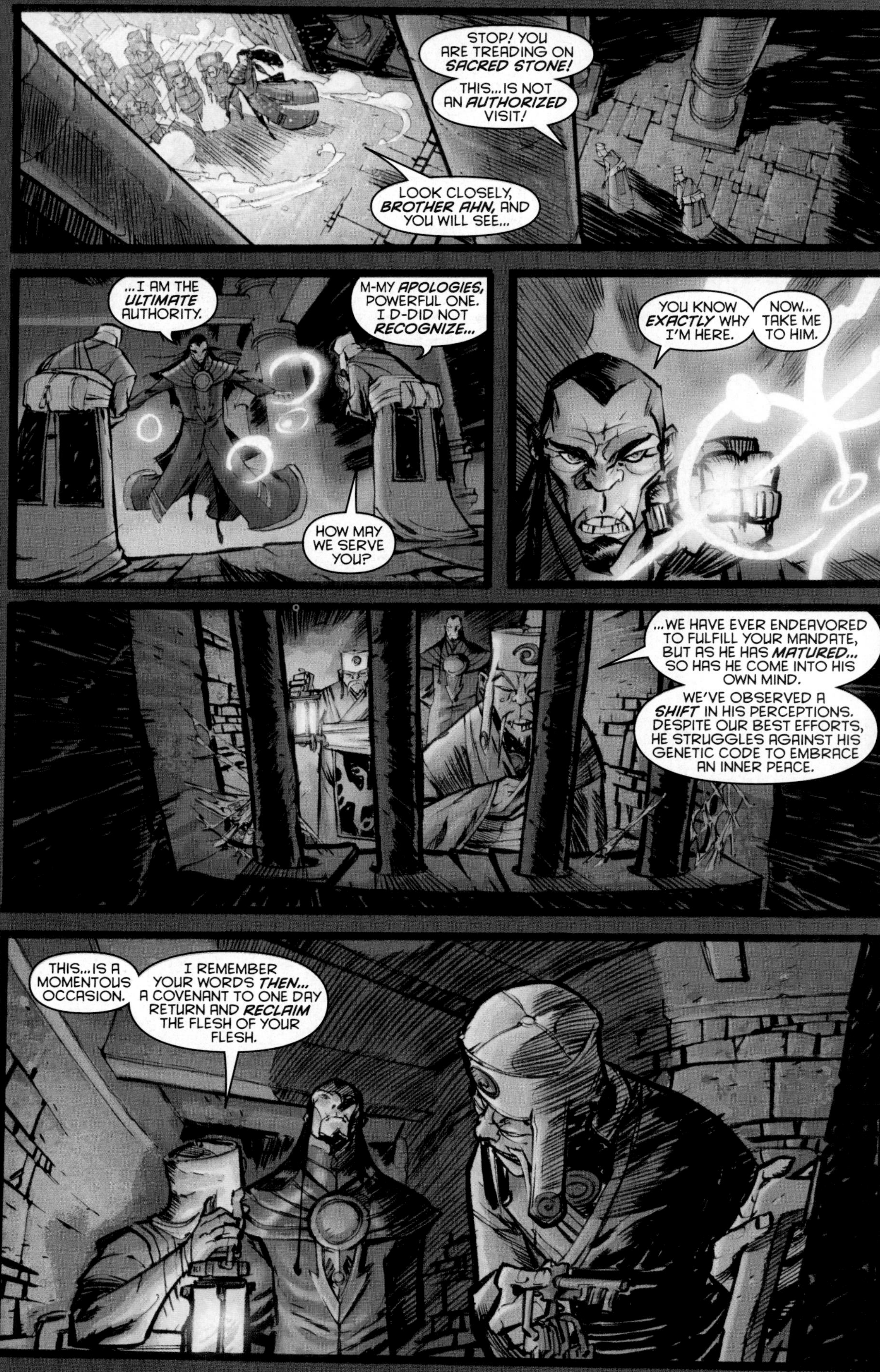
STOP! YOU ARE TREADING ON SACRED STONE!
THIS... IS NOT AN AUTHORIZED VISIT!
LOOK CLOSELY, BROTHER AHN, AND YOU WILL SEE...
...I AM THE ULTIMATE AUTHORITY.
M-MY APOLOGIES, POWERFUL ONE. I D-DID NOT RECOGNIZE...
HOW MAY WE SERVE YOU?
YOU KNOW EXACTLY WHY I'M HERE.
NOW... TAKE ME TO HIM.
...WE HAVE EVER ENDEAVORED TO FULFILL YOUR MANDATE, BUT AS HE HAS MATURED... SO HAS HE COME INTO HIS OWN MIND.
WE'VE OBSERVED A SHIFT IN HIS PERCEPTIONS. DESPITE OUR BEST EFFORTS, HE STRUGGLES AGAINST HIS GENETIC CODE TO EMBRACE AN INNER PEACE.
THIS... IS A MOMENTOUS OCCASION.
I REMEMBER YOUR WORDS THEN... A COVENANT TO ONE DAY RETURN AND RECLAIM THE FLESH OF YOUR FLESH.

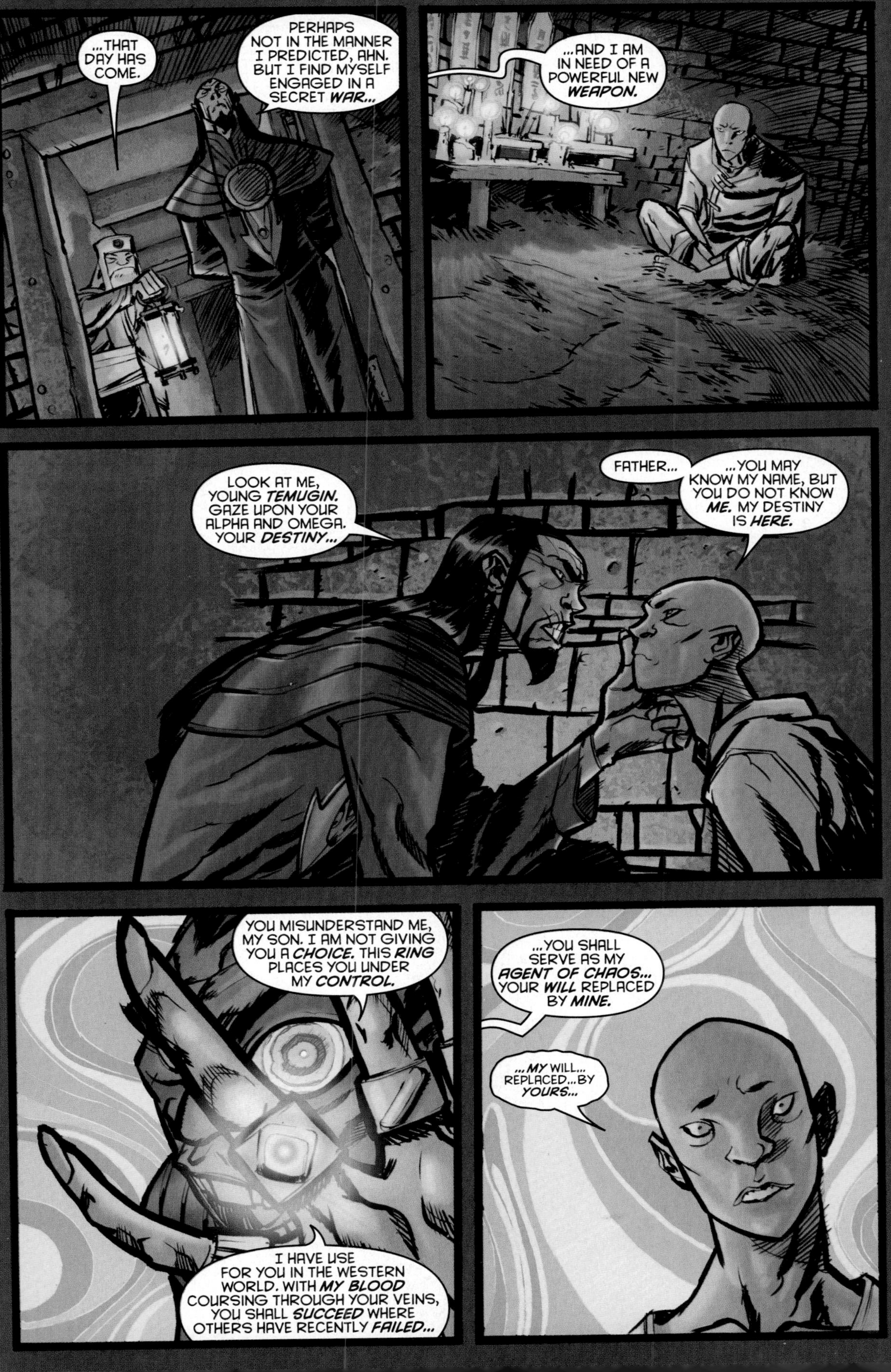
...THAT DAY HAS COME.
PERHAPS NOT IN THE MANNER I PREDICTED, AHN. BUT I FIND MYSELF ENGAGED IN A SECRET WAR...
...AND I AM IN NEED OF A POWERFUL NEW WEAPON.
LOOK AT ME, YOUNG TEMUGIN. GAZE UPON YOUR ALPHA AND OMEGA. YOUR DESTINY...
FATHER...
...YOU MAY KNOW MY NAME, BUT YOU DO NOT KNOW ME. MY DESTINY IS HERE.
YOU MISUNDERSTAND ME, MY SON. I AM NOT GIVING YOU A CHOICE. THIS RING PLACES YOU UNDER MY CONTROL.
I HAVE USE FOR YOU IN THE WESTERN WORLD. WITH MY BLOOD COURSING THROUGH YOUR VEINS, YOU SHALL SUCCEED WHERE OTHERS HAVE RECENTLY FAILED...
...YOU SHALL SERVE AS MY AGENT OF CHAOS... YOUR WILL REPLACED BY MINE.
...MY WILL... REPLACED...BY YOURS...

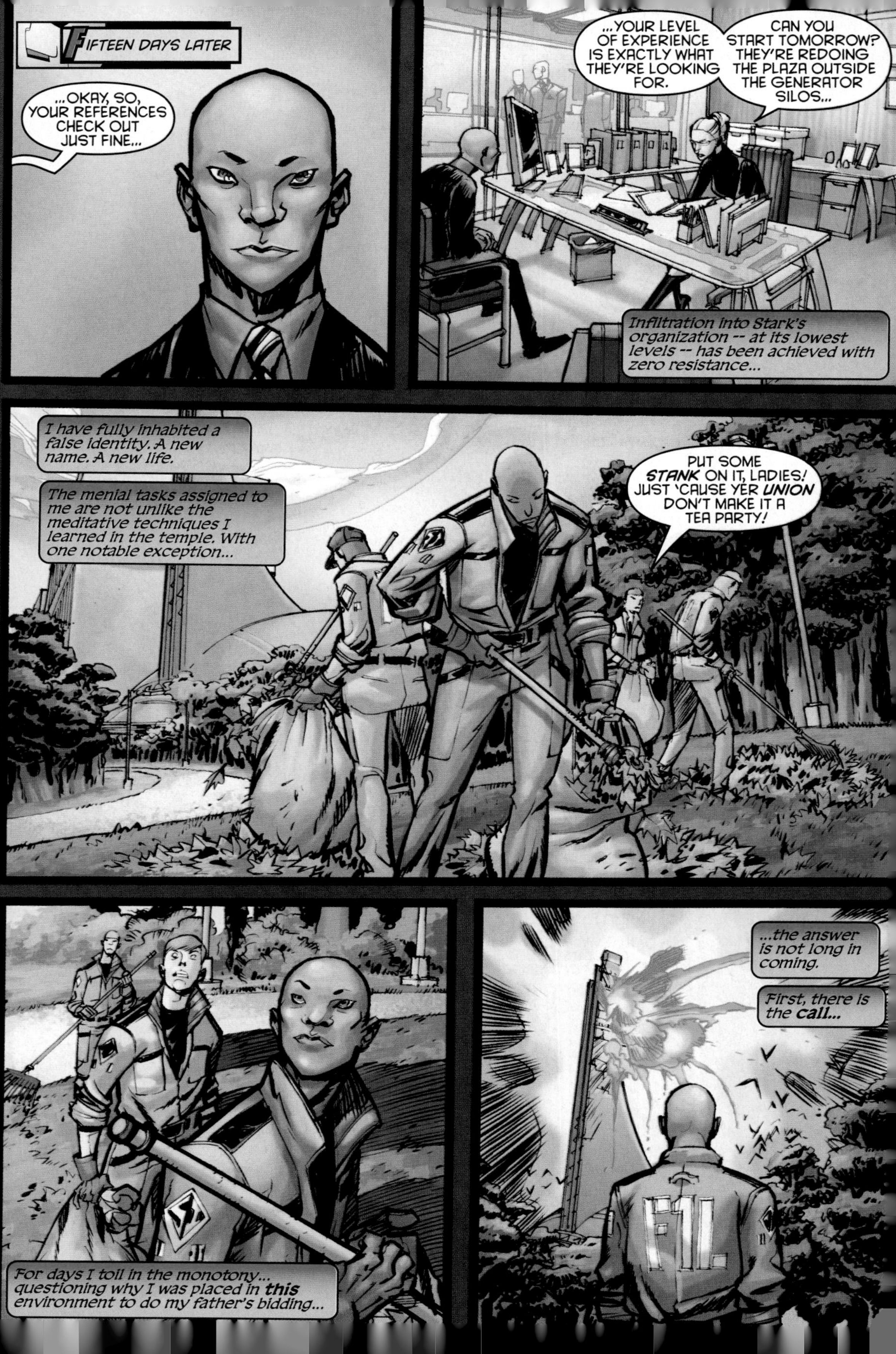
FIFTEEN DAYS LATER
...OKAY, SO, YOUR REFERENCES CHECK OUT JUST FINE...
...YOUR LEVEL OF EXPERIENCE IS EXACTLY WHAT THEY'RE LOOKING FOR.
CAN YOU START TOMORROW? THEY'RE REDOING THE PLAZA OUTSIDE THE GENERATOR SILOS...
Infiltration into Stark's organization -- at its lowest levels -- has been achieved with zero resistance...
I have fully inhabited a false identity. A new name. A new life.
The menial tasks assigned to me are not unlike the meditative techniques I learned in the temple. With one notable exception...
PUT SOME STANK ON IT, LADIES! JUST 'CAUSE YER UNION DON'T MAKE IT A TEA PARTY!
For days I toil in the monotony... questioning why I was placed in this environment to do my father's bidding...
...the answer is not long in coming.
First, there is the call...

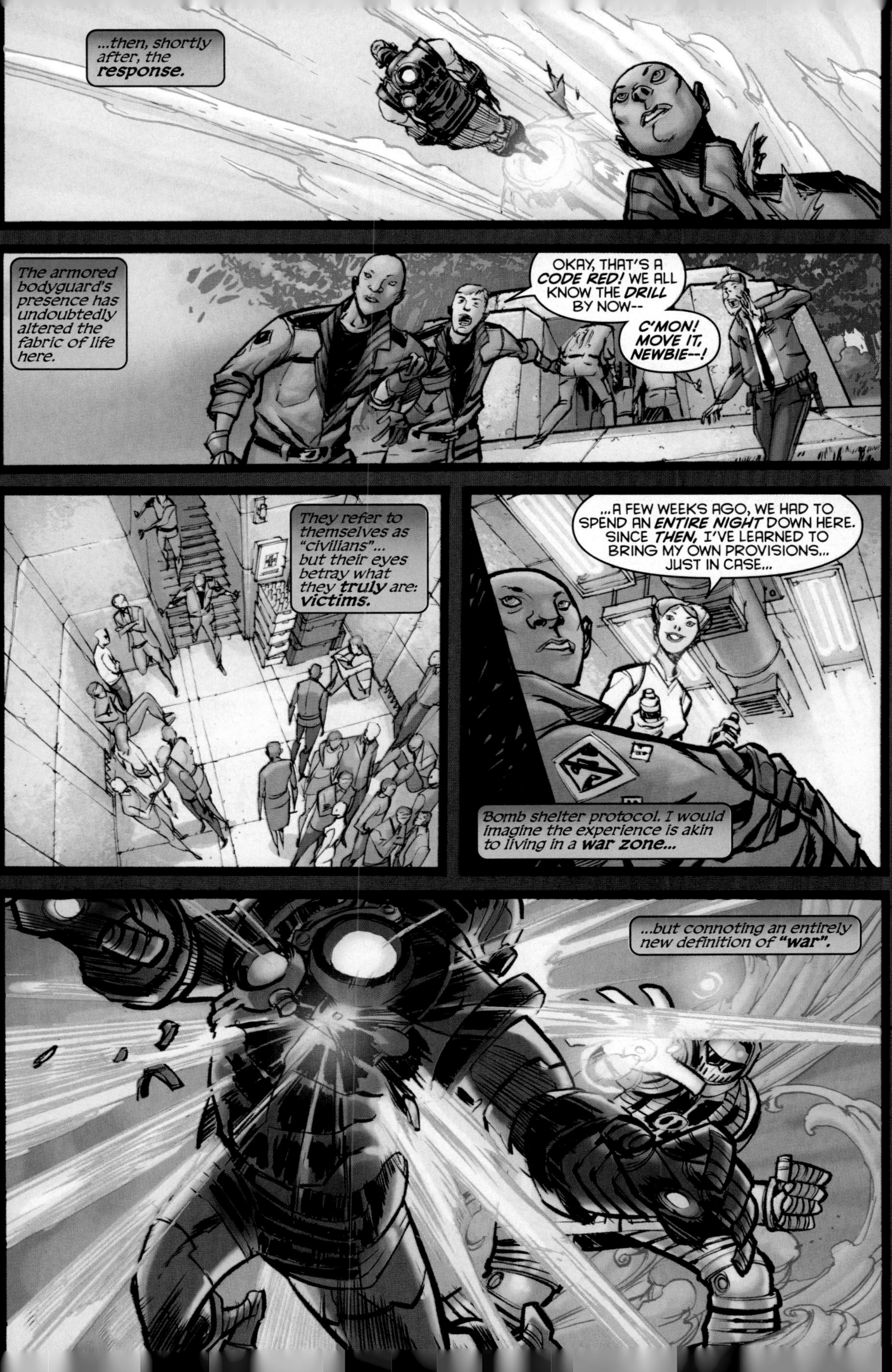
...then, shortly after, the **response.**
The armored bodyguard's presence has undoubtedly altered the fabric of life here.
OKAY, THAT'S A ***CODE RED!*** WE ALL KNOW THE ***DRILL*** BY NOW--
C'MON! MOVE IT, NEWBIE--!
They refer to themselves as "civilians"... but their eyes betray what they **truly** are: **victims.**
...A FEW WEEKS AGO, WE HAD TO SPEND AN ***ENTIRE NIGHT*** DOWN HERE. SINCE ***THEN,*** I'VE LEARNED TO BRING MY OWN PROVISIONS... JUST IN CASE...
Bomb shelter protocol. I would imagine the experience is akin to living in a **war zone...**
...but connoting an entirely new definition of **"war".**

-- NICE, STEADY PACE, PEOPLE. BUT KEEP IT MOVING.

WE'RE STILL IN CODE RED BUT WE'VE GOT THE ORDER TO EVACUATE THE FACTORY GROUNDS. STAY CLEAR OF SECTION NINE --

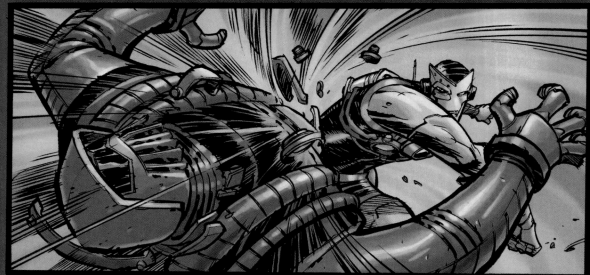

I am compelled to gaze upon the face of my father's enemy...

HUHN--!

WHU--?! WHAT ARE YOU *DOING* HERE?! IT IS TOO *DANGEROUS* FOR CIVILIAN EMPLOYEES--!

FIND THE NEAREST EXIT OFF THE GROUNDS! THIS SITUATION WILL SURELY *ESCALATE!* NOW GO--!

I will not be deterred.

I will look into Anthony Stark's eyes today.

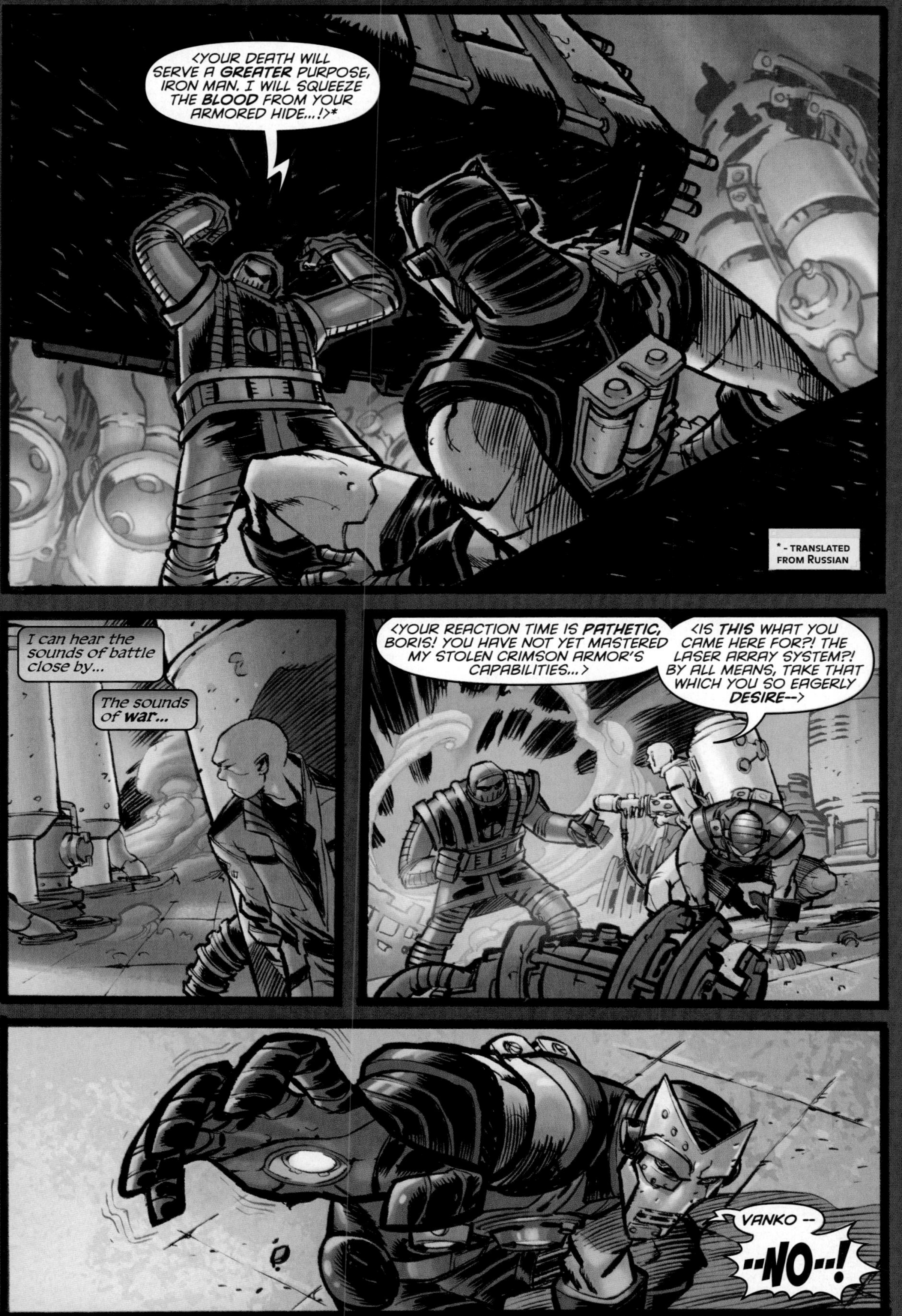
<YOUR DEATH WILL SERVE A GREATER PURPOSE, IRON MAN. I WILL SQUEEZE THE BLOOD FROM YOUR ARMORED HIDE...!>*
* - TRANSLATED FROM RUSSIAN
I can hear the sounds of battle close by...
The sounds of war...
<YOUR REACTION TIME IS PATHETIC, BORIS! YOU HAVE NOT YET MASTERED MY STOLEN CRIMSON ARMOR'S CAPABILITIES...>
<IS THIS WHAT YOU CAME HERE FOR?! THE LASER ARRAY SYSTEM?! BY ALL MEANS, TAKE THAT WHICH YOU SO EAGERLY DESIRE-->
VANKO --
--NO--!

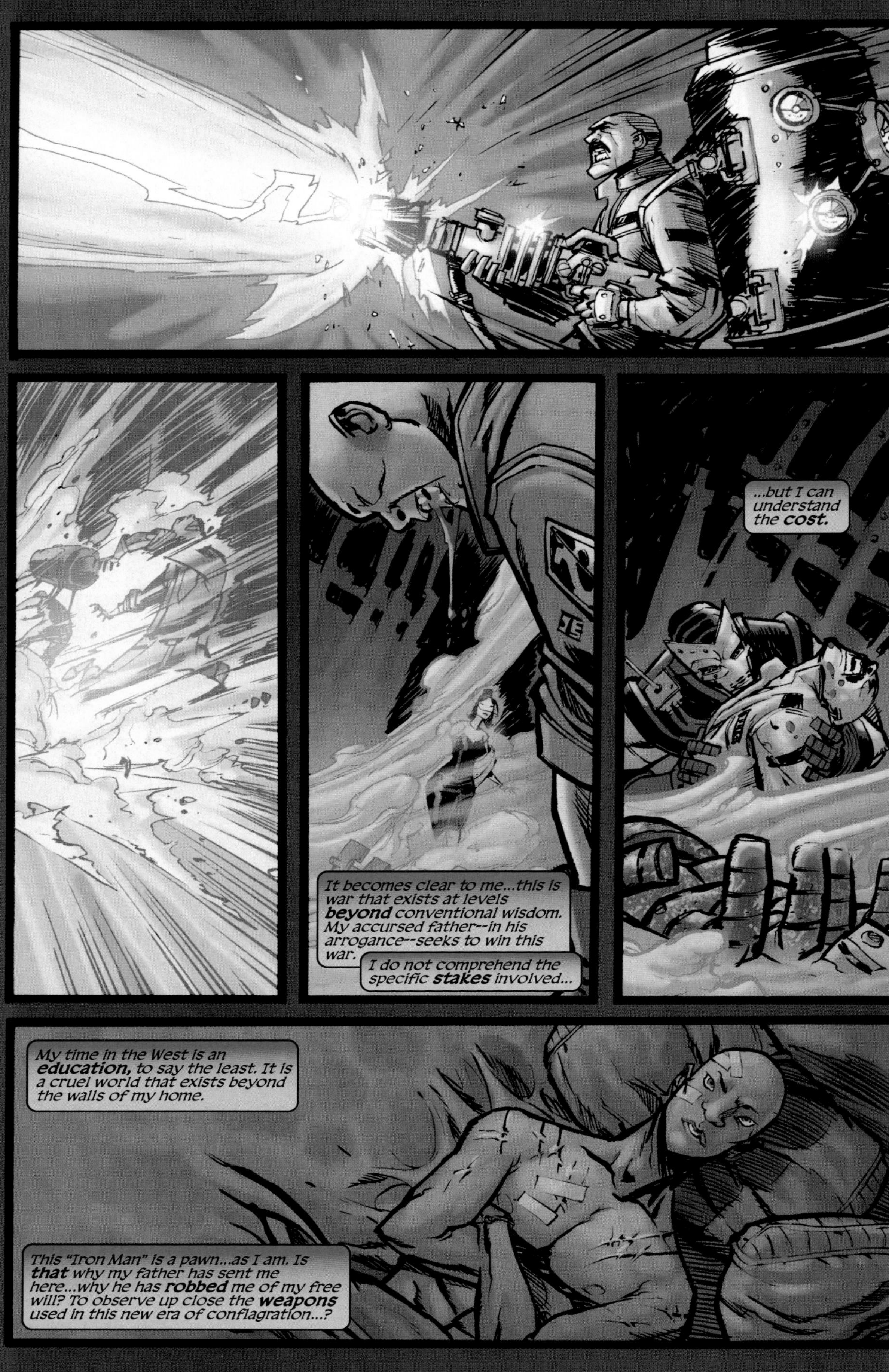
...but I can understand the cost.
It becomes clear to me...this is war that exists at levels beyond conventional wisdom. My accursed father--in his arrogance--seeks to win this war.
I do not comprehend the specific stakes involved...
My time in the West is an education, to say the least. It is a cruel world that exists beyond the walls of my home.
This "Iron Man" is a pawn...as I am. Is that why my father has sent me here...why he has robbed me of my free will? To observe up close the weapons used in this new era of conflagration...?

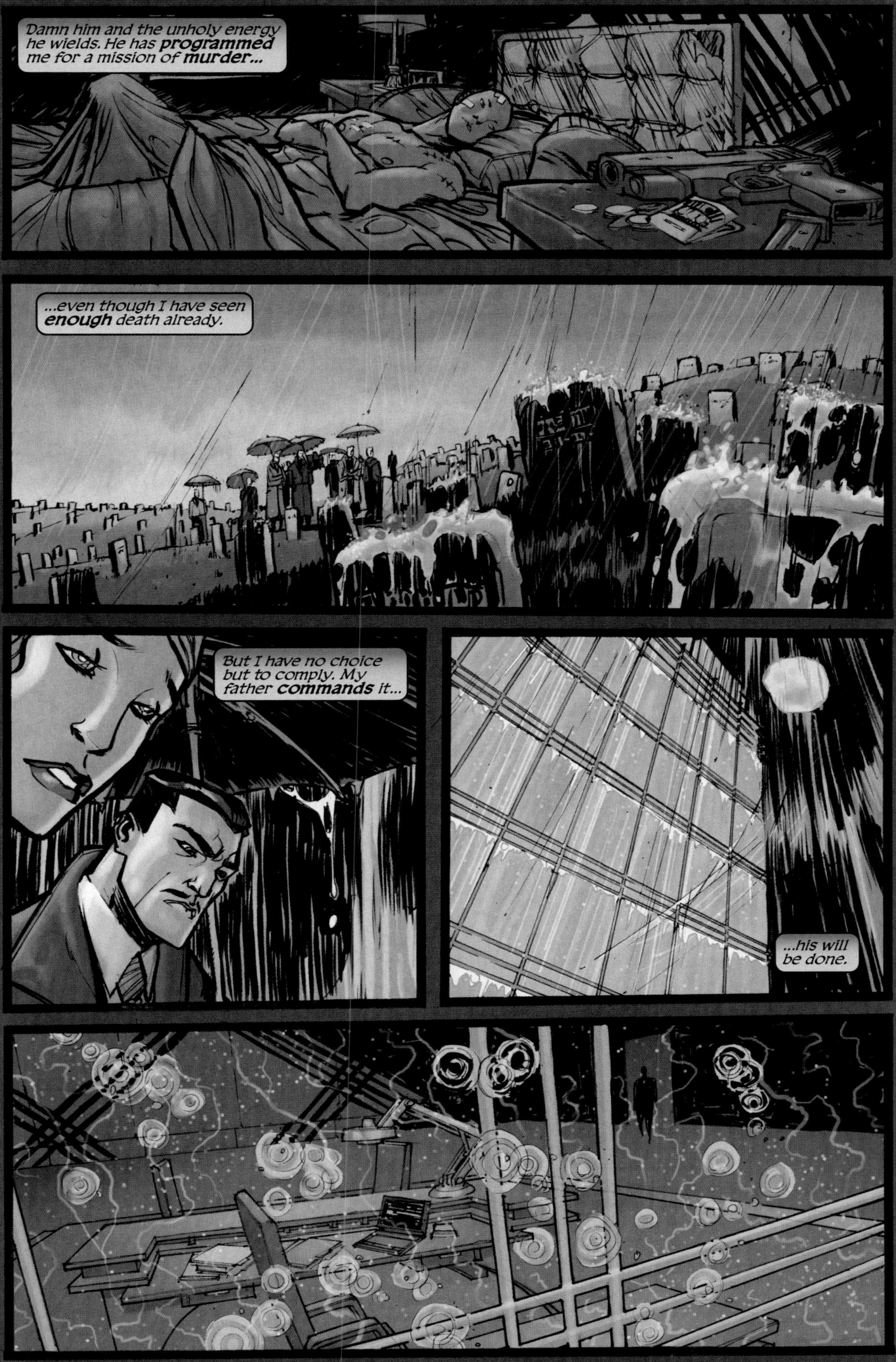
Damn him and the unholy energy he wields. He has **programmed** me for a mission of **murder...**
...even though I have seen **enough** death already.
But I have no choice but to comply. My father **commands** it...
...his will be done.

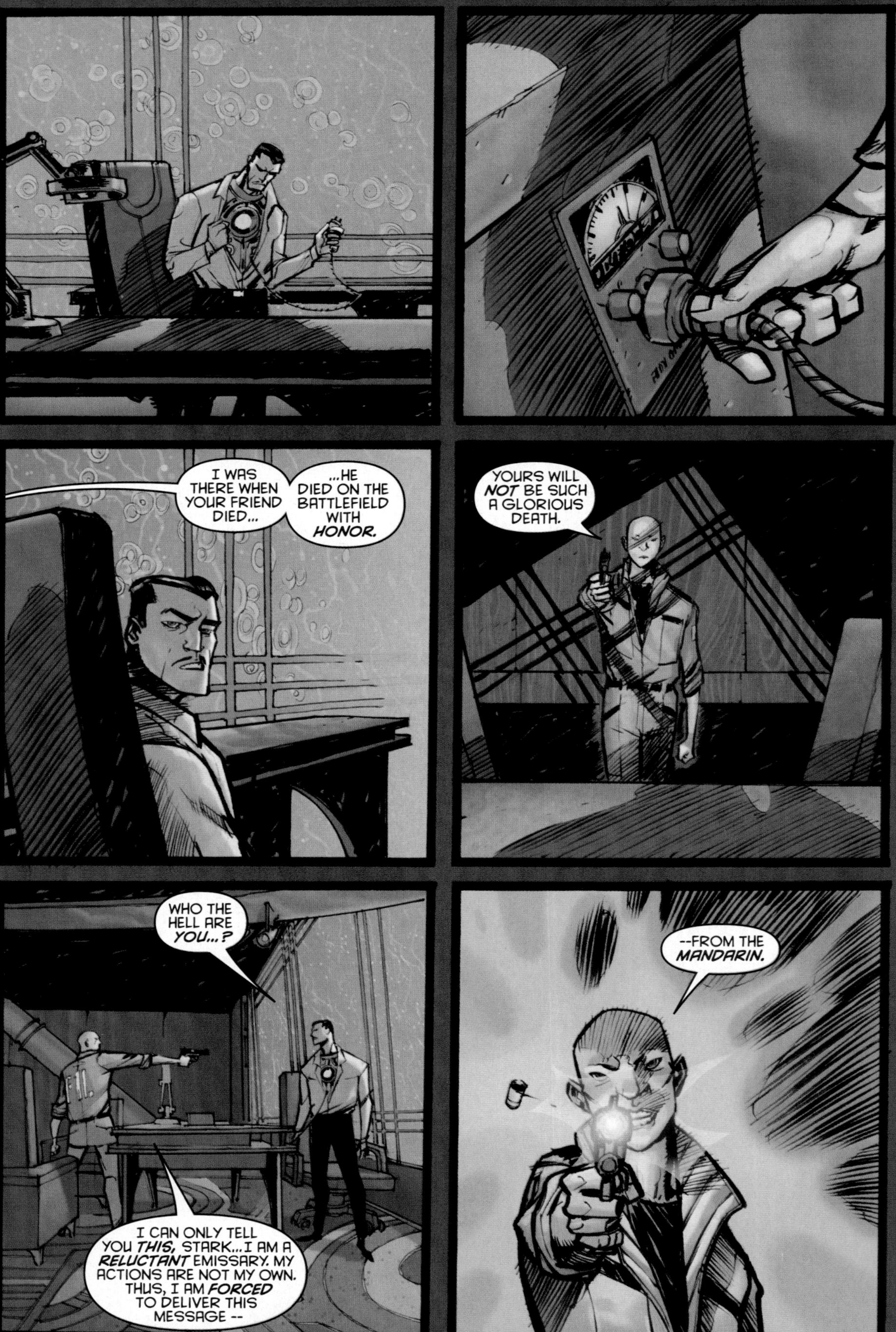
I WAS THERE WHEN YOUR FRIEND DIED...
...HE DIED ON THE BATTLEFIELD WITH HONOR.
YOURS WILL NOT BE SUCH A GLORIOUS DEATH.
WHO THE HELL ARE YOU...?
I CAN ONLY TELL YOU THIS, STARK... I AM A RELUCTANT EMISSARY. MY ACTIONS ARE NOT MY OWN. THUS, I AM FORCED TO DELIVER THIS MESSAGE --
--FROM THE MANDARIN.

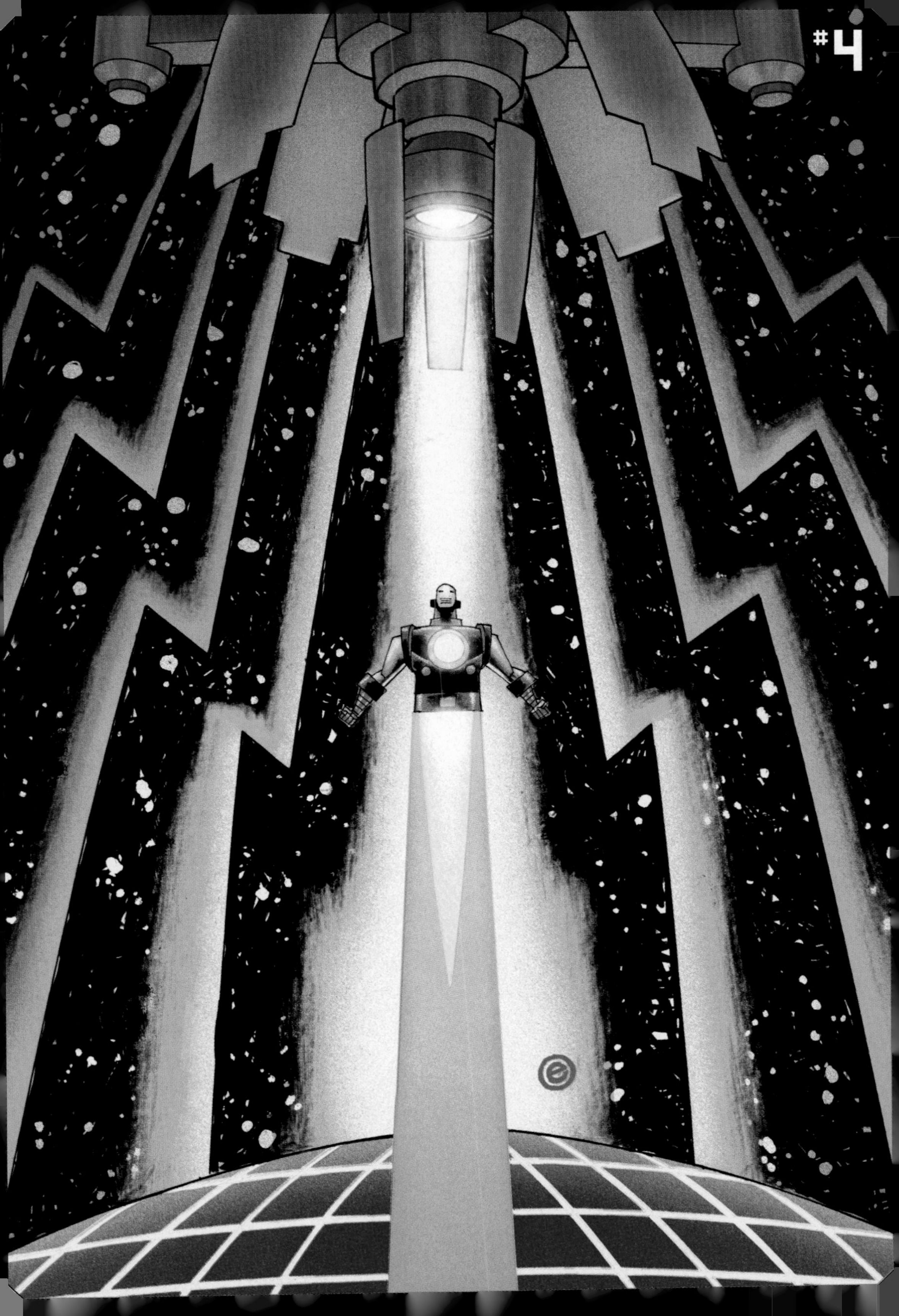
#4

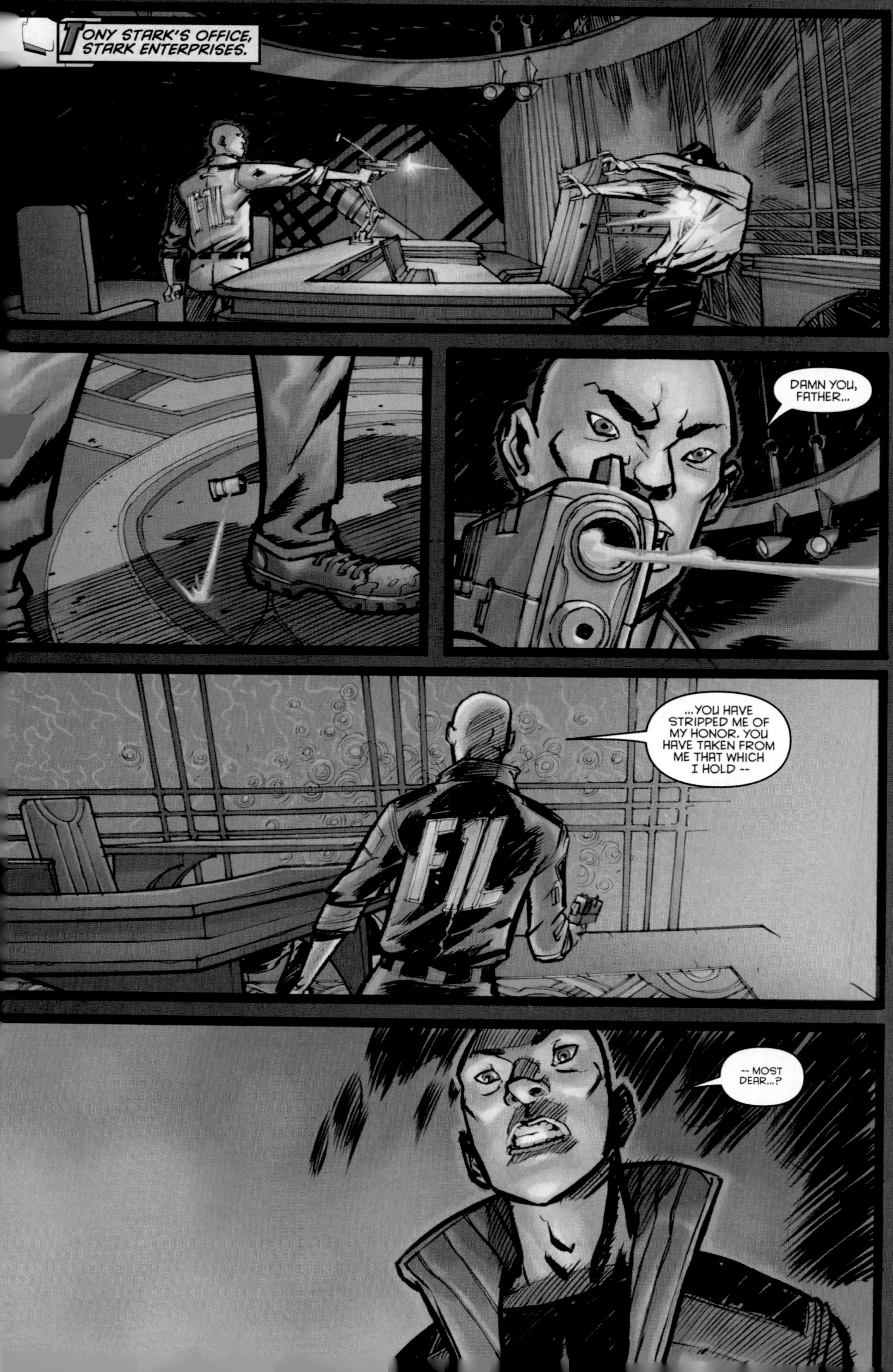
TONY STARK'S OFFICE, STARK ENTERPRISES.
DAMN YOU, FATHER...
...YOU HAVE STRIPPED ME OF MY HONOR. YOU HAVE TAKEN FROM ME THAT WHICH I HOLD --
-- MOST DEAR...?

OF COURSE. IT MAKES PERFECT SENSE...

WHO *ELSE* COULD MASTER SUCH A WEAPON BUT ITS *INVENTOR...*?

UNFORTUNATELY, A CHEST PLATE CAN ONLY PROTECT *SO MUCH,* MR. STARK...

RIGHT.

01001011 / / / /
CHEST BEAMER: ENGAGE PHOTOSTROBE --

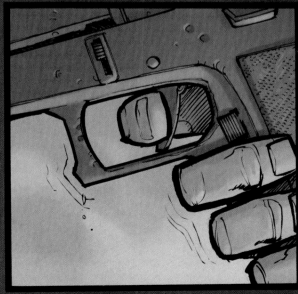

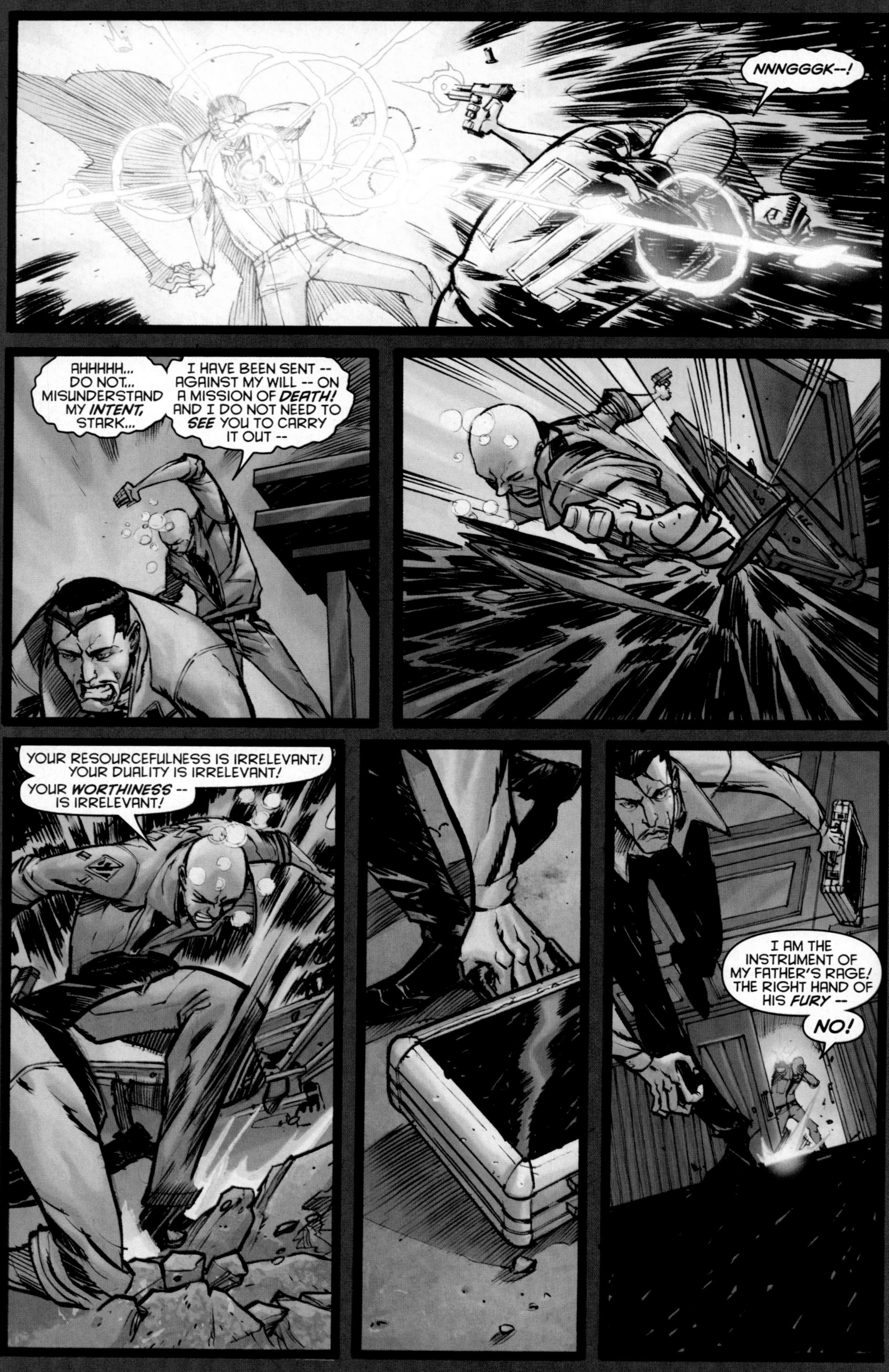
NNNGGGK--!
AHHHHH... DO NOT... MISUNDERSTAND MY *INTENT,* STARK...
I HAVE BEEN SENT -- AGAINST MY WILL -- ON A MISSION OF *DEATH!* AND I DO NOT NEED TO *SEE* YOU TO CARRY IT OUT --
YOUR RESOURCEFULNESS IS IRRELEVANT! YOUR DUALITY IS IRRELEVANT!
YOUR *WORTHINESS* -- IS IRRELEVANT!
I AM THE INSTRUMENT OF MY FATHER'S RAGE! THE RIGHT HAND OF HIS *FURY* --
NO!

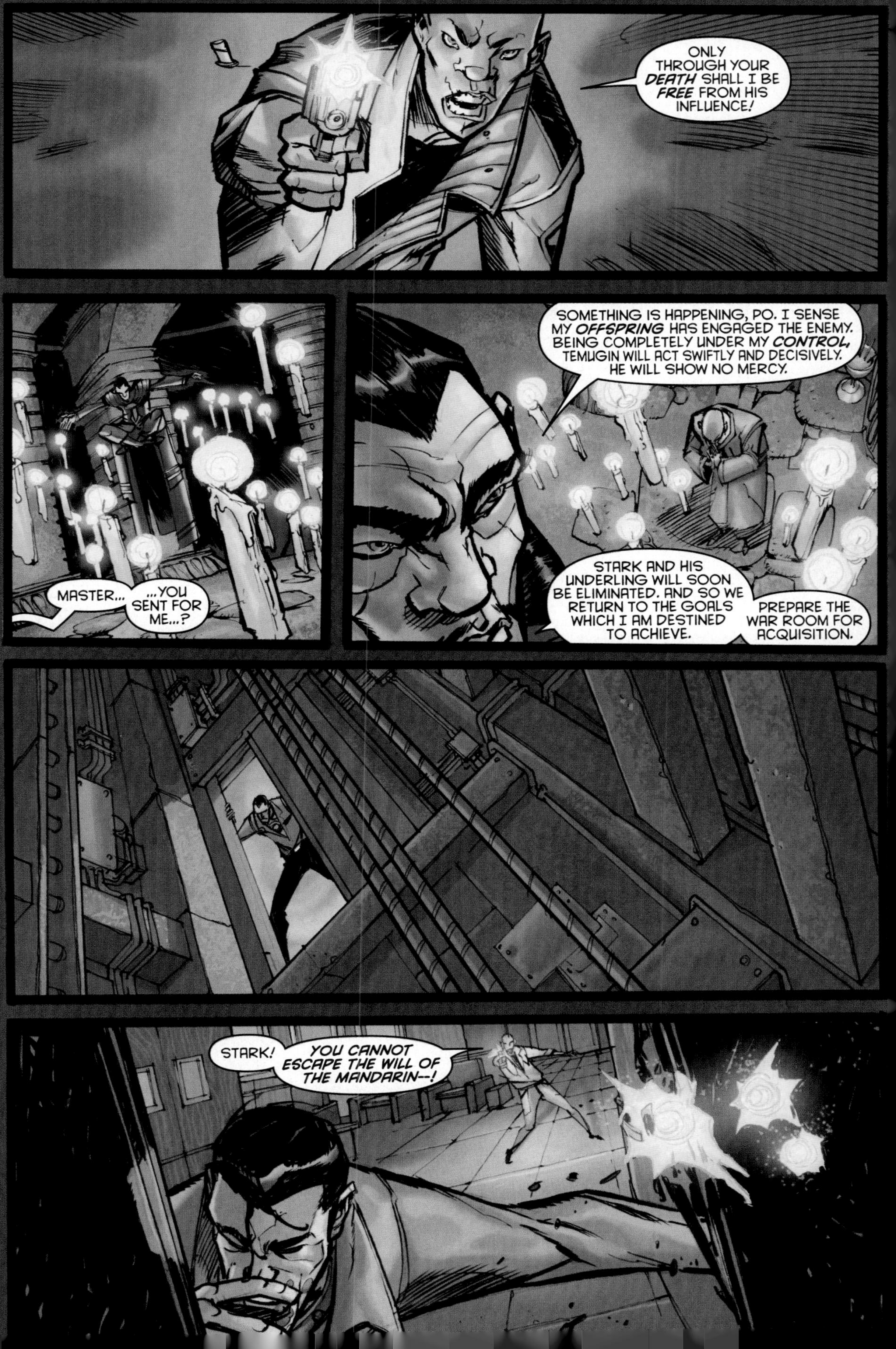
ONLY THROUGH YOUR DEATH SHALL I BE FREE FROM HIS INFLUENCE!
MASTER...
...YOU SENT FOR ME...?
SOMETHING IS HAPPENING, PO. I SENSE MY OFFSPRING HAS ENGAGED THE ENEMY. BEING COMPLETELY UNDER MY CONTROL, TEMUGIN WILL ACT SWIFTLY AND DECISIVELY. HE WILL SHOW NO MERCY.
STARK AND HIS UNDERLING WILL SOON BE ELIMINATED. AND SO WE RETURN TO THE GOALS WHICH I AM DESTINED TO ACHIEVE.
PREPARE THE WAR ROOM FOR ACQUISITION.
STARK!
YOU CANNOT ESCAPE THE WILL OF THE MANDARIN--!

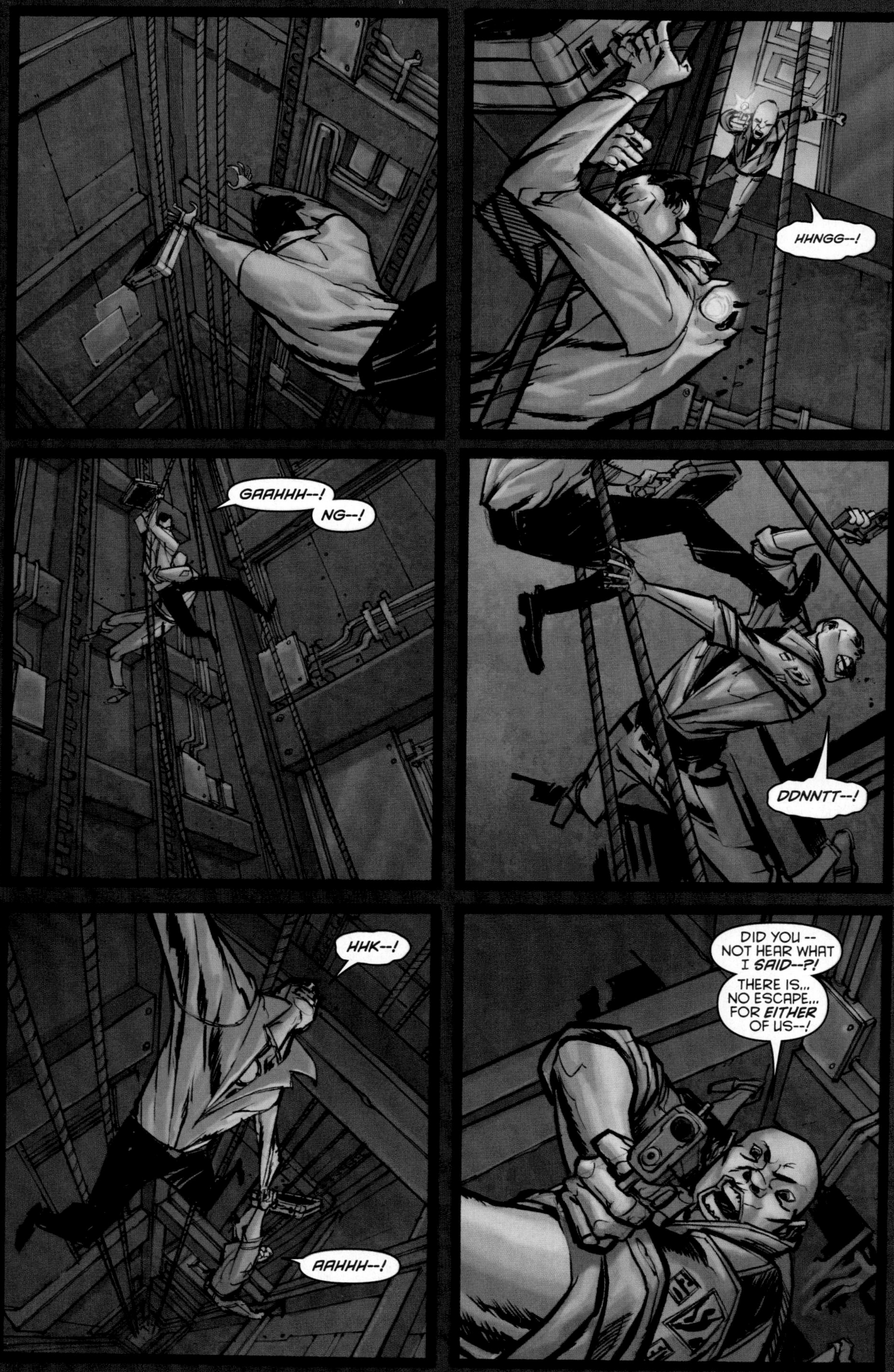
HHNGG--!
GAAHHH--!
NG--!
DDNNTT--!
HHK--!
AAHHH--!
DID YOU -- NOT HEAR WHAT I SAID--?! THERE IS... NO ESCAPE... FOR EITHER OF US--!

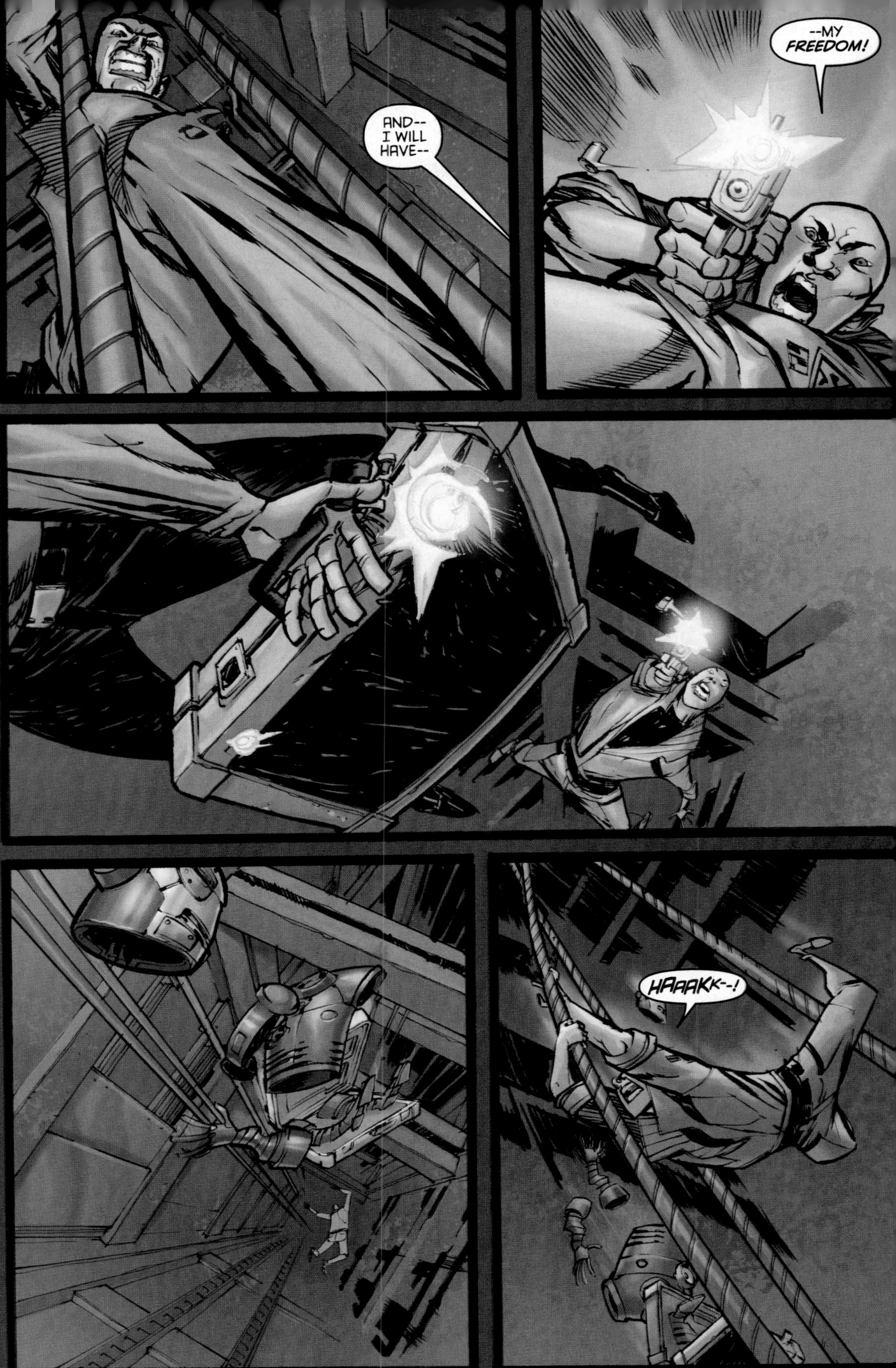
AND-- I WILL HAVE--
--MY FREEDOM!
HAAAKK--!

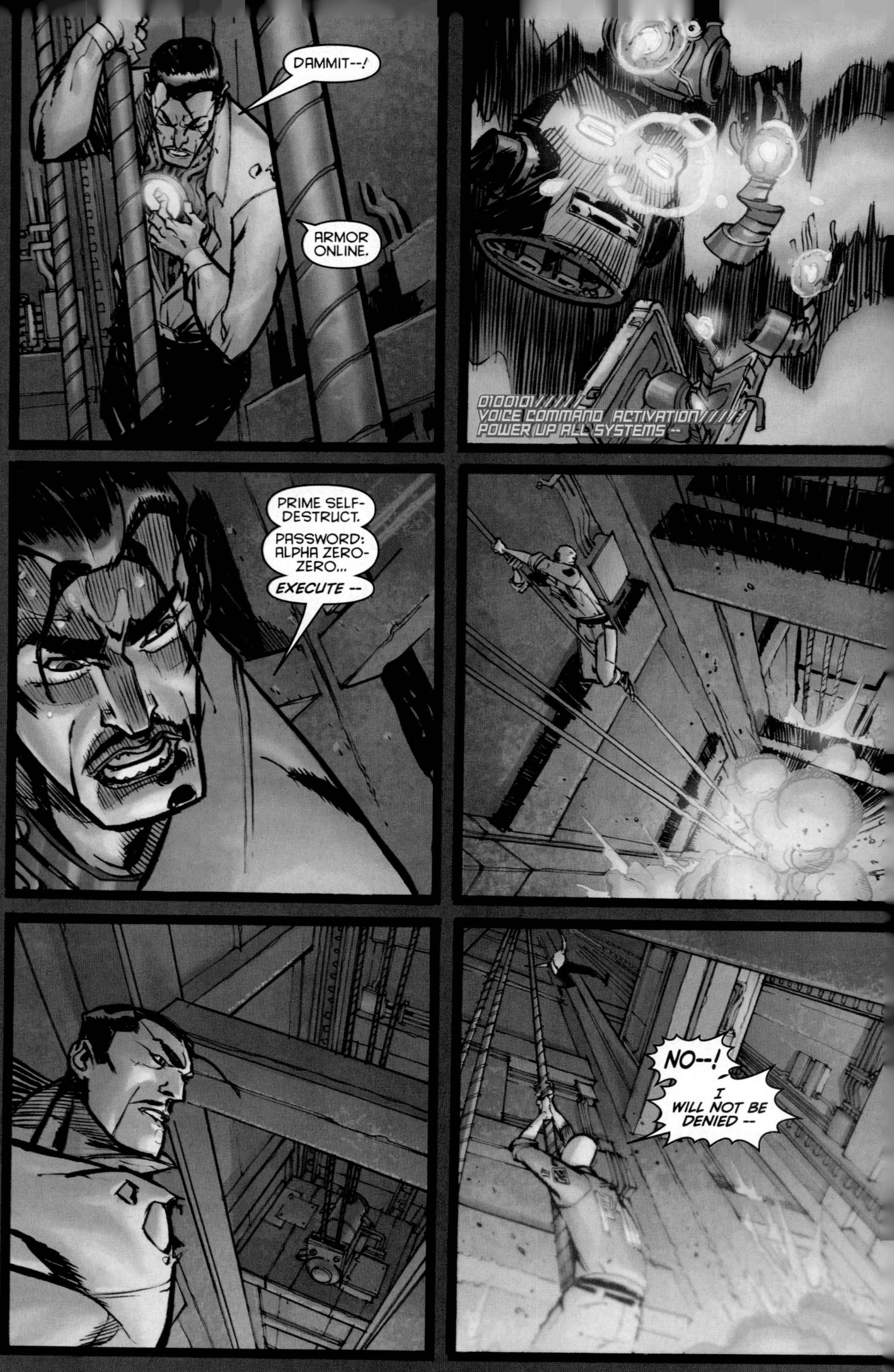
DAMMIT--!
ARMOR ONLINE.
0100101//////
VOICE COMMAND ACTIVATION//////
POWER UP ALL SYSTEMS --
PRIME SELF-DESTRUCT.
PASSWORD: ALPHA ZERO-ZERO...
EXECUTE --
NO--!
I WILL NOT BE DENIED --

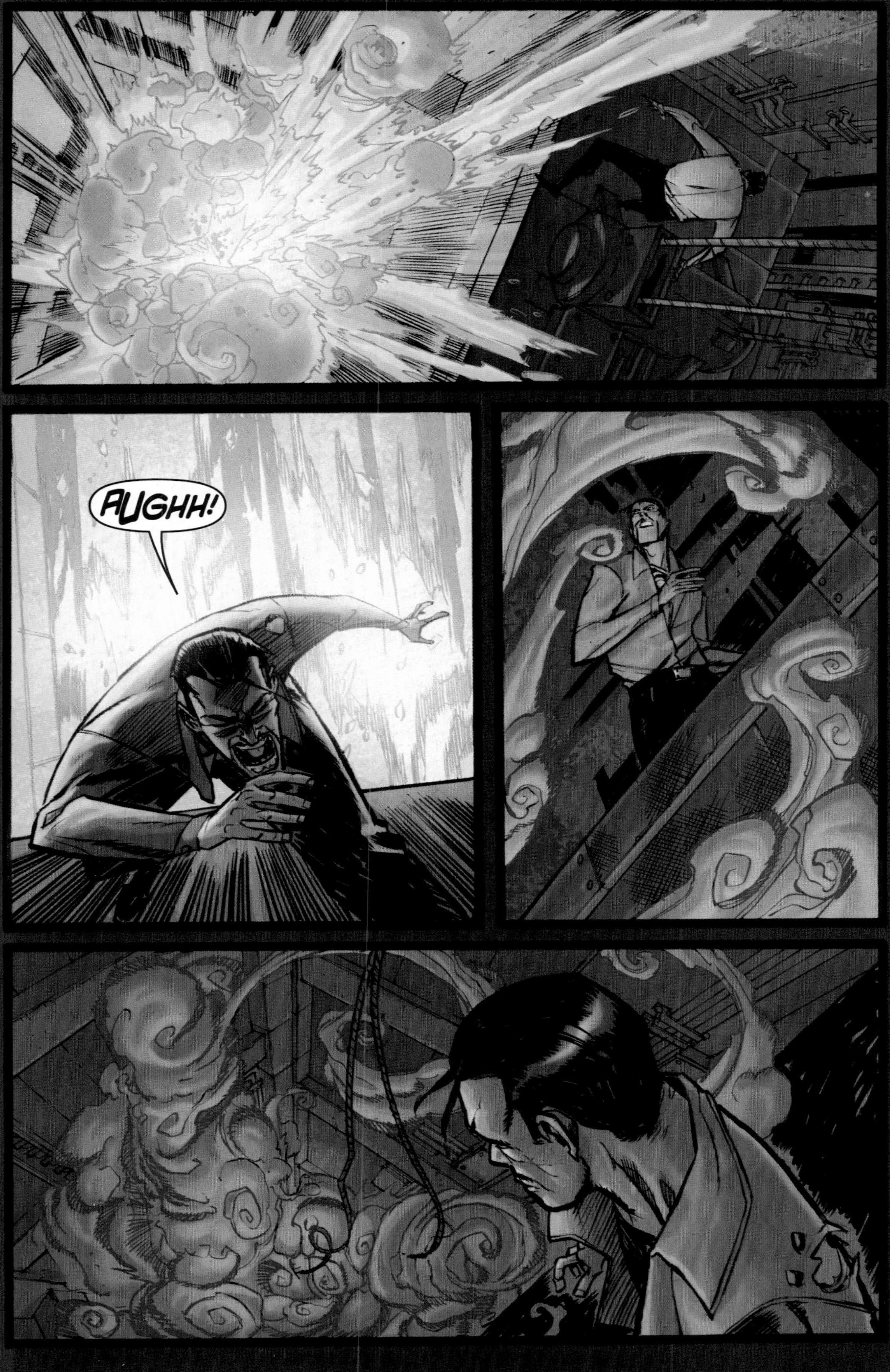
AUGHH!

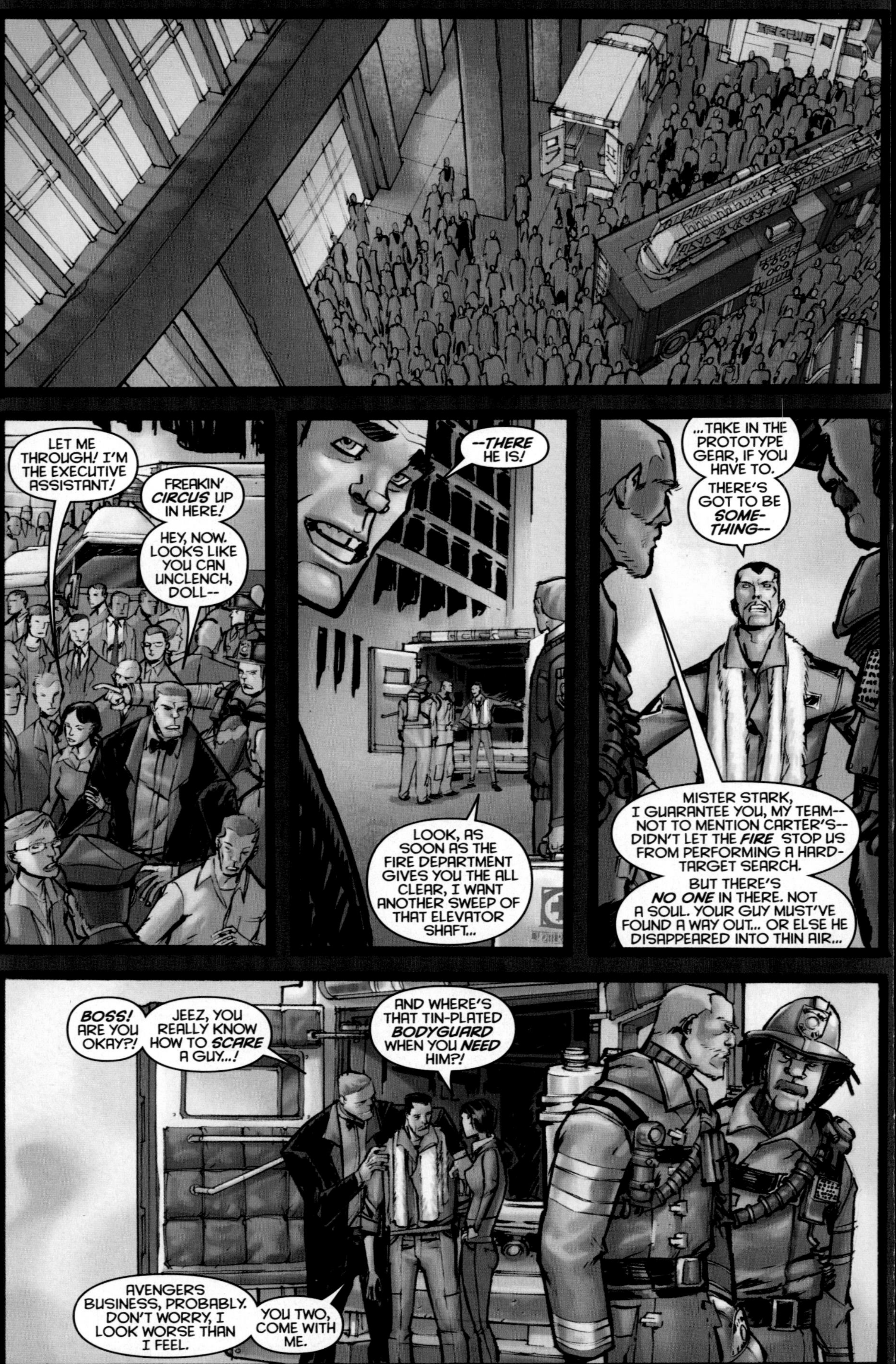
LET ME THROUGH! I'M THE EXECUTIVE ASSISTANT!
FREAKIN' *CIRCUS* UP IN HERE!
HEY, NOW. LOOKS LIKE YOU CAN UNCLENCH, DOLL--
--*THERE* HE IS!
LOOK, AS SOON AS THE FIRE DEPARTMENT GIVES YOU THE ALL CLEAR, I WANT ANOTHER SWEEP OF THAT ELEVATOR SHAFT...
...TAKE IN THE PROTOTYPE GEAR, IF YOU HAVE TO.
THERE'S GOT TO BE *SOME-THING*--
MISTER STARK, I GUARANTEE YOU, MY TEAM-- NOT TO MENTION CARTER'S-- DIDN'T LET THE *FIRE* STOP US FROM PERFORMING A HARD-TARGET SEARCH.
BUT THERE'S *NO ONE* IN THERE. NOT A SOUL. YOUR GUY MUST'VE FOUND A WAY OUT... OR ELSE HE DISAPPEARED INTO THIN AIR...
BOSS! ARE YOU OKAY?!
JEEZ, YOU REALLY KNOW HOW TO *SCARE* A GUY...!
AND WHERE'S THAT TIN-PLATED *BODYGUARD* WHEN YOU *NEED* HIM?!
AVENGERS BUSINESS, PROBABLY. DON'T WORRY, I LOOK WORSE THAN I FEEL.
YOU TWO, COME WITH ME.

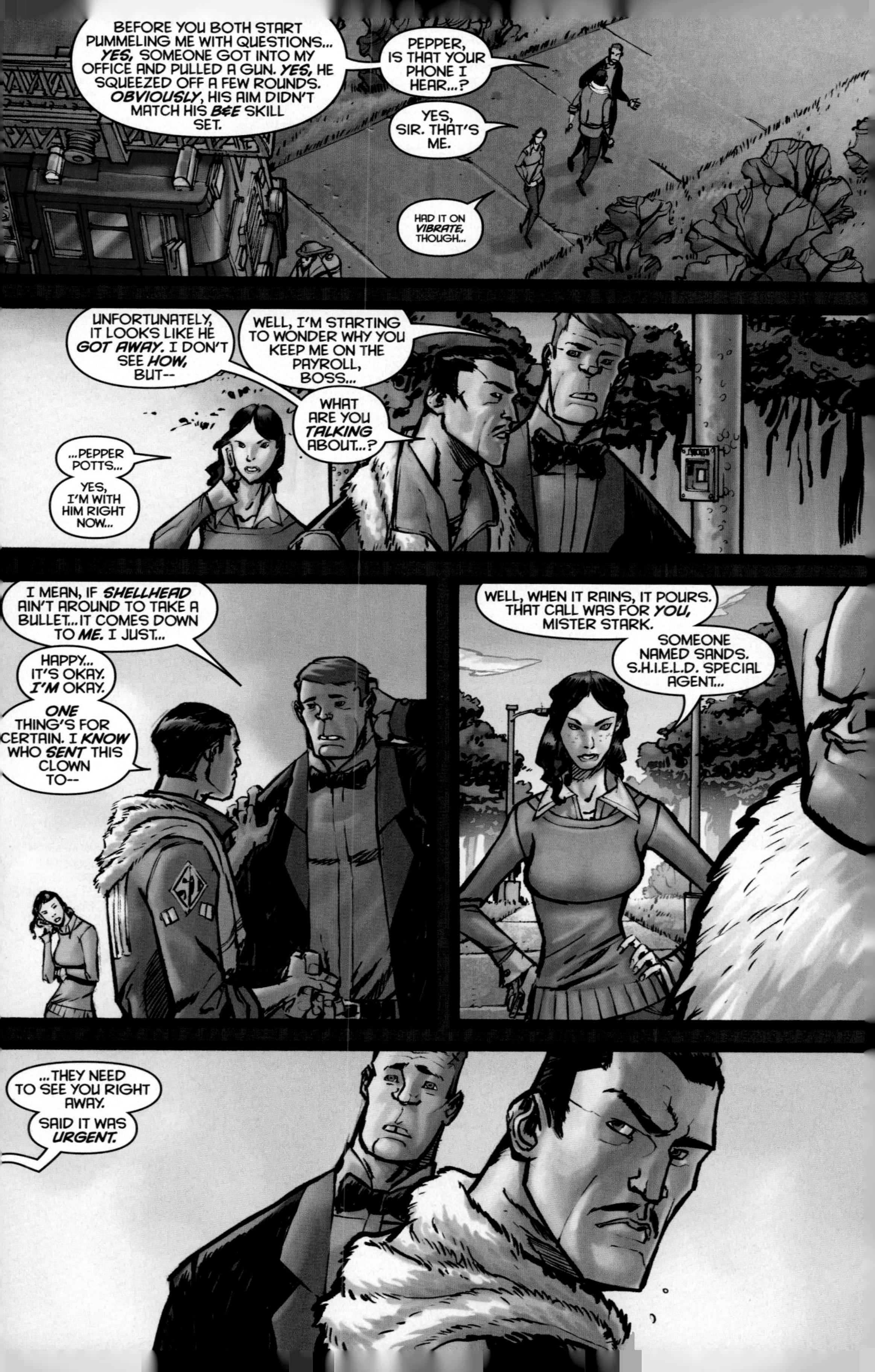
BEFORE YOU BOTH START PUMMELING ME WITH QUESTIONS... *YES,* SOMEONE GOT INTO MY OFFICE AND PULLED A GUN. *YES,* HE SQUEEZED OFF A FEW ROUNDS. *OBVIOUSLY,* HIS AIM DIDN'T MATCH HIS *B&E* SKILL SET.
PEPPER, IS THAT YOUR PHONE I HEAR...?
YES, SIR. THAT'S ME.
HAD IT ON *VIBRATE,* THOUGH...
UNFORTUNATELY, IT LOOKS LIKE HE *GOT AWAY.* I DON'T SEE *HOW,* BUT--
WELL, I'M STARTING TO WONDER WHY YOU KEEP ME ON THE PAYROLL, BOSS...
WHAT ARE YOU *TALKING* ABOUT...?
...PEPPER POTTS...
YES, I'M WITH HIM RIGHT NOW...
I MEAN, IF *SHELLHEAD* AIN'T AROUND TO TAKE A BULLET...IT COMES DOWN TO *ME.* I JUST...
HAPPY... IT'S OKAY. *I'M* OKAY.
ONE THING'S FOR CERTAIN. I *KNOW* WHO *SENT* THIS CLOWN TO--
WELL, WHEN IT RAINS, IT POURS. THAT CALL WAS FOR *YOU,* MISTER STARK.
SOMEONE NAMED SANDS. S.H.I.E.L.D. SPECIAL AGENT...
...THEY NEED TO SEE YOU RIGHT AWAY.
SAID IT WAS *URGENT.*

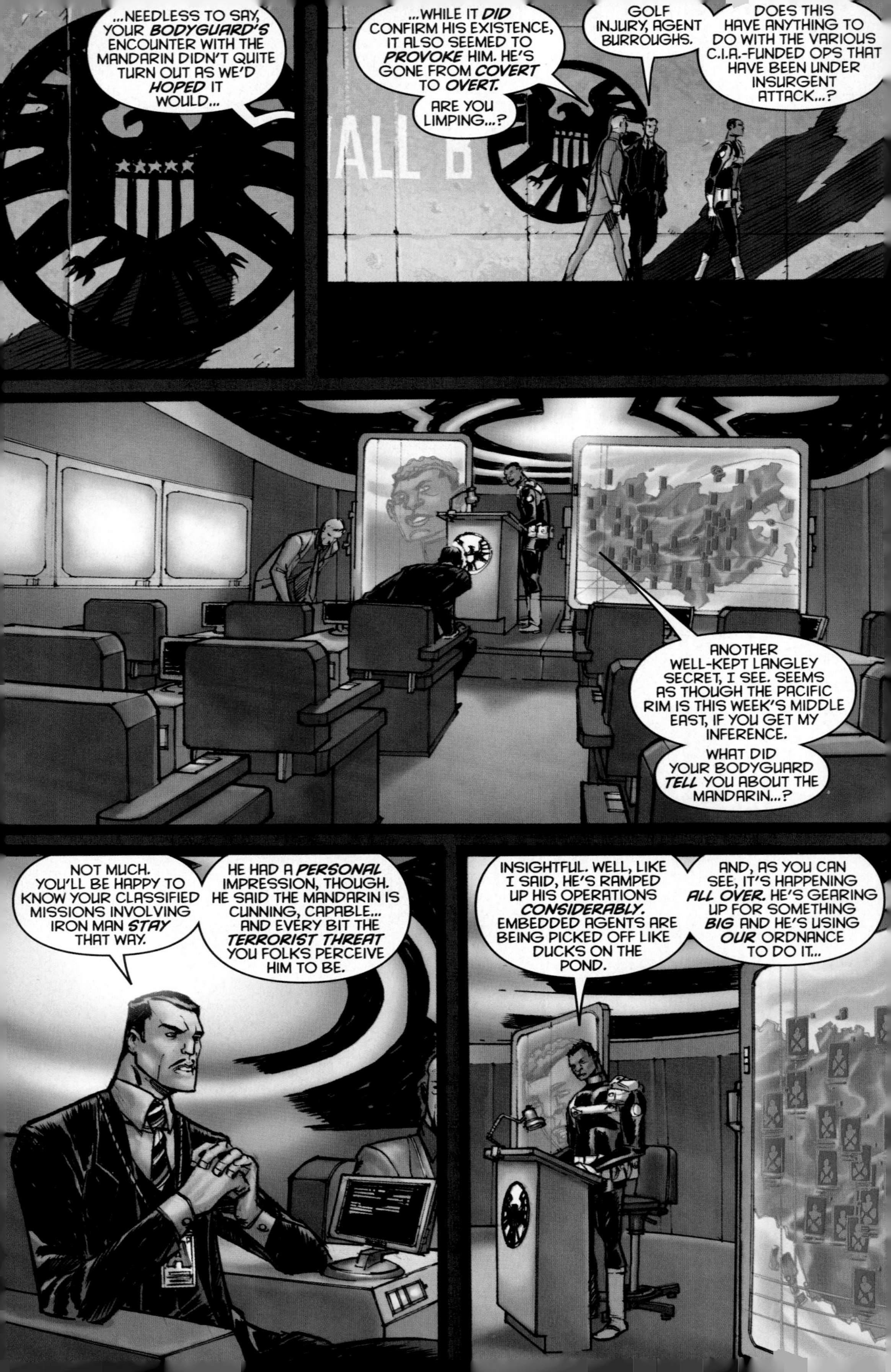
...NEEDLESS TO SAY, YOUR BODYGUARD'S ENCOUNTER WITH THE MANDARIN DIDN'T QUITE TURN OUT AS WE'D HOPED IT WOULD...
...WHILE IT DID CONFIRM HIS EXISTENCE, IT ALSO SEEMED TO PROVOKE HIM. HE'S GONE FROM COVERT TO OVERT.
ARE YOU LIMPING...?
GOLF INJURY, AGENT BURROUGHS.
DOES THIS HAVE ANYTHING TO DO WITH THE VARIOUS C.I.A.-FUNDED OPS THAT HAVE BEEN UNDER INSURGENT ATTACK...?
ALL B
ANOTHER WELL-KEPT LANGLEY SECRET, I SEE. SEEMS AS THOUGH THE PACIFIC RIM IS THIS WEEK'S MIDDLE EAST, IF YOU GET MY INFERENCE.
WHAT DID YOUR BODYGUARD TELL YOU ABOUT THE MANDARIN...?
NOT MUCH. YOU'LL BE HAPPY TO KNOW YOUR CLASSIFIED MISSIONS INVOLVING IRON MAN STAY THAT WAY.
HE HAD A PERSONAL IMPRESSION, THOUGH. HE SAID THE MANDARIN IS CUNNING, CAPABLE... AND EVERY BIT THE TERRORIST THREAT YOU FOLKS PERCEIVE HIM TO BE.
INSIGHTFUL. WELL, LIKE I SAID, HE'S RAMPED UP HIS OPERATIONS CONSIDERABLY. EMBEDDED AGENTS ARE BEING PICKED OFF LIKE DUCKS ON THE POND.
AND, AS YOU CAN SEE, IT'S HAPPENING ALL OVER. HE'S GEARING UP FOR SOMETHING BIG AND HE'S USING OUR ORDNANCE TO DO IT...

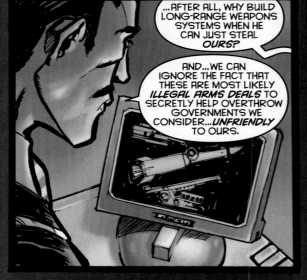

...AFTER ALL, WHY BUILD LONG-RANGE WEAPONS SYSTEMS WHEN HE CAN JUST STEAL *OURS?*

AND...WE CAN IGNORE THE FACT THAT THESE ARE MOST LIKELY *ILLEGAL ARMS DEALS* TO SECRETLY HELP OVERTHROW GOVERNMENTS WE CONSIDER...*UNFRIENDLY* TO OURS.

WE CAN IGNORE THAT, YES. BECAUSE *NOW* HE'S TRYING TO LAND THE *BIG FISH.*

THIS S.H.I.E.L.D. *ORBITAL PLATFORM*, CONTAINING THE LATEST IN STATE-OF-THE-ART SURVEILLANCE TECH...

...*LOOK FAMILIAR...?*

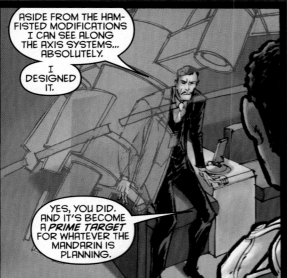

ASIDE FROM THE HAM-FISTED MODIFICATIONS I CAN SEE ALONG THE AXIS SYSTEMS... ABSOLUTELY.

I DESIGNED IT.

YES, YOU DID. AND IT'S BECOME A *PRIME TARGET* FOR WHATEVER THE MANDARIN IS PLANNING.

GROUND SYSTEMS HAVE BEEN REGISTERING SIGNIFICANT FLUCTUATIONS IN THE ULTRA-MAG SPECTRAL FIELD.

SOMETHING-- OR SOME*ONE*-- IS TRYING TO *PULL* THE PLATFORM OUT OF ITS ORBITAL PATH...AND OUT OF OUR CONTROL.

RIGHT.

GET ME TO A CONNECTING TERMINAL.

MASTER, YOUR SON IS EN ROUTE...

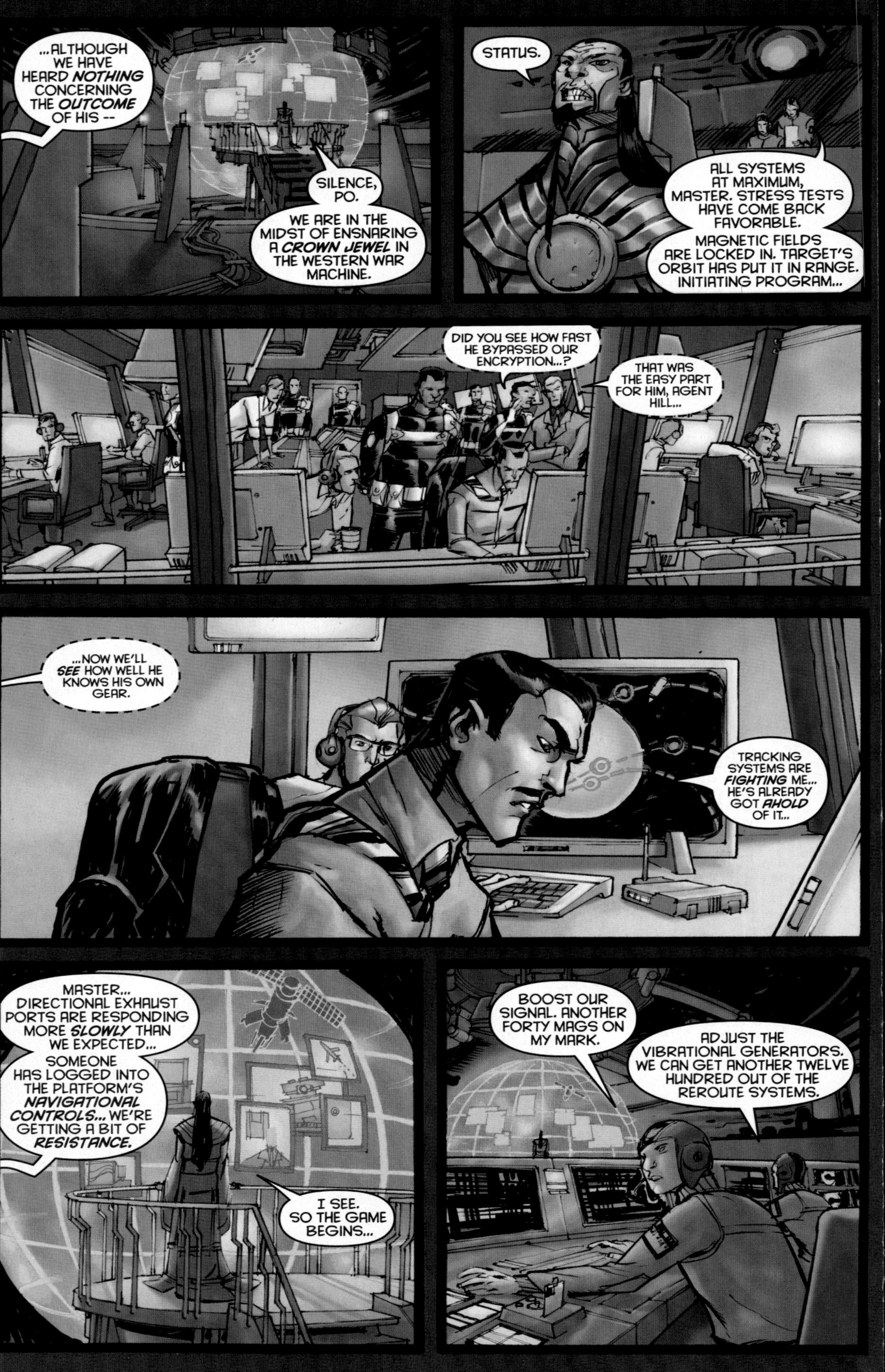
...ALTHOUGH WE HAVE HEARD NOTHING CONCERNING THE OUTCOME OF HIS --
SILENCE, PO.
WE ARE IN THE MIDST OF ENSNARING A CROWN JEWEL IN THE WESTERN WAR MACHINE.
STATUS.
ALL SYSTEMS AT MAXIMUM, MASTER. STRESS TESTS HAVE COME BACK FAVORABLE.
MAGNETIC FIELDS ARE LOCKED IN. TARGET'S ORBIT HAS PUT IT IN RANGE. INITIATING PROGRAM...
DID YOU SEE HOW FAST HE BYPASSED OUR ENCRYPTION...?
THAT WAS THE EASY PART FOR HIM, AGENT HILL...
...NOW WE'LL SEE HOW WELL HE KNOWS HIS OWN GEAR.
TRACKING SYSTEMS ARE FIGHTING ME... HE'S ALREADY GOT AHOLD OF IT...
MASTER... DIRECTIONAL EXHAUST PORTS ARE RESPONDING MORE SLOWLY THAN WE EXPECTED...
SOMEONE HAS LOGGED INTO THE PLATFORM'S NAVIGATIONAL CONTROLS... WE'RE GETTING A BIT OF RESISTANCE.
I SEE. SO THE GAME BEGINS...
BOOST OUR SIGNAL. ANOTHER FORTY MAGS ON MY MARK.
ADJUST THE VIBRATIONAL GENERATORS. WE CAN GET ANOTHER TWELVE HUNDRED OUT OF THE REROUTE SYSTEMS.

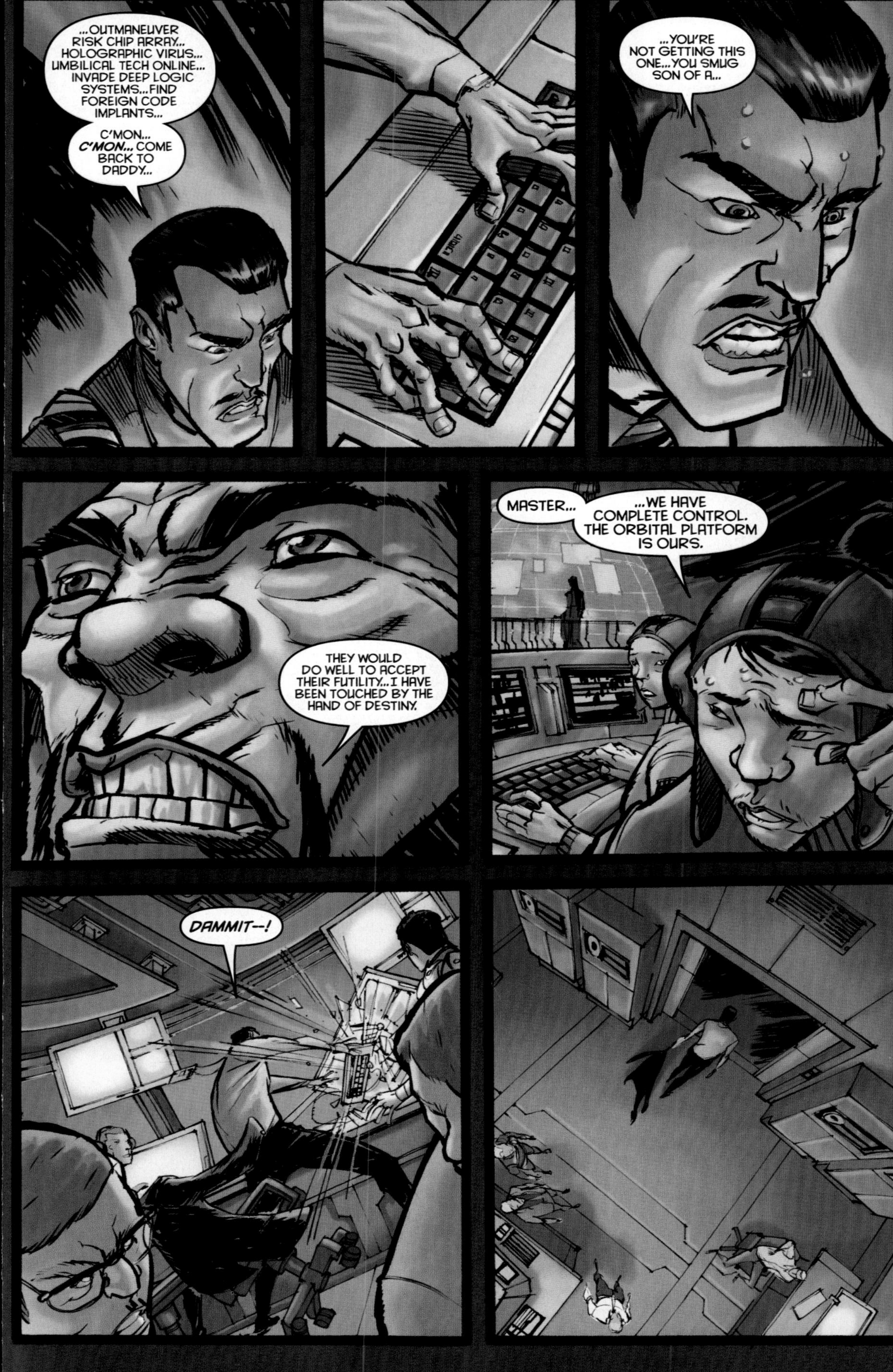
...OUTMANEUVER RISK CHIP ARRAY... HOLOGRAPHIC VIRUS... UMBILICAL TECH ONLINE... INVADE DEEP LOGIC SYSTEMS...FIND FOREIGN CODE IMPLANTS...
C'MON... C'MON... COME BACK TO DADDY...
...YOU'RE NOT GETTING THIS ONE...YOU SMUG SON OF A...
THEY WOULD DO WELL TO ACCEPT THEIR FUTILITY...I HAVE BEEN TOUCHED BY THE HAND OF DESTINY.
MASTER...
...WE HAVE COMPLETE CONTROL. THE ORBITAL PLATFORM IS OURS.
DAMMIT--!

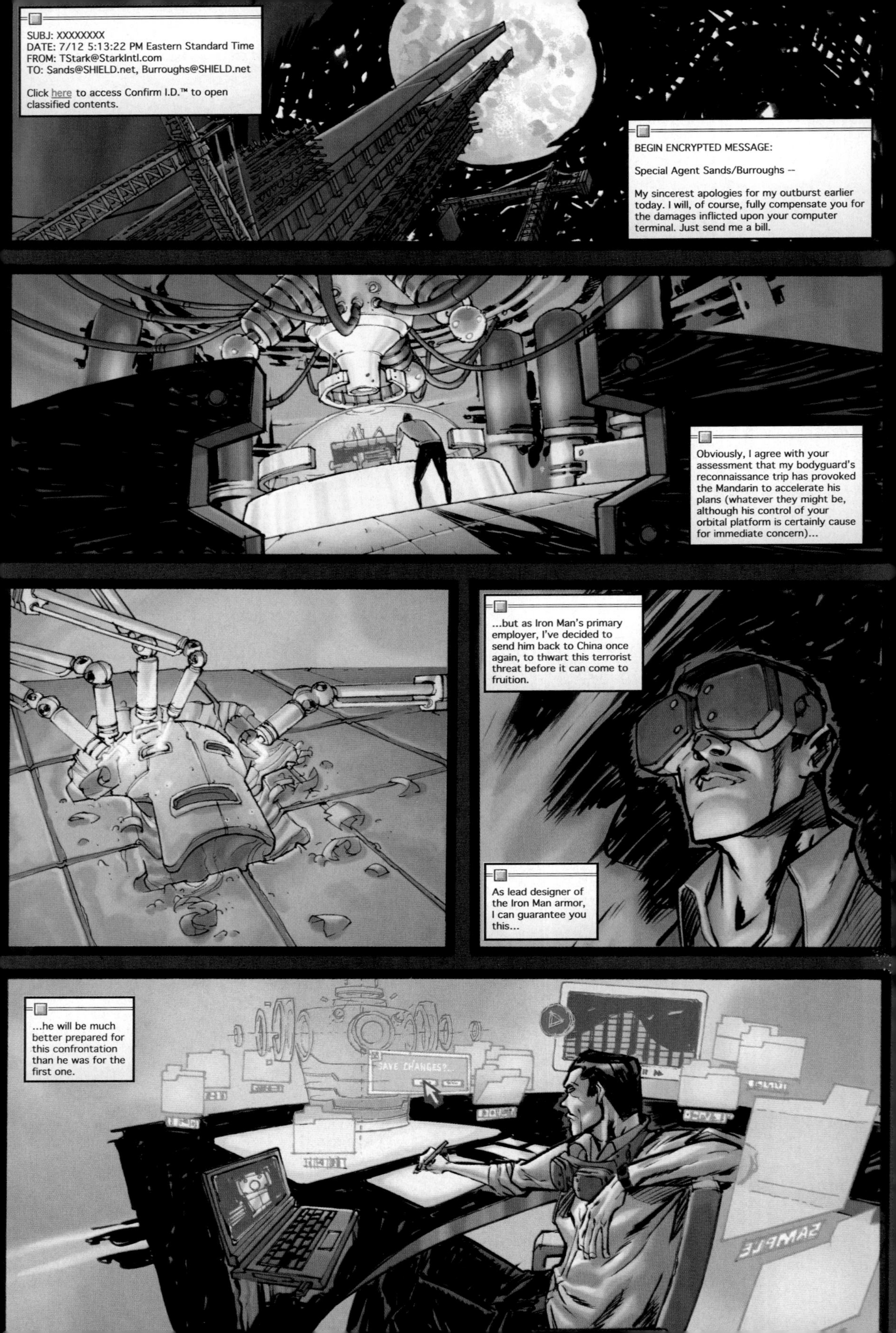
SUBJ: XXXXXXXX
DATE: 7/12 5:13:22 PM Eastern Standard Time
FROM: TStark@StarkIntl.com
TO: Sands@SHIELD.net, Burroughs@SHIELD.net
Click here to access Confirm I.D.™ to open classified contents.
BEGIN ENCRYPTED MESSAGE:
Special Agent Sands/Burroughs --
My sincerest apologies for my outburst earlier today. I will, of course, fully compensate you for the damages inflicted upon your computer terminal. Just send me a bill.
Obviously, I agree with your assessment that my bodyguard's reconnaissance trip has provoked the Mandarin to accelerate his plans (whatever they might be, although his control of your orbital platform is certainly cause for immediate concern)...
...but as Iron Man's primary employer, I've decided to send him back to China once again, to thwart this terrorist threat before it can come to fruition.
As lead designer of the Iron Man armor, I can guarantee you this...
...he will be much better prepared for this confrontation than he was for the first one.
SAVE CHANGES?..

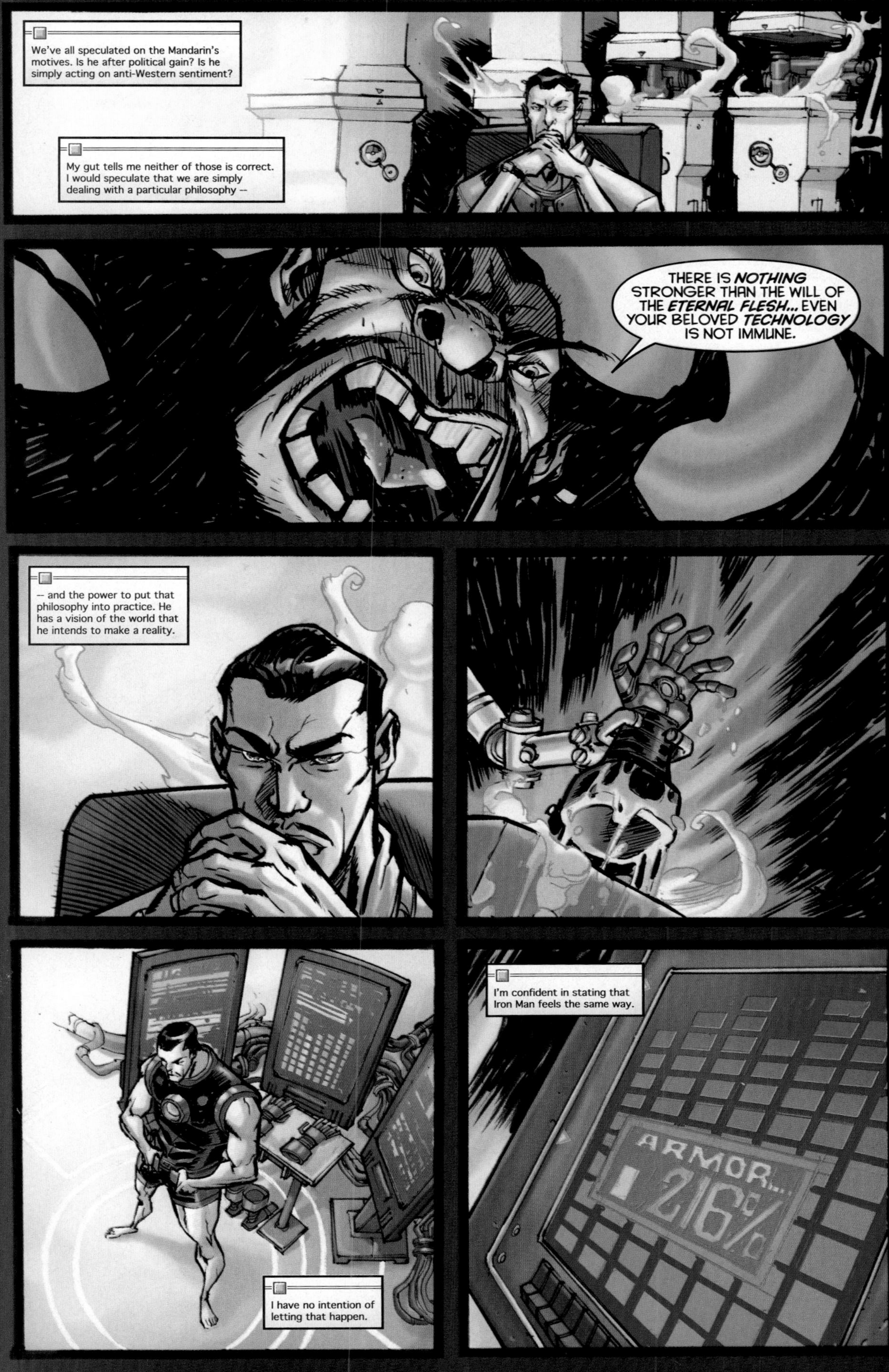
We've all speculated on the Mandarin's motives. Is he after political gain? Is he simply acting on anti-Western sentiment?
My gut tells me neither of those is correct. I would speculate that we are simply dealing with a particular philosophy --
THERE IS NOTHING STRONGER THAN THE WILL OF THE ETERNAL FLESH... EVEN YOUR BELOVED TECHNOLOGY IS NOT IMMUNE.
-- and the power to put that philosophy into practice. He has a vision of the world that he intends to make a reality.
I have no intention of letting that happen.
I'm confident in stating that Iron Man feels the same way.
ARMOR... 26%

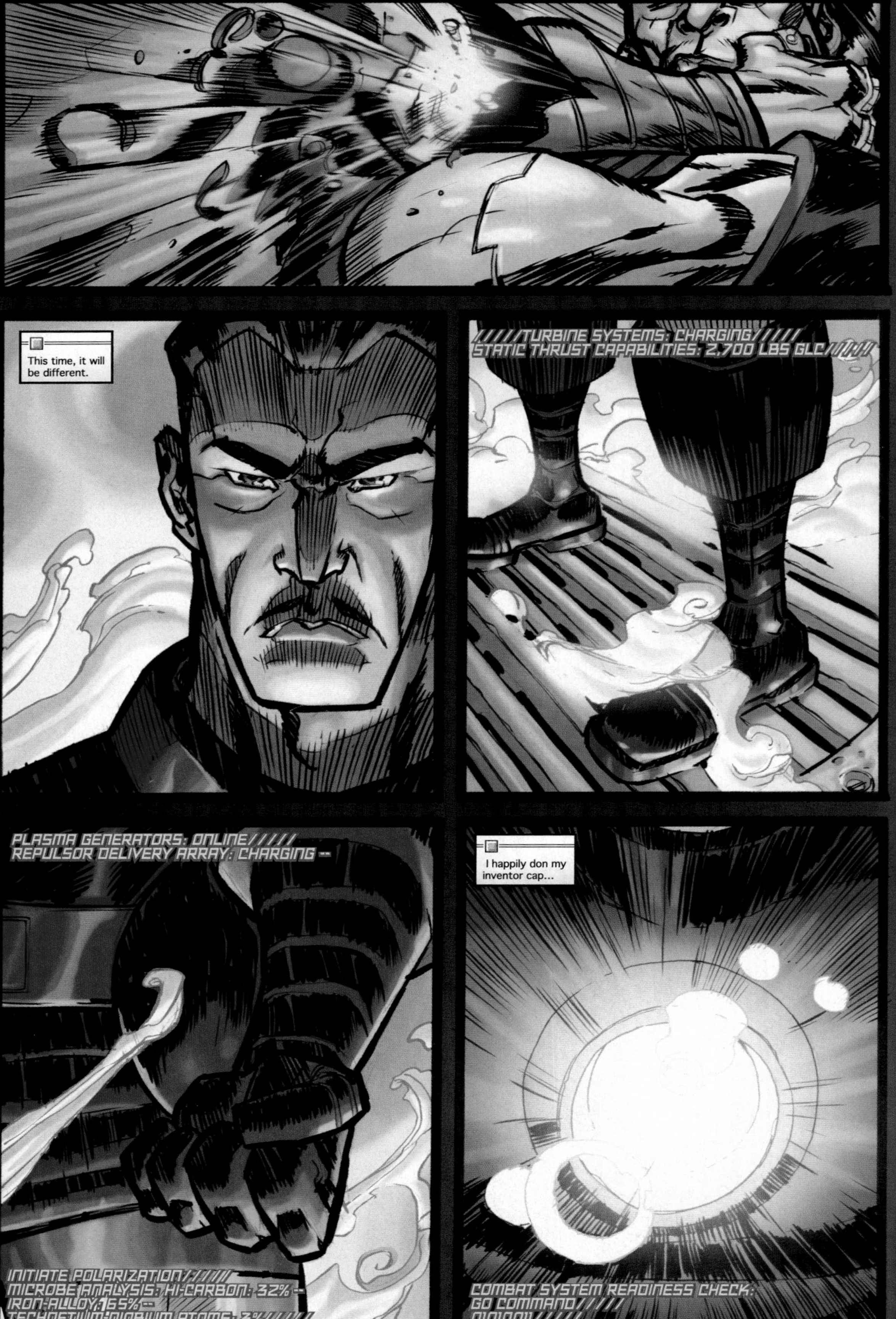

This time, it will be different.
//////TURBINE SYSTEMS: CHARGING//////
STATIC THRUST CAPABILITIES: 2,700 LBS GLC//////
PLASMA GENERATORS: ONLINE//////
REPULSOR DELIVERY ARRAY: CHARGING --
INITIATE POLARIZATION//////
MICROBE ANALYSIS: HI-CARBON: 32% --
IRON-ALLOY: 65% --
TECHNETIUM-NIOBIUM ATOMS: 3%//////
CONFIRMED
I happily don my inventor cap...
COMBAT SYSTEM READINESS CHECK:
GO COMMAND//////
01010011//////
IRON MAN SYSTEMS OPERATIONAL

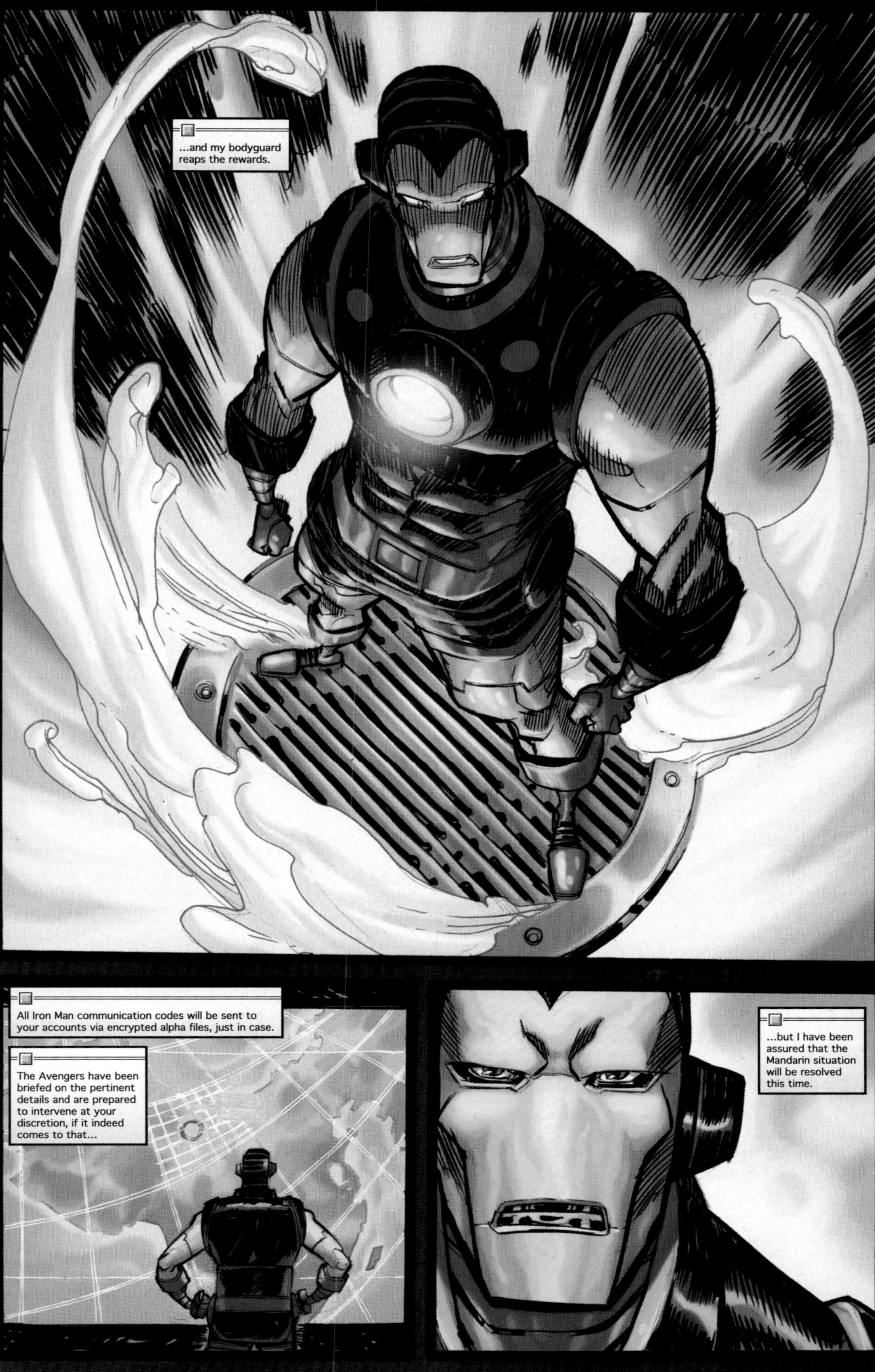
...and my bodyguard reaps the rewards.
All Iron Man communication codes will be sent to your accounts via encrypted alpha files, just in case.
The Avengers have been briefed on the pertinent details and are prepared to intervene at your discretion, if it indeed comes to that...
...but I have been assured that the Mandarin situation will be resolved this time.

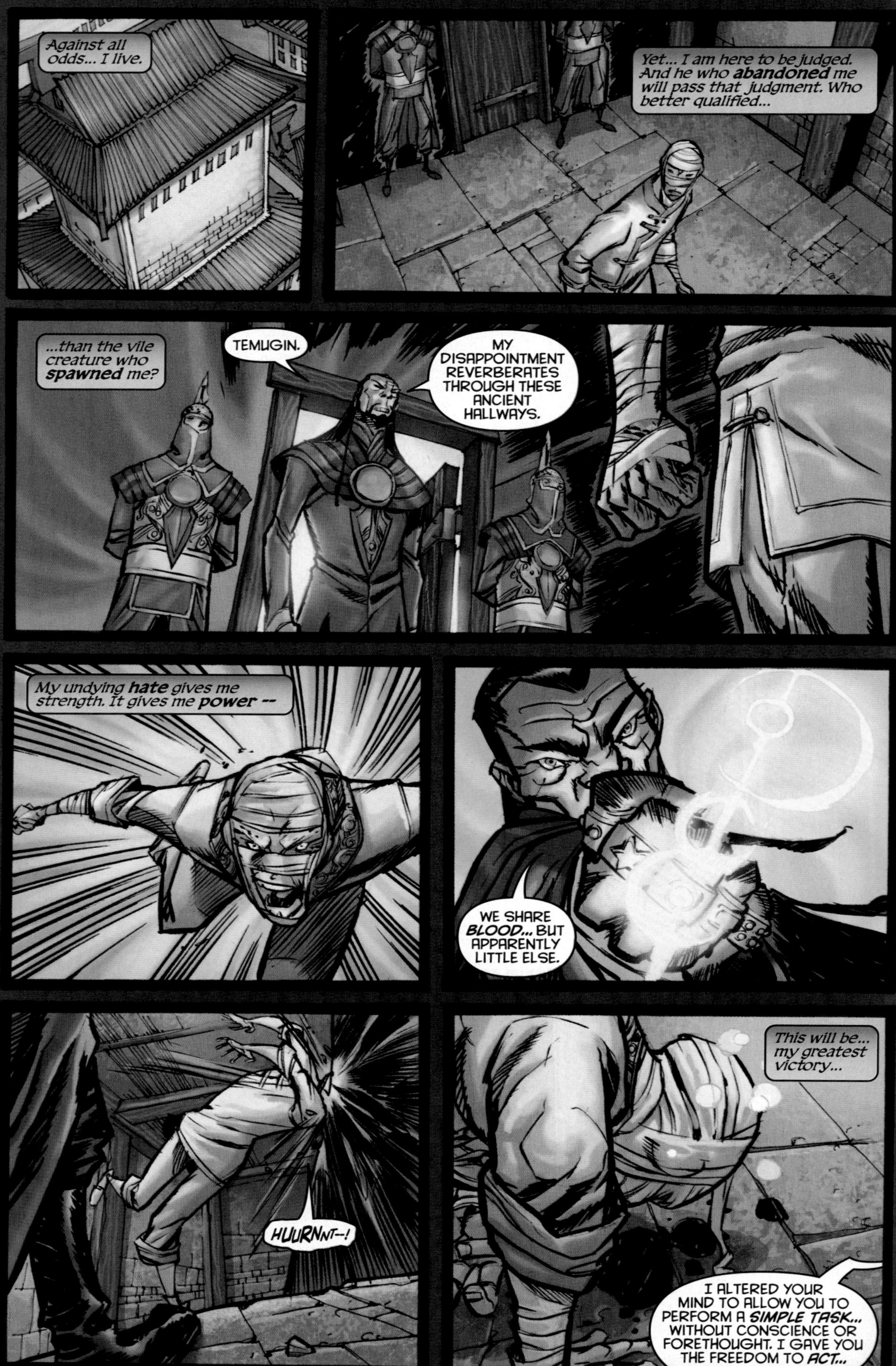
Against all odds... I live.
Yet... I am here to be judged. And he who **abandoned** me will pass that judgment. Who better qualified...
...than the vile creature who **spawned** me?
TEMUGIN.
MY DISAPPOINTMENT REVERBERATES THROUGH THESE ANCIENT HALLWAYS.
My undying **hate** gives me strength. It gives me **power** --
WE SHARE ***BLOOD...*** BUT APPARENTLY LITTLE ELSE.
HUURNNT--!
This will be... my greatest victory...
I ALTERED YOUR MIND TO ALLOW YOU TO PERFORM A ***SIMPLE TASK...*** WITHOUT CONSCIENCE OR FORETHOUGHT. I GAVE YOU THE FREEDOM TO ***ACT...***

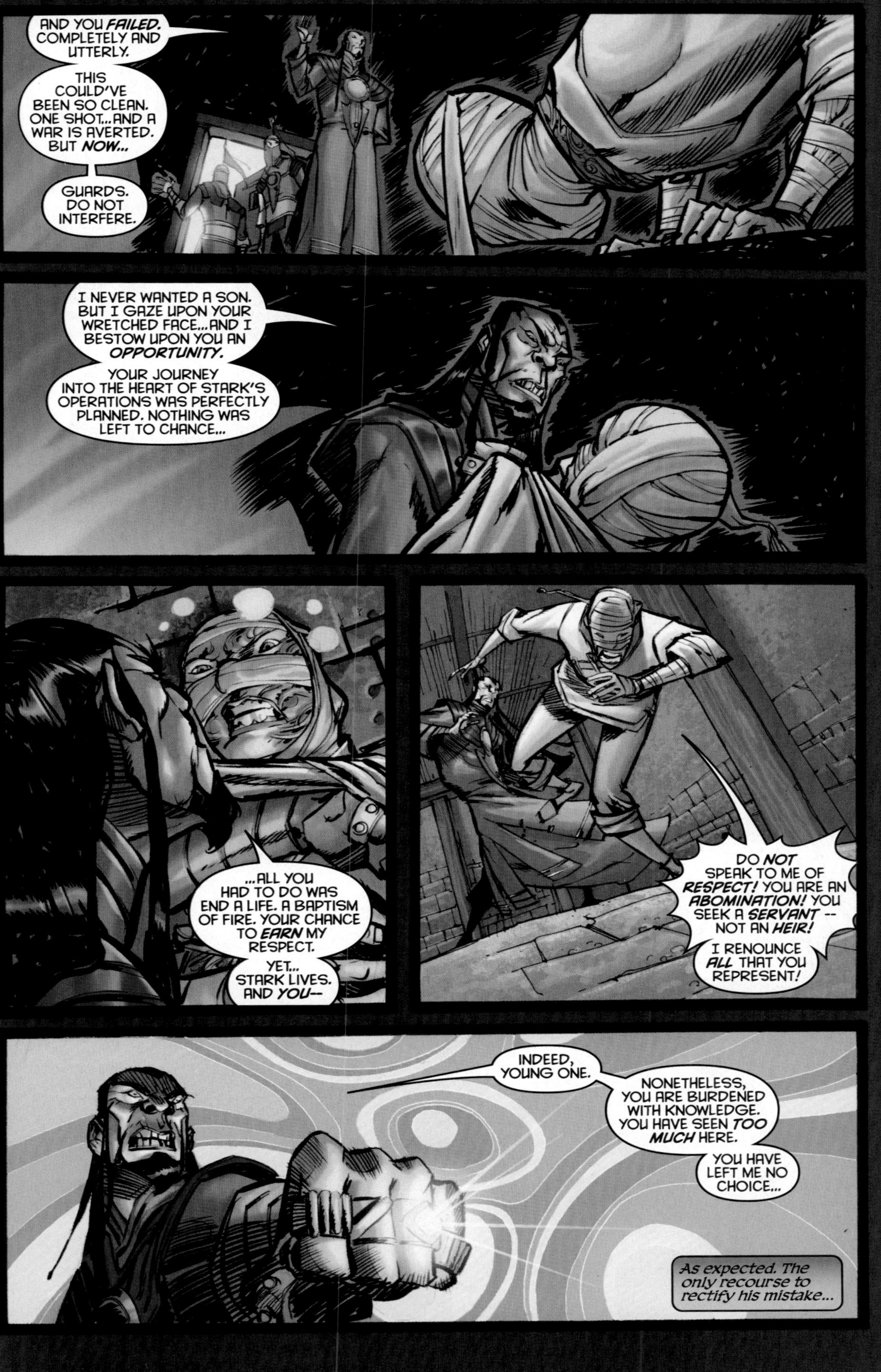
AND YOU FAILED. COMPLETELY AND UTTERLY.
THIS COULD'VE BEEN SO CLEAN. ONE SHOT...AND A WAR IS AVERTED. BUT NOW...
GUARDS. DO NOT INTERFERE.
I NEVER WANTED A SON. BUT I GAZE UPON YOUR WRETCHED FACE...AND I BESTOW UPON YOU AN OPPORTUNITY.
YOUR JOURNEY INTO THE HEART OF STARK'S OPERATIONS WAS PERFECTLY PLANNED. NOTHING WAS LEFT TO CHANCE...
...ALL YOU HAD TO DO WAS END A LIFE. A BAPTISM OF FIRE. YOUR CHANCE TO EARN MY RESPECT.
YET... STARK LIVES. AND YOU--
DO NOT SPEAK TO ME OF RESPECT! YOU ARE AN ABOMINATION! YOU SEEK A SERVANT -- NOT AN HEIR!
I RENOUNCE ALL THAT YOU REPRESENT!
INDEED, YOUNG ONE.
NONETHELESS, YOU ARE BURDENED WITH KNOWLEDGE. YOU HAVE SEEN TOO MUCH HERE.
YOU HAVE LEFT ME NO CHOICE...
As expected. The only recourse to rectify his mistake...

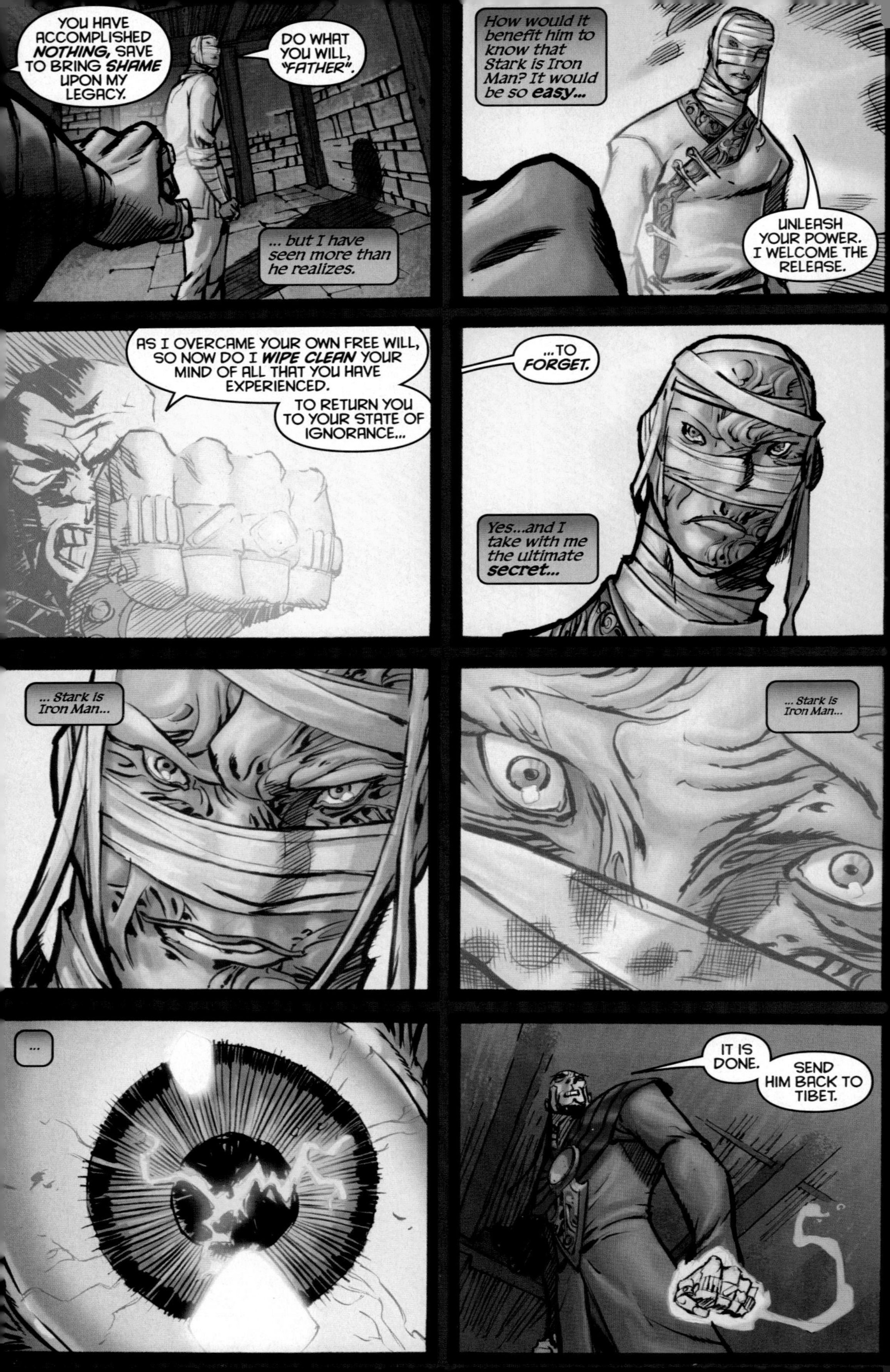
YOU HAVE ACCOMPLISHED NOTHING, SAVE TO BRING SHAME UPON MY LEGACY.
DO WHAT YOU WILL, "FATHER".
... but I have seen more than he realizes.
How would it benefit him to know that Stark is Iron Man? It would be so easy...
UNLEASH YOUR POWER. I WELCOME THE RELEASE.
AS I OVERCAME YOUR OWN FREE WILL, SO NOW DO I WIPE CLEAN YOUR MIND OF ALL THAT YOU HAVE EXPERIENCED.
TO RETURN YOU TO YOUR STATE OF IGNORANCE...
...TO FORGET.
Yes...and I take with me the ultimate secret...
... Stark is Iron Man...
... Stark is Iron Man...
...
IT IS DONE.
SEND HIM BACK TO TIBET.

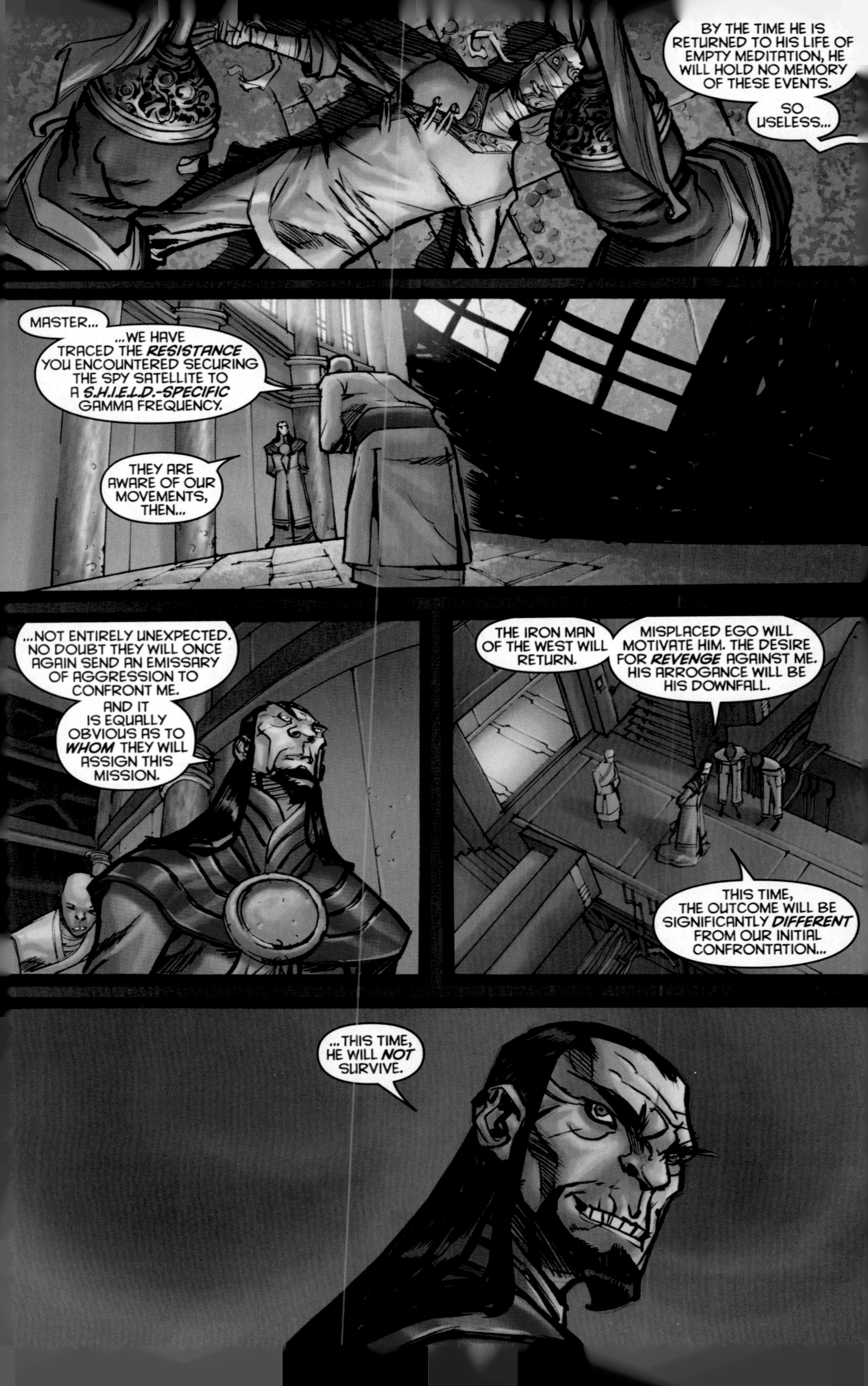
BY THE TIME HE IS RETURNED TO HIS LIFE OF EMPTY MEDITATION, HE WILL HOLD NO MEMORY OF THESE EVENTS.
SO USELESS...
MASTER...
...WE HAVE TRACED THE RESISTANCE YOU ENCOUNTERED SECURING THE SPY SATELLITE TO A S.H.I.E.L.D.-SPECIFIC GAMMA FREQUENCY.
THEY ARE AWARE OF OUR MOVEMENTS, THEN...
...NOT ENTIRELY UNEXPECTED. NO DOUBT THEY WILL ONCE AGAIN SEND AN EMISSARY OF AGGRESSION TO CONFRONT ME.
AND IT IS EQUALLY OBVIOUS AS TO WHOM THEY WILL ASSIGN THIS MISSION.
THE IRON MAN OF THE WEST WILL RETURN.
MISPLACED EGO WILL MOTIVATE HIM. THE DESIRE FOR REVENGE AGAINST ME. HIS ARROGANCE WILL BE HIS DOWNFALL.
THIS TIME, THE OUTCOME WILL BE SIGNIFICANTLY DIFFERENT FROM OUR INITIAL CONFRONTATION...
...THIS TIME, HE WILL NOT SURVIVE.

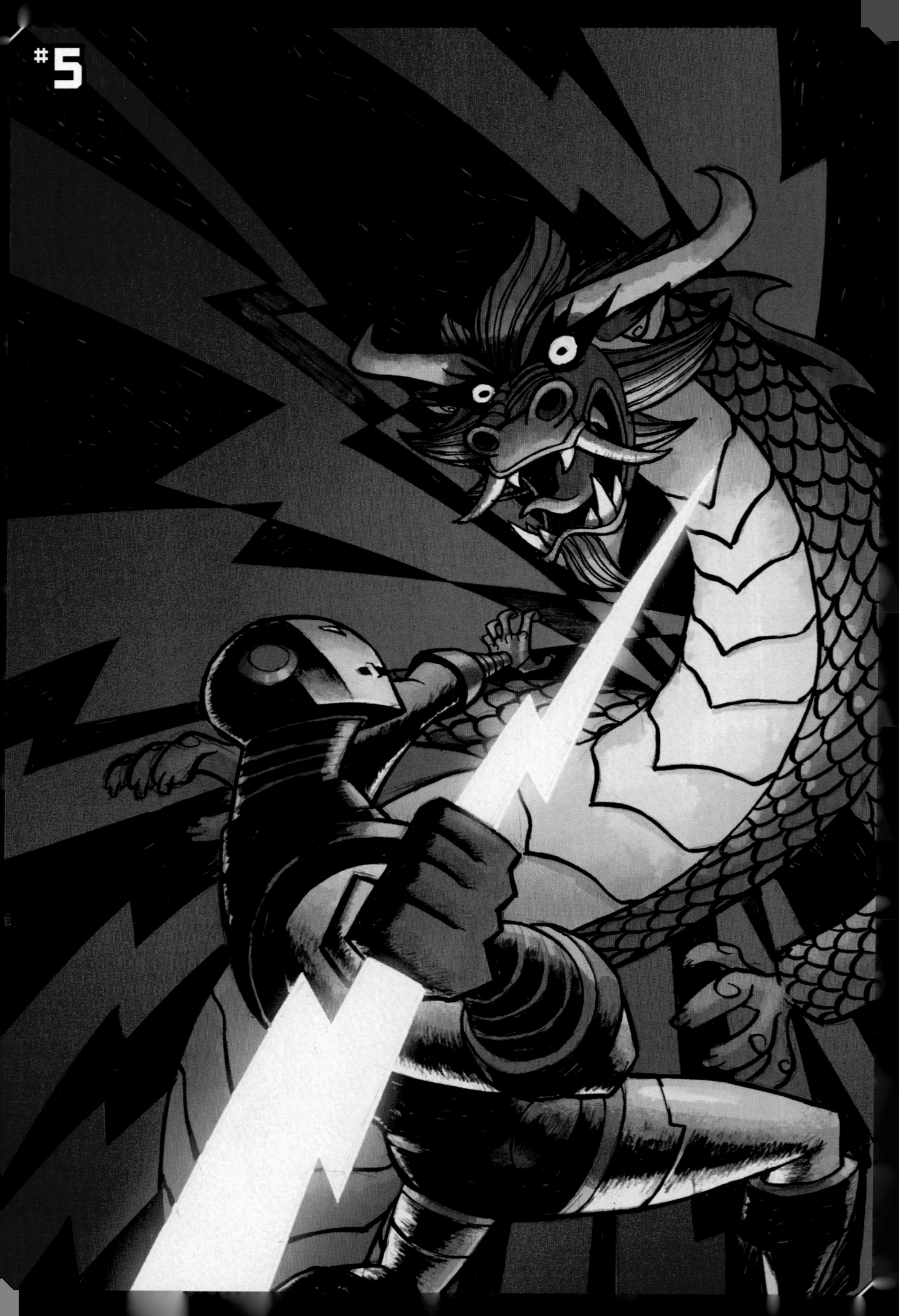
#5

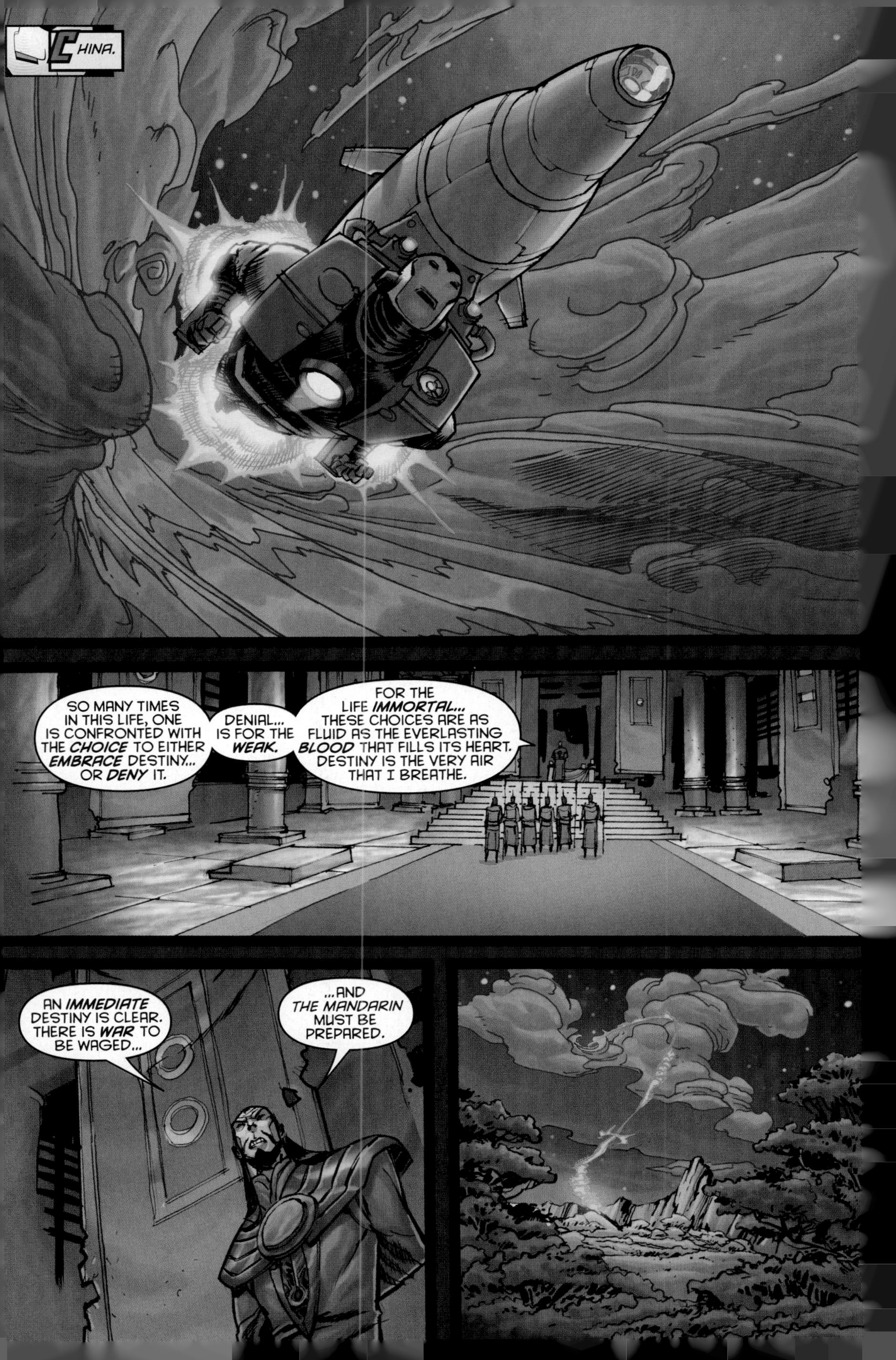
CHINA.
SO MANY TIMES IN THIS LIFE, ONE IS CONFRONTED WITH THE CHOICE TO EITHER EMBRACE DESTINY... OR DENY IT.
DENIAL... IS FOR THE WEAK.
FOR THE LIFE IMMORTAL... THESE CHOICES ARE AS FLUID AS THE EVERLASTING BLOOD THAT FILLS ITS HEART. DESTINY IS THE VERY AIR THAT I BREATHE.
AN IMMEDIATE DESTINY IS CLEAR. THERE IS WAR TO BE WAGED...
...AND THE MANDARIN MUST BE PREPARED.

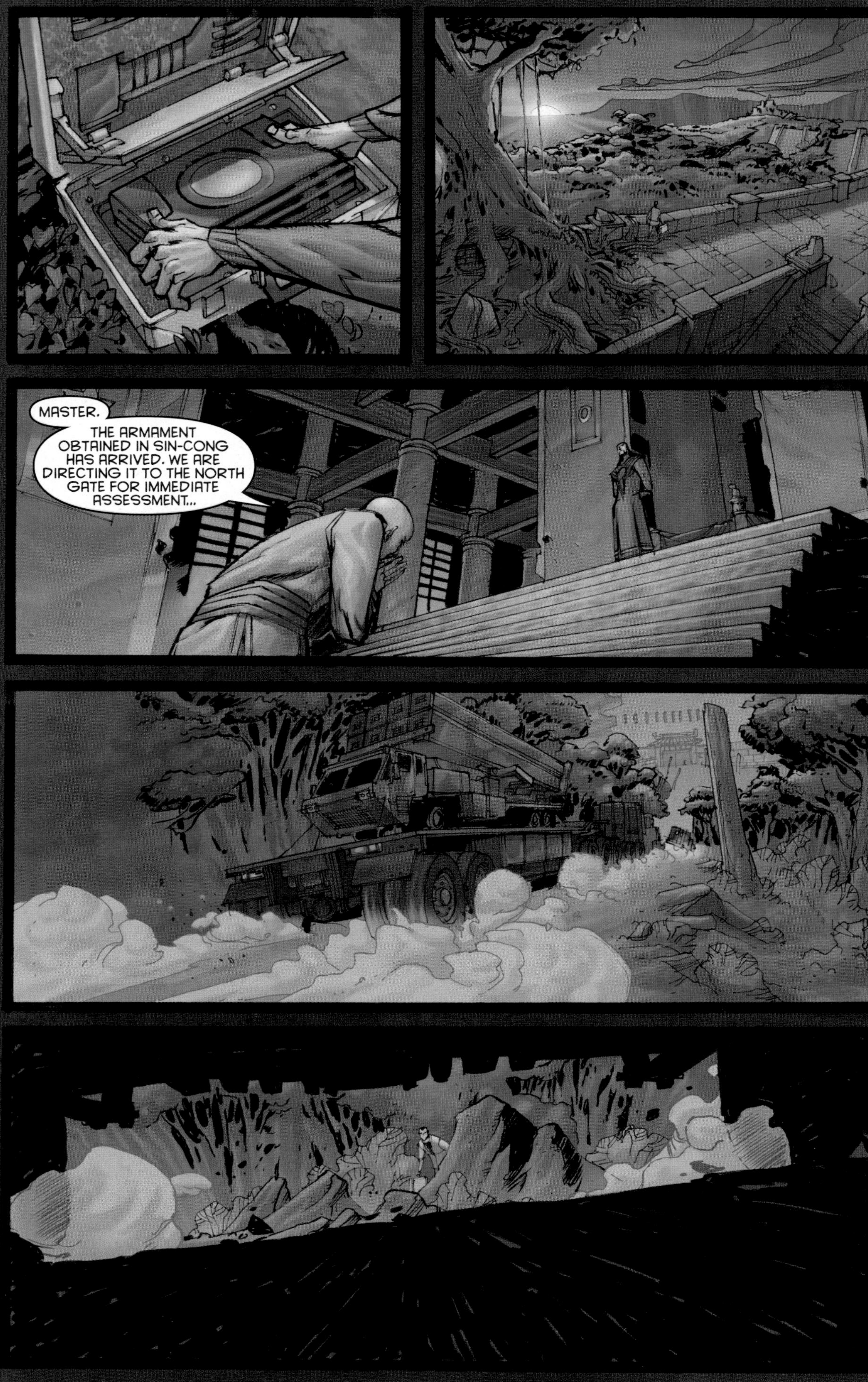
MASTER.
THE ARMAMENT OBTAINED IN SIN-CONG HAS ARRIVED. WE ARE DIRECTING IT TO THE NORTH GATE FOR IMMEDIATE ASSESSMENT...

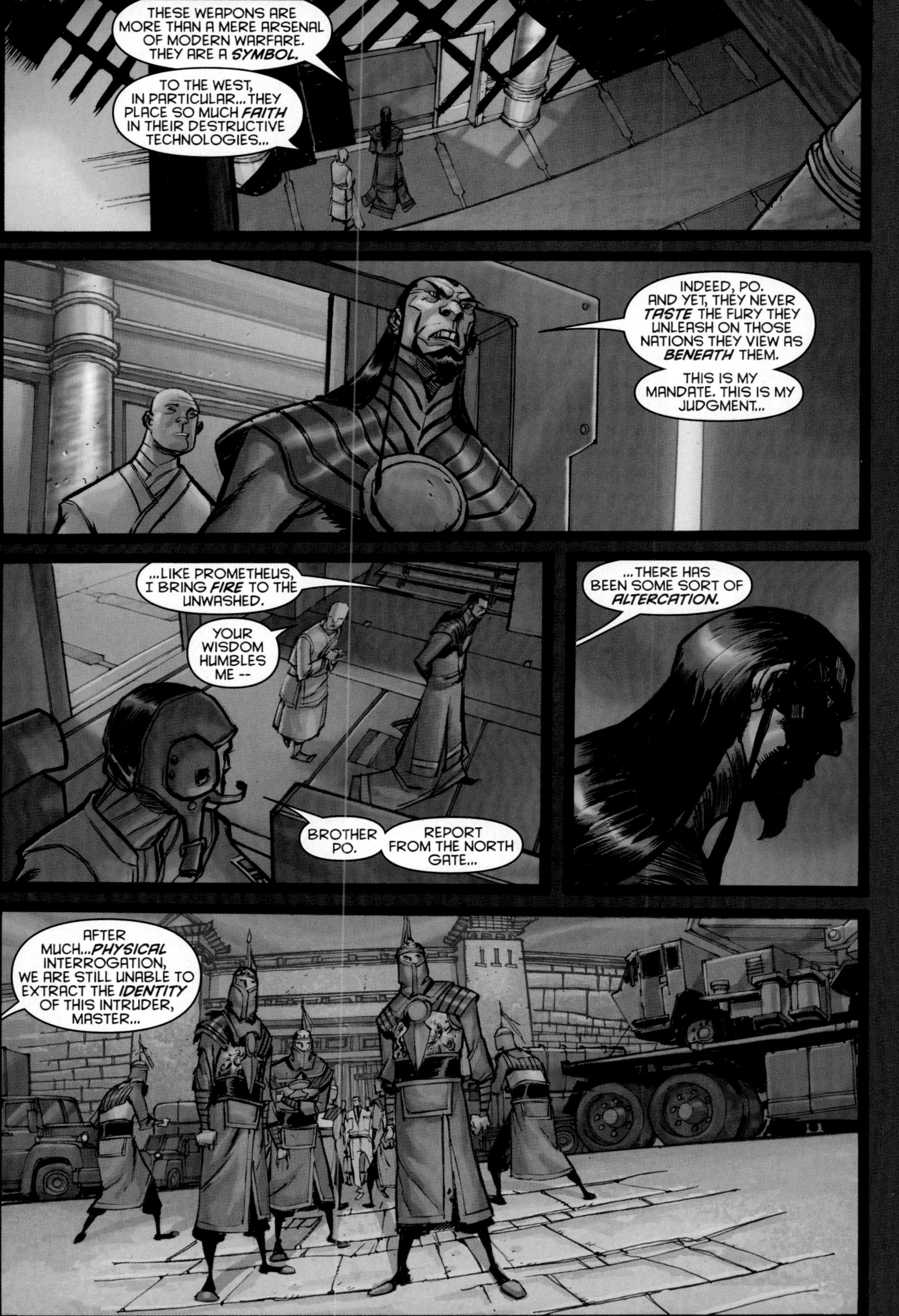
THESE WEAPONS ARE MORE THAN A MERE ARSENAL OF MODERN WARFARE. THEY ARE A *SYMBOL.*
TO THE WEST, IN PARTICULAR... THEY PLACE SO MUCH *FAITH* IN THEIR DESTRUCTIVE TECHNOLOGIES...
INDEED, PO. AND YET, THEY NEVER *TASTE* THE FURY THEY UNLEASH ON THOSE NATIONS THEY VIEW AS *BENEATH* THEM.
THIS IS MY MANDATE. THIS IS MY JUDGMENT...
...LIKE PROMETHEUS, I BRING *FIRE* TO THE UNWASHED.
YOUR WISDOM HUMBLES ME --
BROTHER PO.
REPORT FROM THE NORTH GATE...
...THERE HAS BEEN SOME SORT OF *ALTERCATION.*
AFTER MUCH... *PHYSICAL* INTERROGATION, WE ARE STILL UNABLE TO EXTRACT THE *IDENTITY* OF THIS INTRUDER, MASTER...

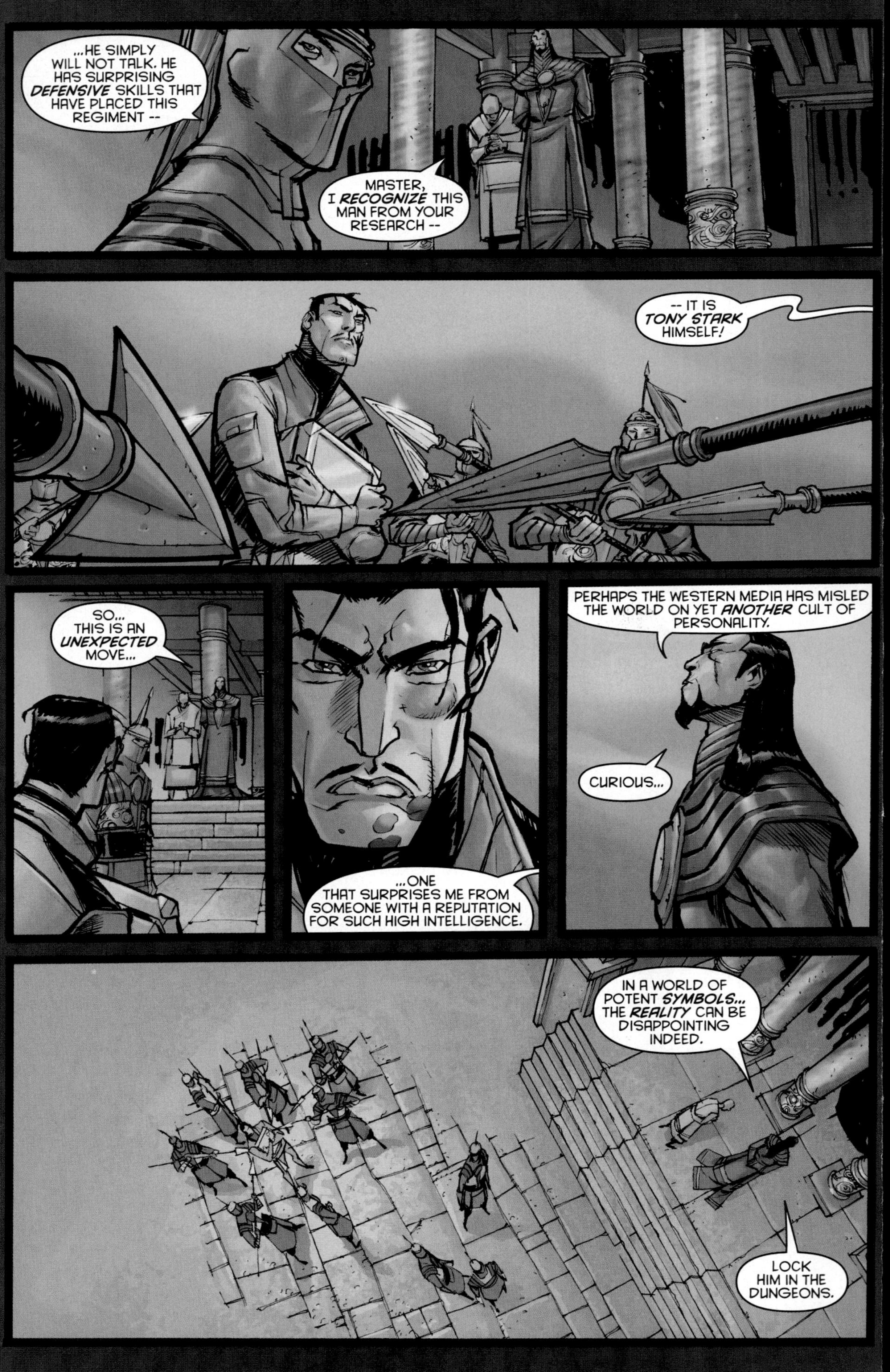
...HE SIMPLY WILL NOT TALK. HE HAS SURPRISING DEFENSIVE SKILLS THAT HAVE PLACED THIS REGIMENT --
MASTER, I RECOGNIZE THIS MAN FROM YOUR RESEARCH --
-- IT IS TONY STARK HIMSELF!
SO... THIS IS AN UNEXPECTED MOVE...
...ONE THAT SURPRISES ME FROM SOMEONE WITH A REPUTATION FOR SUCH HIGH INTELLIGENCE.
PERHAPS THE WESTERN MEDIA HAS MISLED THE WORLD ON YET ANOTHER CULT OF PERSONALITY.
CURIOUS...
IN A WORLD OF POTENT SYMBOLS... THE REALITY CAN BE DISAPPOINTING INDEED.
LOCK HIM IN THE DUNGEONS.

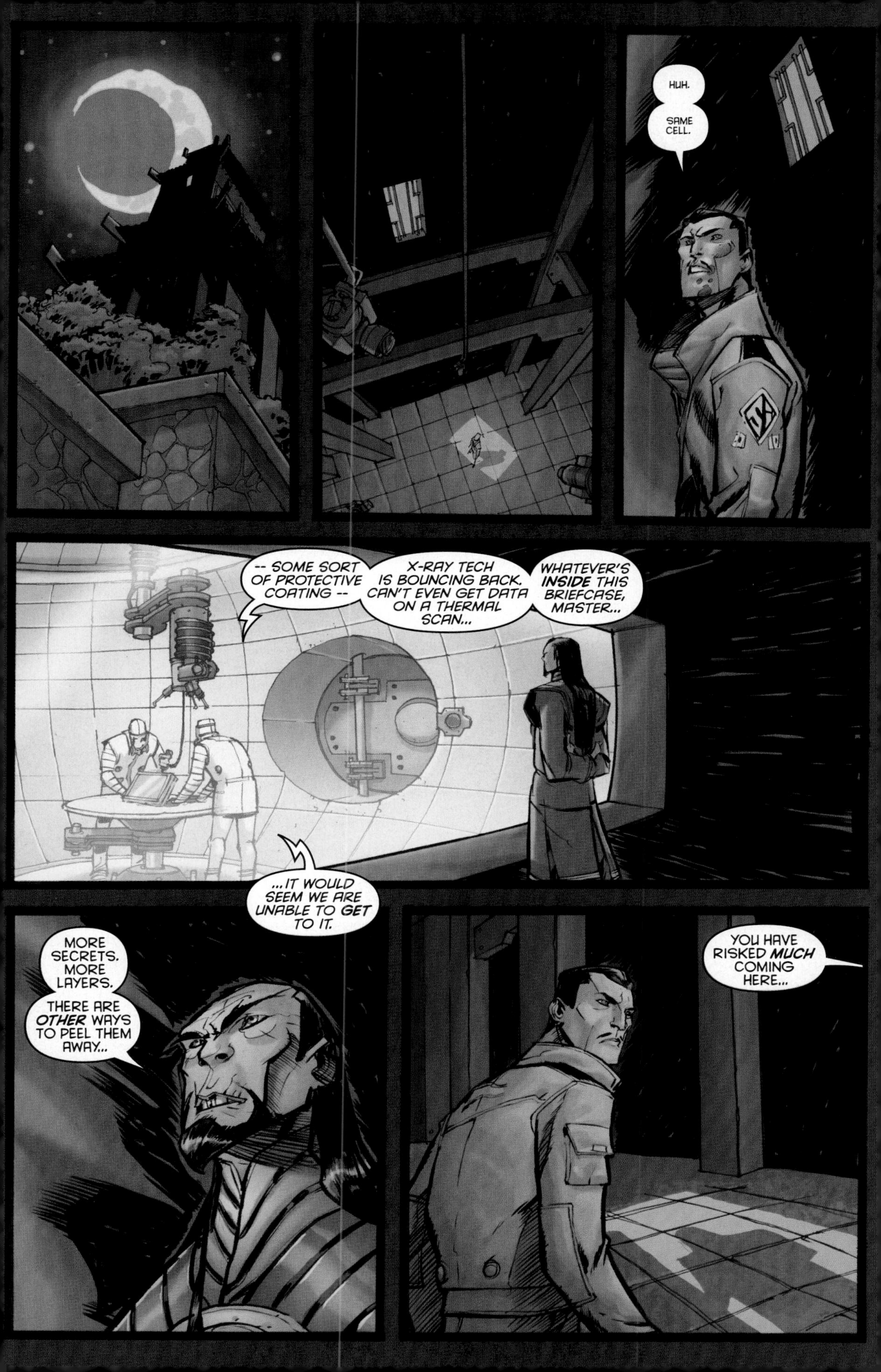
HUH.
SAME CELL.
-- SOME SORT OF PROTECTIVE COATING --
X-RAY TECH IS BOUNCING BACK. CAN'T EVEN GET DATA ON A THERMAL SCAN...
WHATEVER'S INSIDE THIS BRIEFCASE, MASTER...
...IT WOULD SEEM WE ARE UNABLE TO GET TO IT.
MORE SECRETS. MORE LAYERS.
THERE ARE OTHER WAYS TO PEEL THEM AWAY...
YOU HAVE RISKED MUCH COMING HERE...

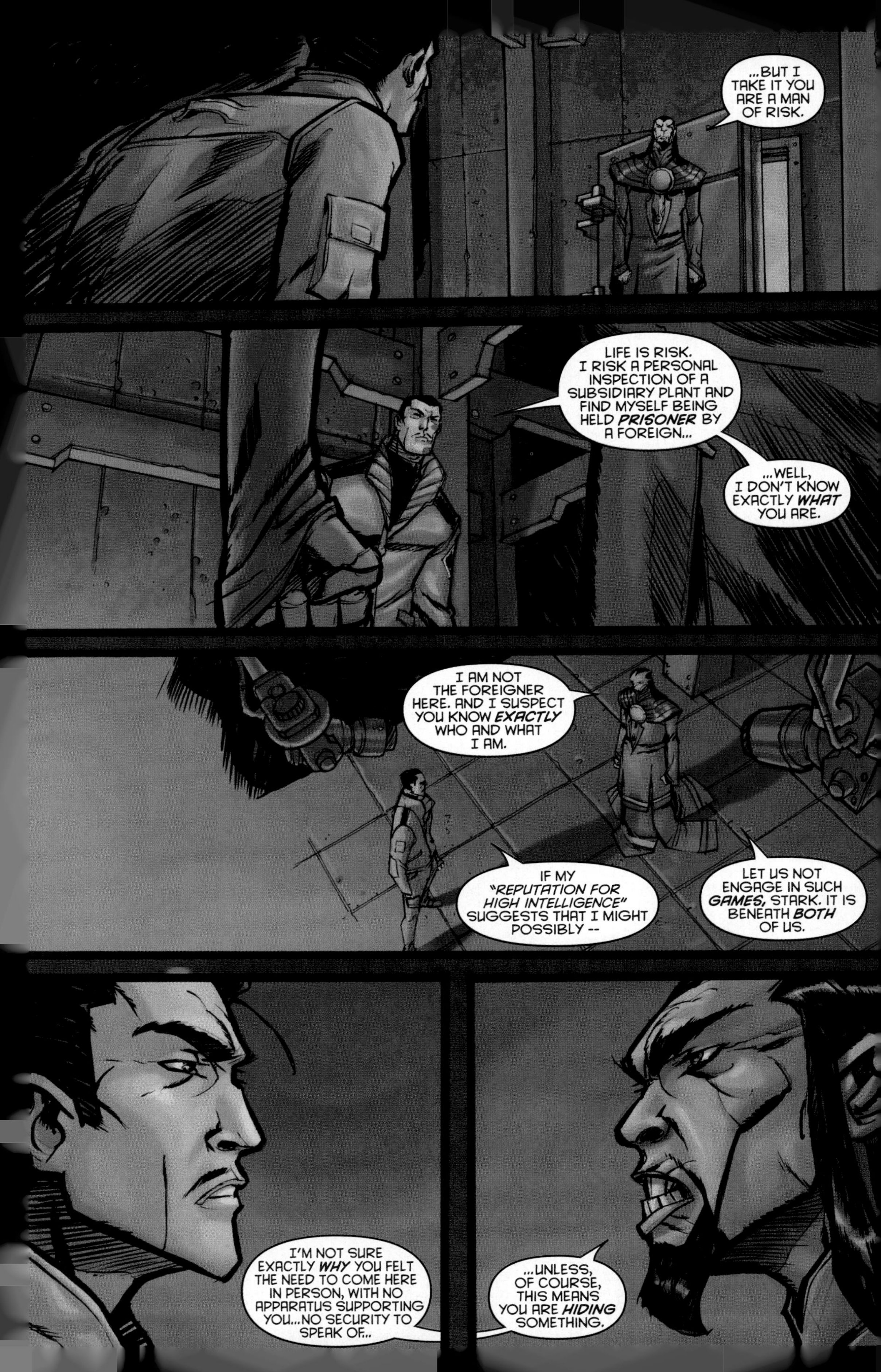
...BUT I TAKE IT YOU ARE A MAN OF RISK.
LIFE IS RISK. I RISK A PERSONAL INSPECTION OF A SUBSIDIARY PLANT AND FIND MYSELF BEING HELD PRISONER BY A FOREIGN...
...WELL, I DON'T KNOW EXACTLY WHAT YOU ARE.
I AM NOT THE FOREIGNER HERE. AND I SUSPECT YOU KNOW EXACTLY WHO AND WHAT I AM.
IF MY "REPUTATION FOR HIGH INTELLIGENCE" SUGGESTS THAT I MIGHT POSSIBLY --
LET US NOT ENGAGE IN SUCH GAMES, STARK. IT IS BENEATH BOTH OF US.
I'M NOT SURE EXACTLY WHY YOU FELT THE NEED TO COME HERE IN PERSON, WITH NO APPARATUS SUPPORTING YOU...NO SECURITY TO SPEAK OF...
...UNLESS, OF COURSE, THIS MEANS YOU ARE HIDING SOMETHING.

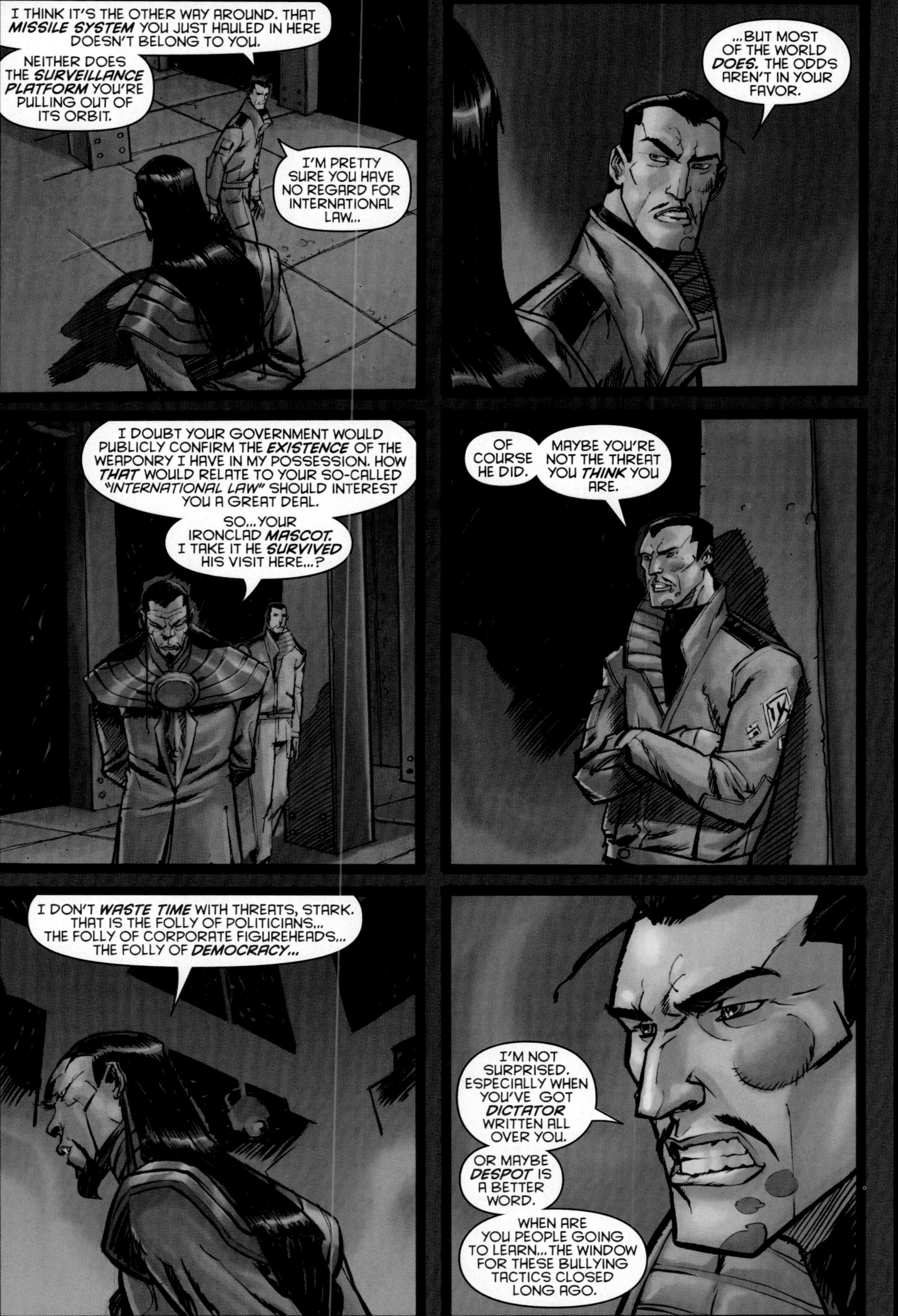
I THINK IT'S THE OTHER WAY AROUND. THAT MISSILE SYSTEM YOU JUST HAULED IN HERE DOESN'T BELONG TO YOU.
NEITHER DOES THE SURVEILLANCE PLATFORM YOU'RE PULLING OUT OF ITS ORBIT.
I'M PRETTY SURE YOU HAVE NO REGARD FOR INTERNATIONAL LAW...
...BUT MOST OF THE WORLD DOES. THE ODDS AREN'T IN YOUR FAVOR.
I DOUBT YOUR GOVERNMENT WOULD PUBLICLY CONFIRM THE EXISTENCE OF THE WEAPONRY I HAVE IN MY POSSESSION. HOW THAT WOULD RELATE TO YOUR SO-CALLED "INTERNATIONAL LAW" SHOULD INTEREST YOU A GREAT DEAL.
SO...YOUR IRONCLAD MASCOT. I TAKE IT HE SURVIVED HIS VISIT HERE...?
OF COURSE HE DID.
MAYBE YOU'RE NOT THE THREAT YOU THINK YOU ARE.
I DON'T WASTE TIME WITH THREATS, STARK. THAT IS THE FOLLY OF POLITICIANS... THE FOLLY OF CORPORATE FIGUREHEADS... THE FOLLY OF DEMOCRACY...
I'M NOT SURPRISED. ESPECIALLY WHEN YOU'VE GOT DICTATOR WRITTEN ALL OVER YOU.
OR MAYBE DESPOT IS A BETTER WORD.
WHEN ARE YOU PEOPLE GOING TO LEARN...THE WINDOW FOR THESE BULLYING TACTICS CLOSED LONG AGO.

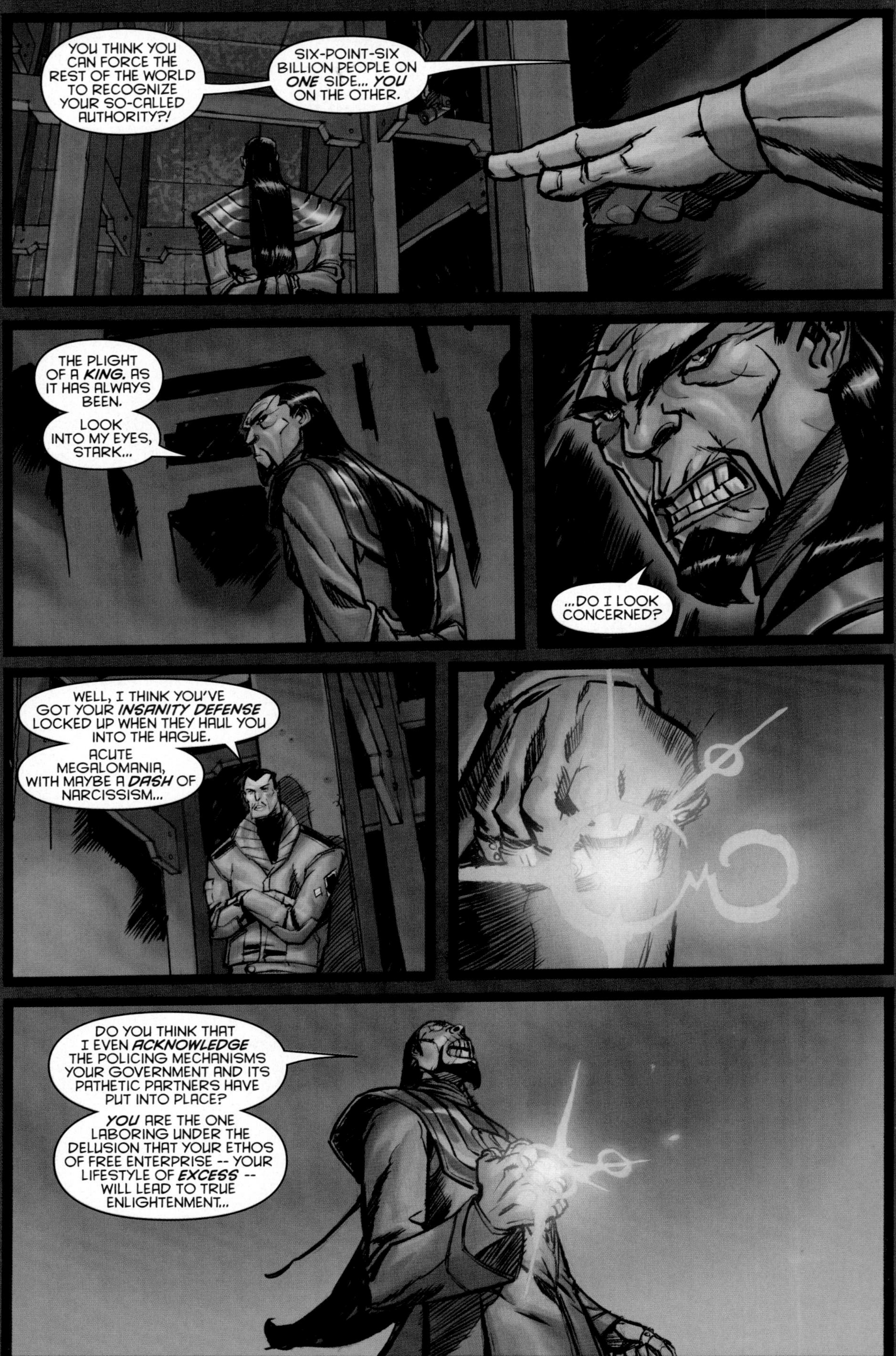
YOU THINK YOU CAN FORCE THE REST OF THE WORLD TO RECOGNIZE YOUR SO-CALLED AUTHORITY?!
SIX-POINT-SIX BILLION PEOPLE ON ONE SIDE... YOU ON THE OTHER.
THE PLIGHT OF A KING. AS IT HAS ALWAYS BEEN.
LOOK INTO MY EYES, STARK...
...DO I LOOK CONCERNED?
WELL, I THINK YOU'VE GOT YOUR INSANITY DEFENSE LOCKED UP WHEN THEY HAUL YOU INTO THE HAGUE.
ACUTE MEGALOMANIA, WITH MAYBE A DASH OF NARCISSISM...
DO YOU THINK THAT I EVEN ACKNOWLEDGE THE POLICING MECHANISMS YOUR GOVERNMENT AND ITS PATHETIC PARTNERS HAVE PUT INTO PLACE?
YOU ARE THE ONE LABORING UNDER THE DELUSION THAT YOUR ETHOS OF FREE ENTERPRISE -- YOUR LIFESTYLE OF EXCESS -- WILL LEAD TO TRUE ENLIGHTENMENT...

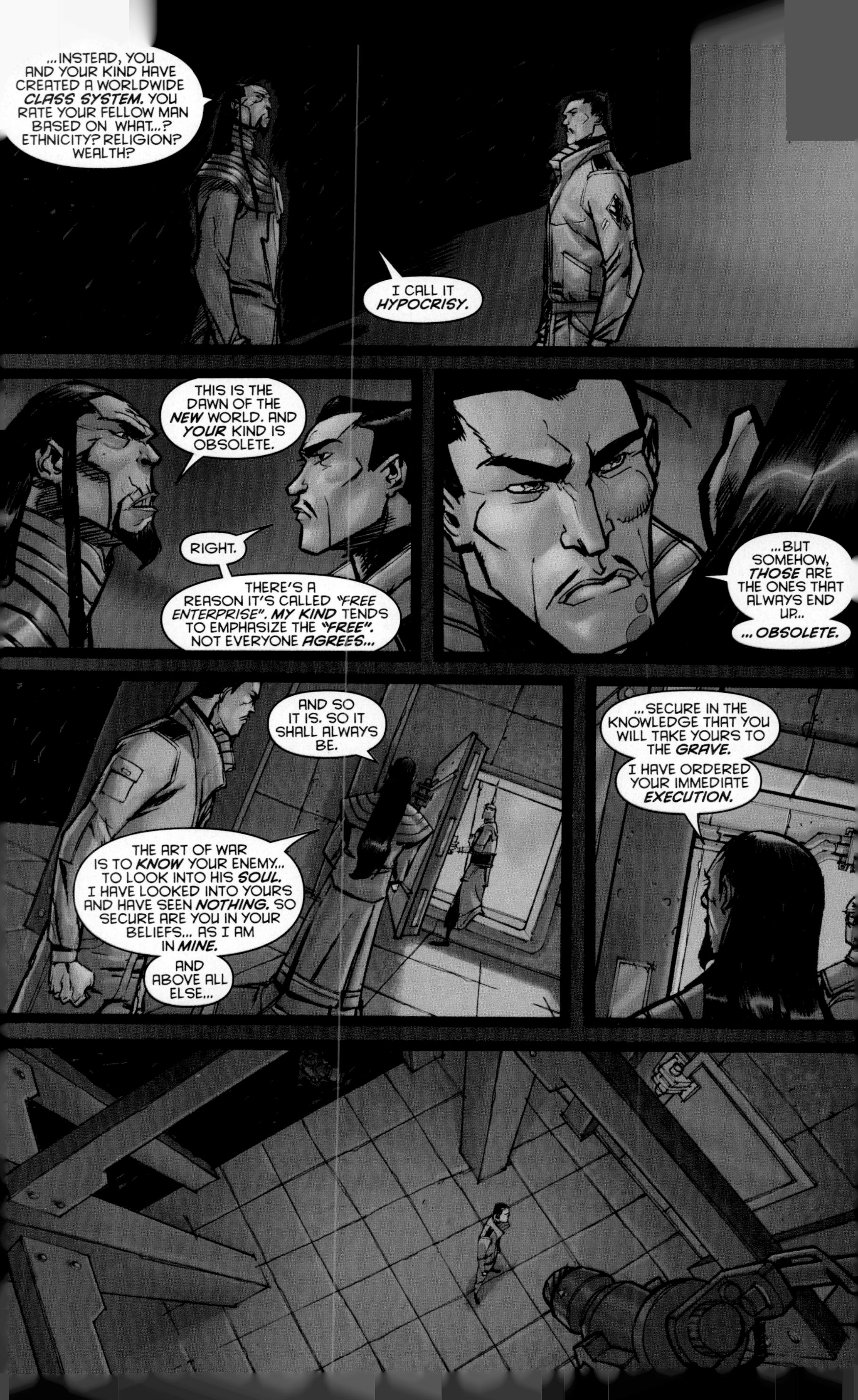
...INSTEAD, YOU AND YOUR KIND HAVE CREATED A WORLDWIDE CLASS SYSTEM. YOU RATE YOUR FELLOW MAN BASED ON WHAT...? ETHNICITY? RELIGION? WEALTH?
I CALL IT HYPOCRISY.
THIS IS THE DAWN OF THE NEW WORLD. AND YOUR KIND IS OBSOLETE.
RIGHT.
THERE'S A REASON IT'S CALLED "FREE ENTERPRISE". MY KIND TENDS TO EMPHASIZE THE "FREE". NOT EVERYONE AGREES...
...BUT SOMEHOW, THOSE ARE THE ONES THAT ALWAYS END UP...
...OBSOLETE.
AND SO IT IS. SO IT SHALL ALWAYS BE.
THE ART OF WAR IS TO KNOW YOUR ENEMY... TO LOOK INTO HIS SOUL. I HAVE LOOKED INTO YOURS AND HAVE SEEN NOTHING. SO SECURE ARE YOU IN YOUR BELIEFS... AS I AM IN MINE.
AND ABOVE ALL ELSE...
...SECURE IN THE KNOWLEDGE THAT YOU WILL TAKE YOURS TO THE GRAVE.
I HAVE ORDERED YOUR IMMEDIATE EXECUTION.

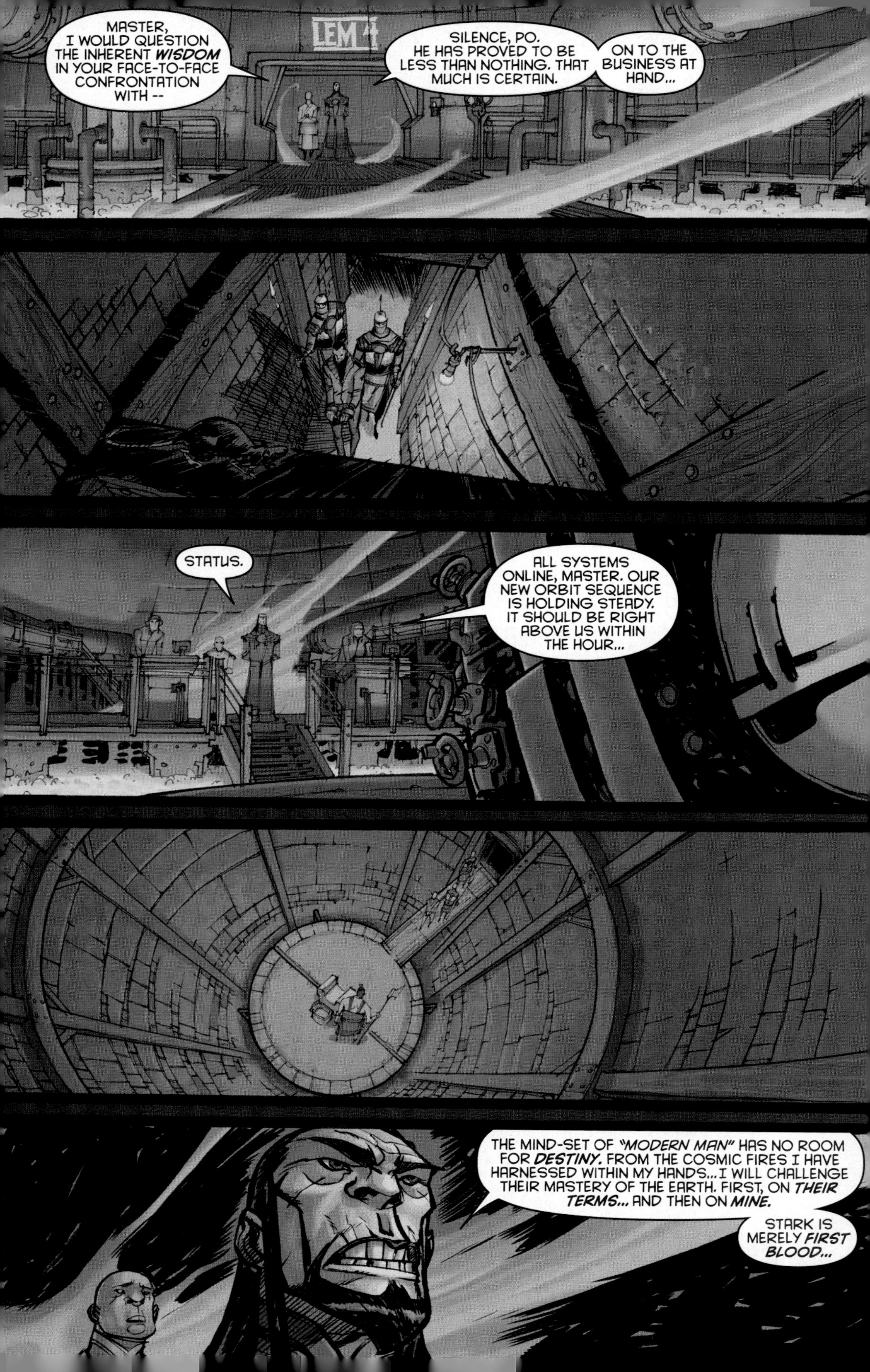
LEM 4
MASTER, I WOULD QUESTION THE INHERENT *WISDOM* IN YOUR FACE-TO-FACE CONFRONTATION WITH --
SILENCE, PO. HE HAS PROVED TO BE LESS THAN NOTHING. THAT MUCH IS CERTAIN.
ON TO THE BUSINESS AT HAND...
STATUS.
ALL SYSTEMS ONLINE, MASTER. OUR NEW ORBIT SEQUENCE IS HOLDING STEADY. IT SHOULD BE RIGHT ABOVE US WITHIN THE HOUR...
THE MIND-SET OF *"MODERN MAN"* HAS NO ROOM FOR *DESTINY.* FROM THE COSMIC FIRES I HAVE HARNESSED WITHIN MY HANDS... I WILL CHALLENGE THEIR MASTERY OF THE EARTH. FIRST, ON *THEIR TERMS...* AND THEN ON *MINE.*
STARK IS MERELY *FIRST BLOOD...*

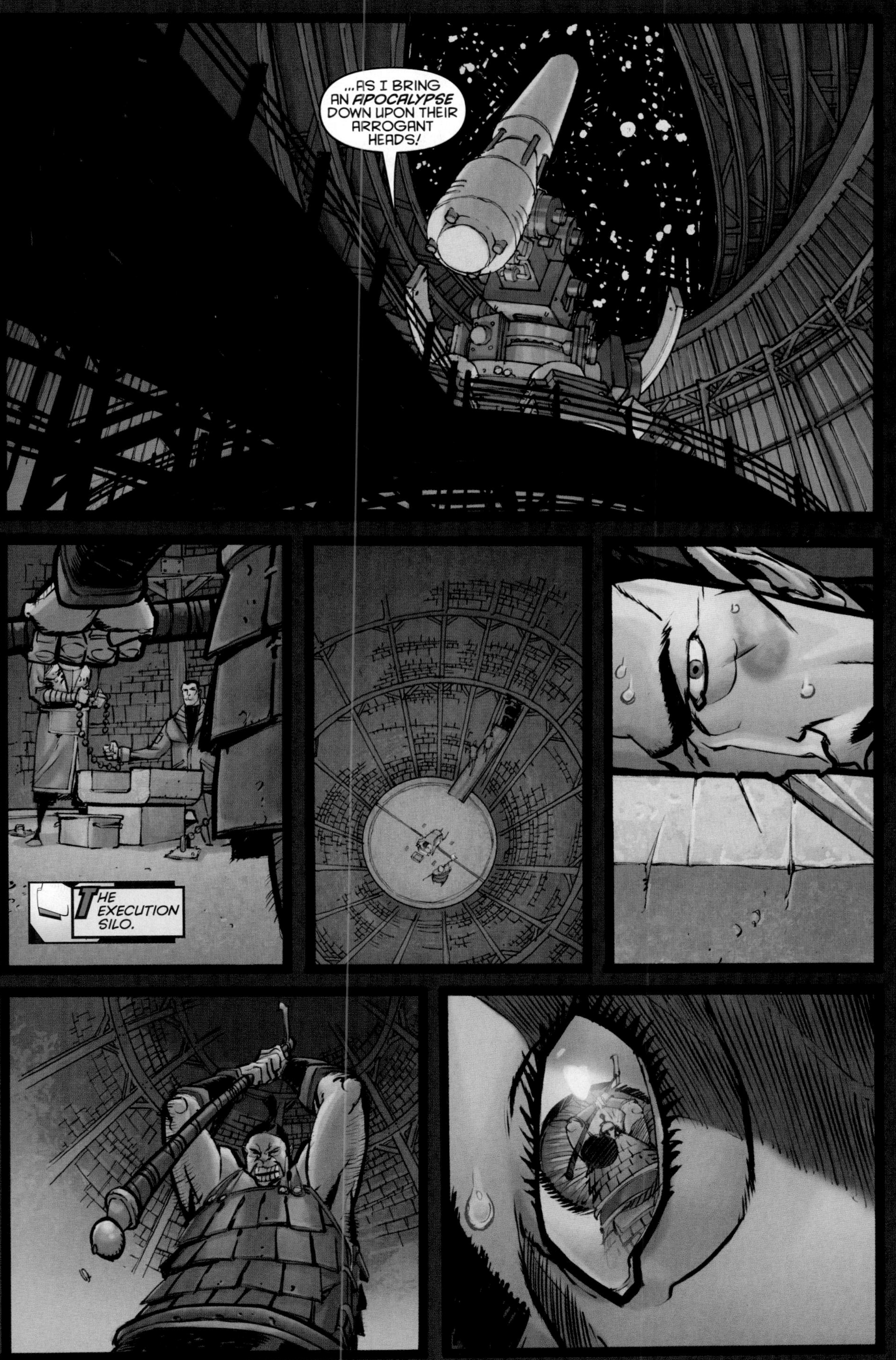
...AS I BRING AN APOCALYPSE DOWN UPON THEIR ARROGANT HEADS!
THE EXECUTION SILO.

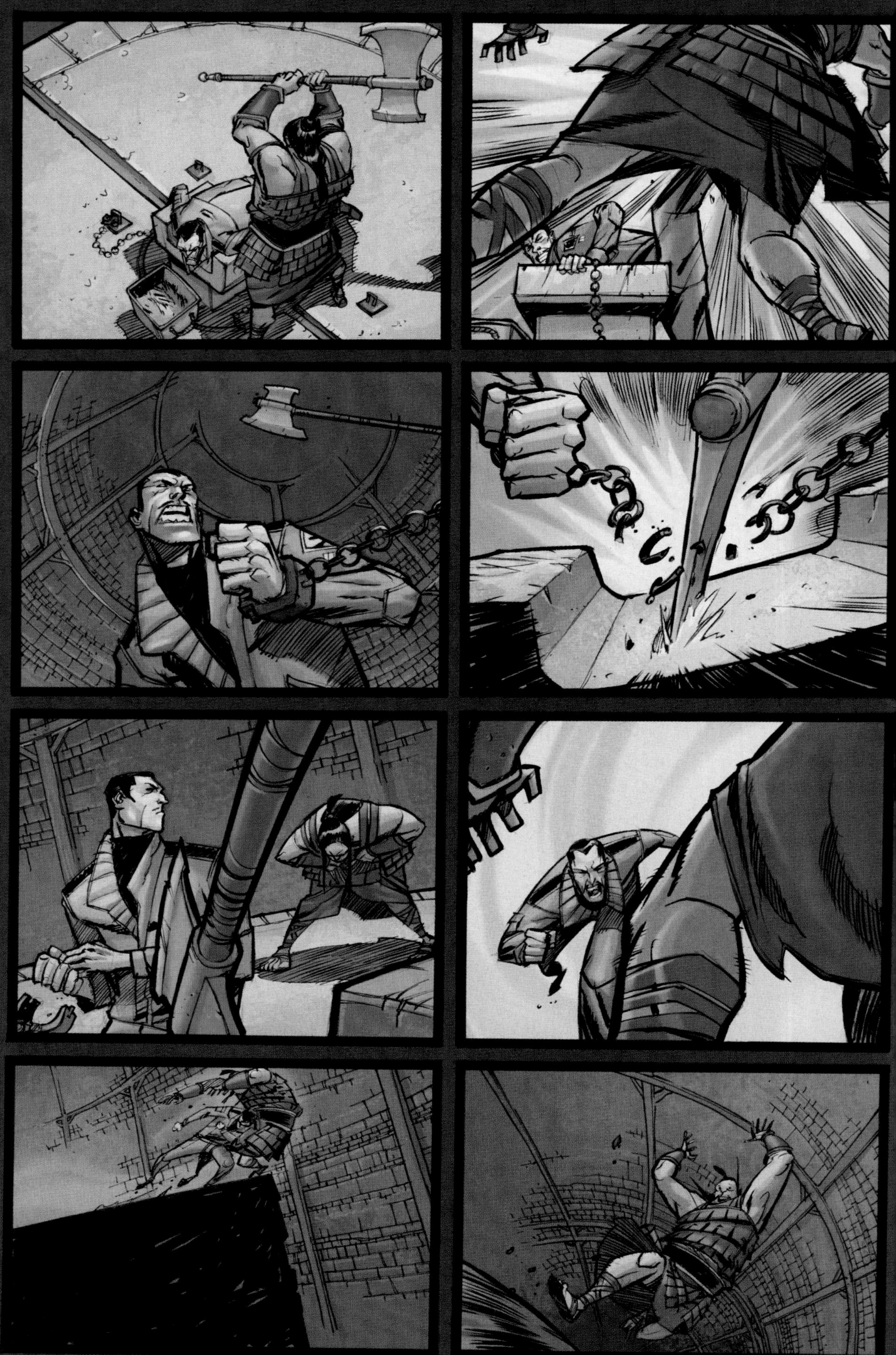

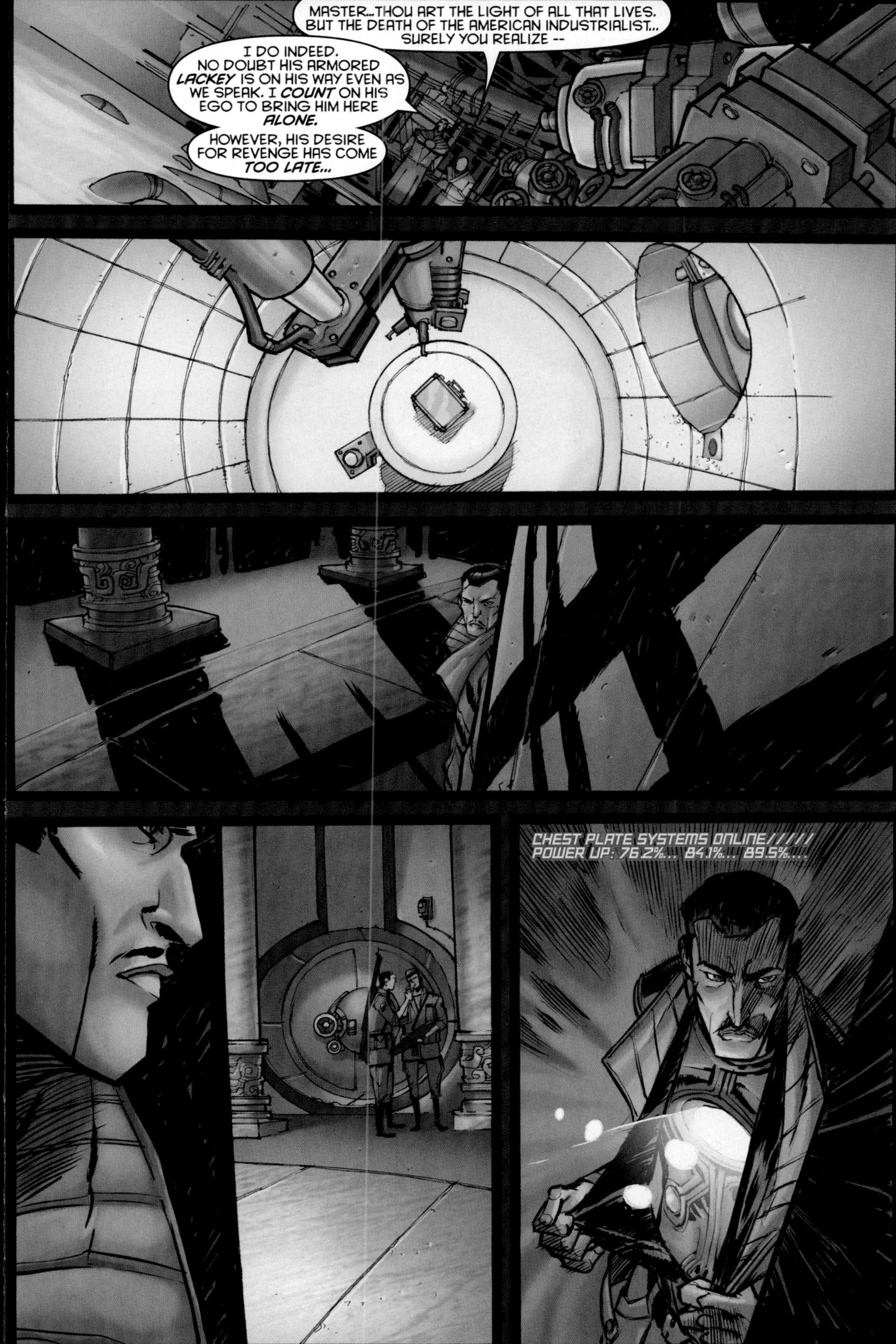
MASTER...THOU ART THE LIGHT OF ALL THAT LIVES. BUT THE DEATH OF THE AMERICAN INDUSTRIALIST... SURELY YOU REALIZE --
I DO INDEED. NO DOUBT HIS ARMORED *LACKEY* IS ON HIS WAY EVEN AS WE SPEAK. I *COUNT* ON HIS EGO TO BRING HIM HERE *ALONE.*
HOWEVER, HIS DESIRE FOR REVENGE HAS COME *TOO LATE...*
CHEST PLATE SYSTEMS ONLINE/////
POWER UP: 76.2%... 84.1%... 89.5%....

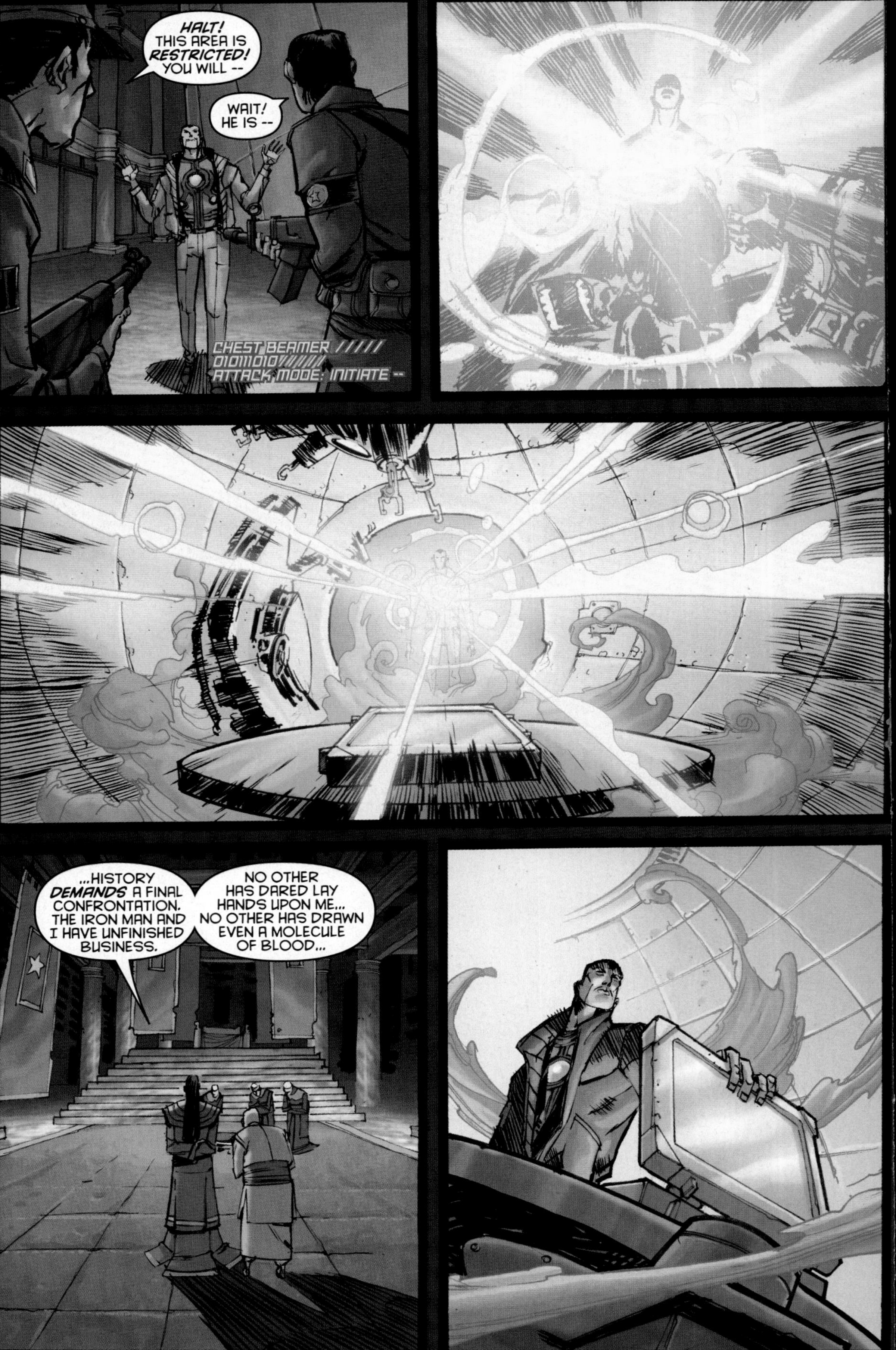
HALT! THIS AREA IS RESTRICTED! YOU WILL --
WAIT! HE IS --
CHEST BEAMER ///// 01011010////// ATTACK MODE: INITIATE --
...HISTORY DEMANDS A FINAL CONFRONTATION. THE IRON MAN AND I HAVE UNFINISHED BUSINESS.
NO OTHER HAS DARED LAY HANDS UPON ME... NO OTHER HAS DRAWN EVEN A MOLECULE OF BLOOD...

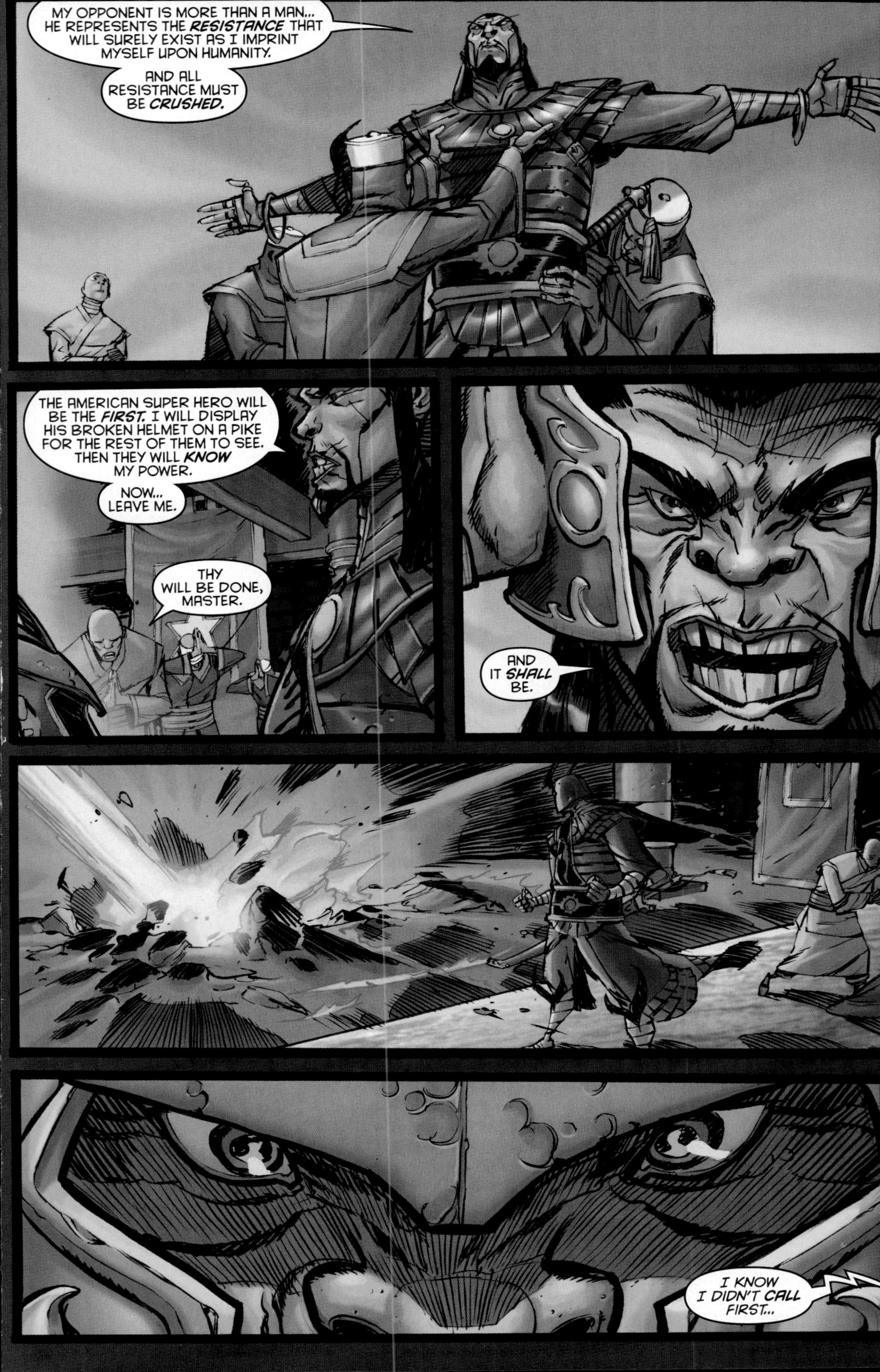
MY OPPONENT IS MORE THAN A MAN... HE REPRESENTS THE RESISTANCE THAT WILL SURELY EXIST AS I IMPRINT MYSELF UPON HUMANITY.
AND ALL RESISTANCE MUST BE CRUSHED.
THE AMERICAN SUPER HERO WILL BE THE FIRST. I WILL DISPLAY HIS BROKEN HELMET ON A PIKE FOR THE REST OF THEM TO SEE. THEN THEY WILL KNOW MY POWER.
NOW... LEAVE ME.
THY WILL BE DONE, MASTER.
AND IT SHALL BE.
I KNOW I DIDN'T CALL FIRST...

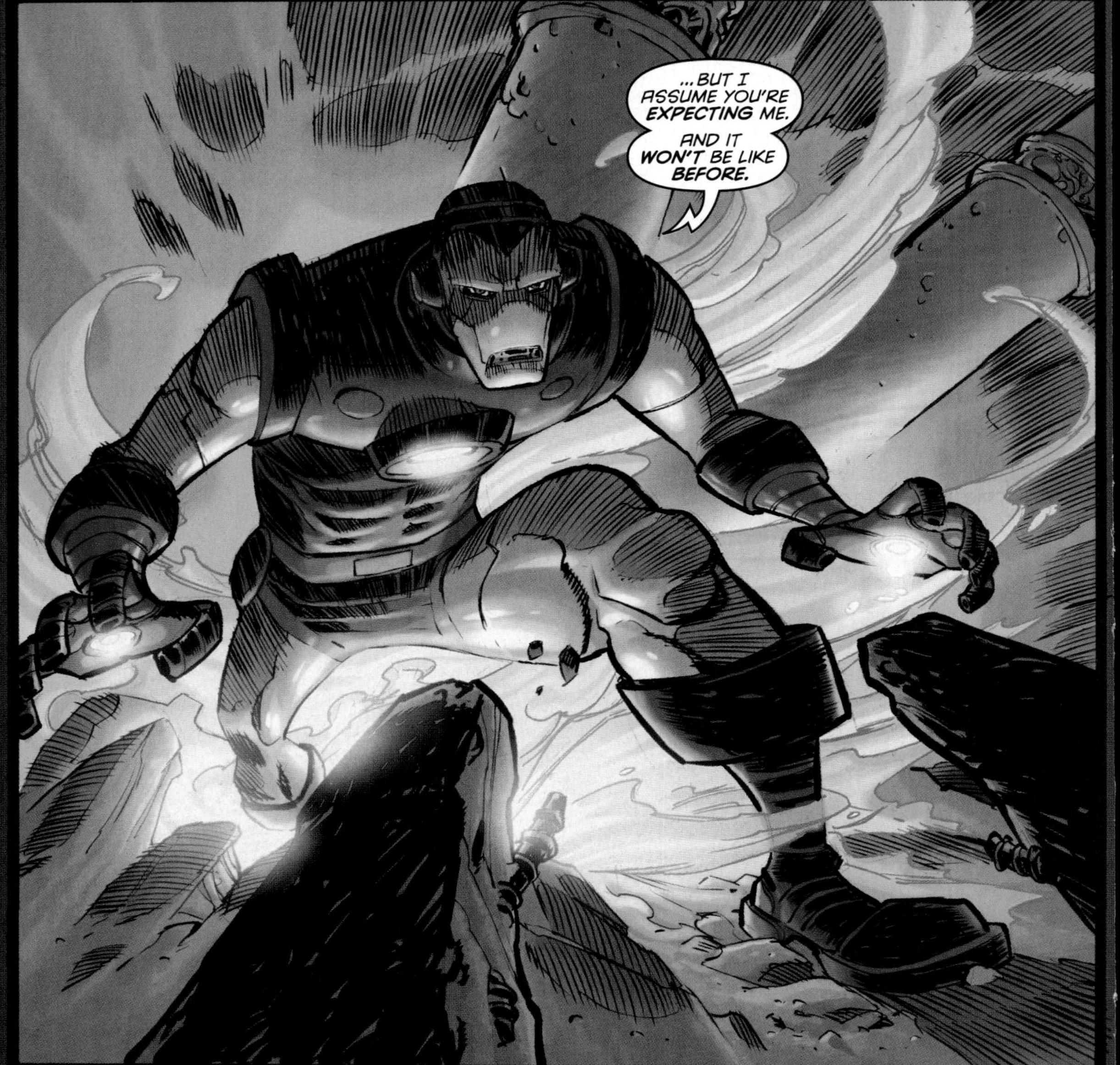
...BUT I ASSUME YOU'RE EXPECTING ME.
AND IT WON'T BE LIKE BEFORE.

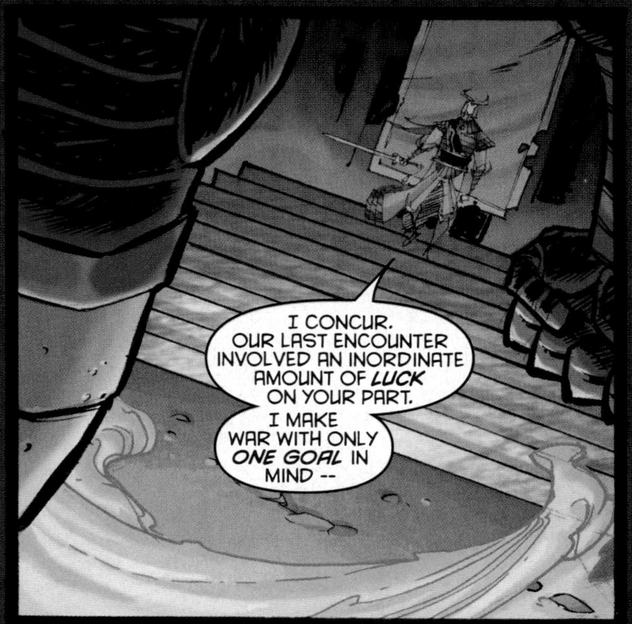
I CONCUR. OUR LAST ENCOUNTER INVOLVED AN INORDINATE AMOUNT OF LUCK ON YOUR PART.
I MAKE WAR WITH ONLY ONE GOAL IN MIND --

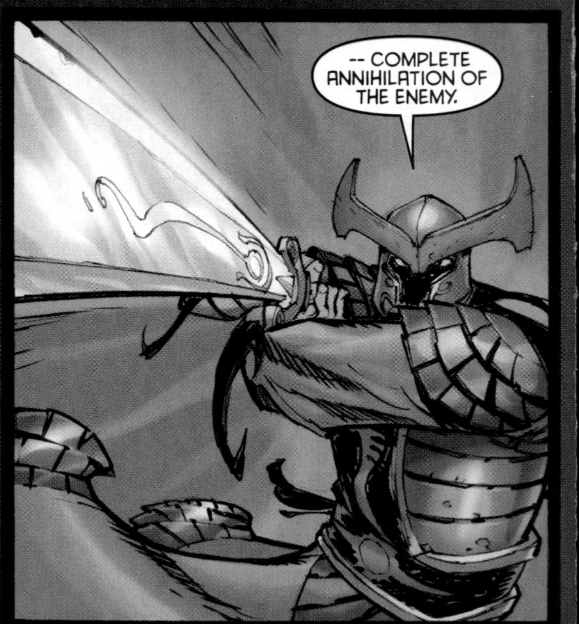
-- COMPLETE ANNIHILATION OF THE ENEMY.

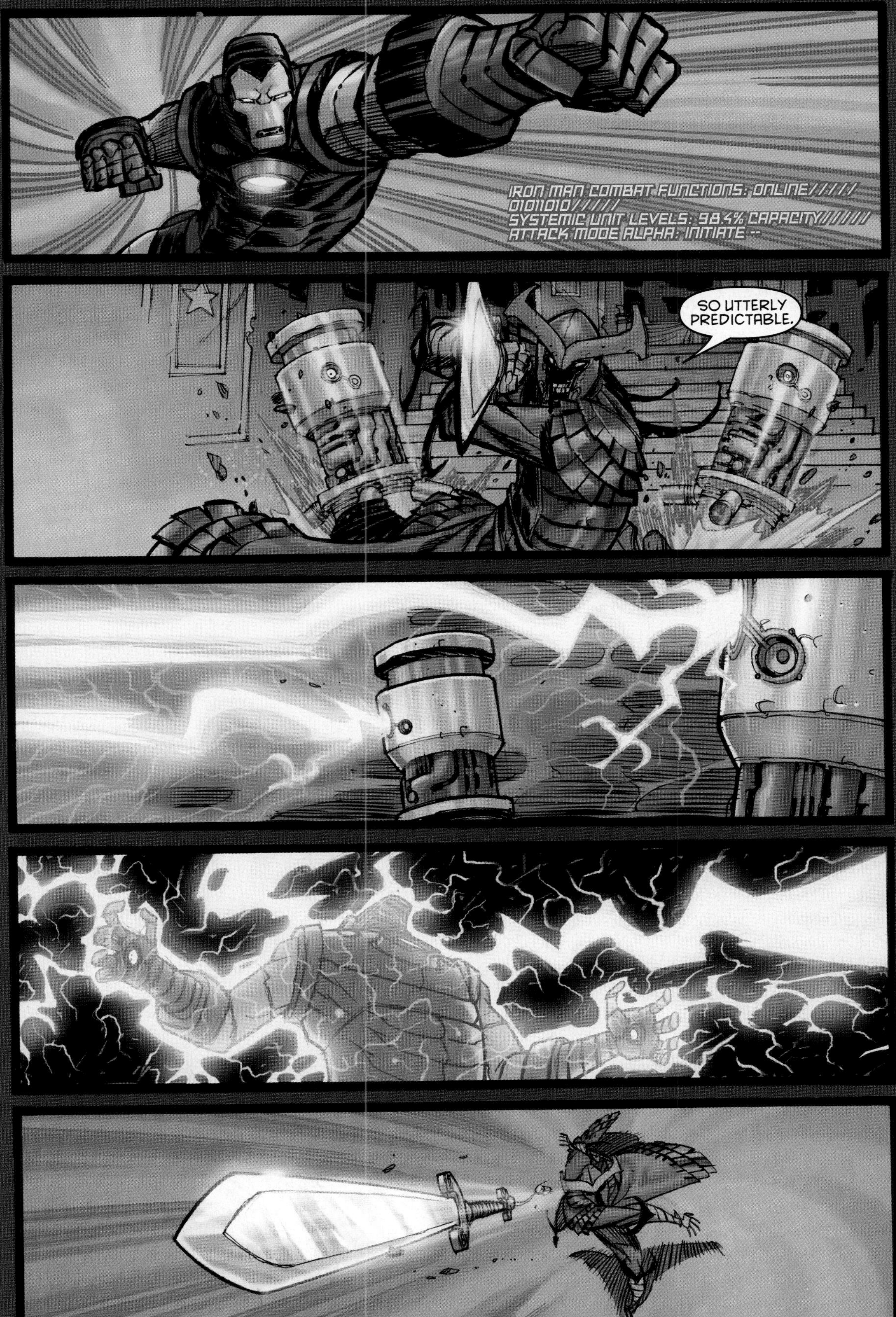
IRON MAN COMBAT FUNCTIONS: ONLINE//////
01011010//////
SYSTEMIC UNIT LEVELS: 98.4% CAPACITY//////
ATTACK MODE ALPHA: INITIATE --
SO UTTERLY PREDICTABLE.

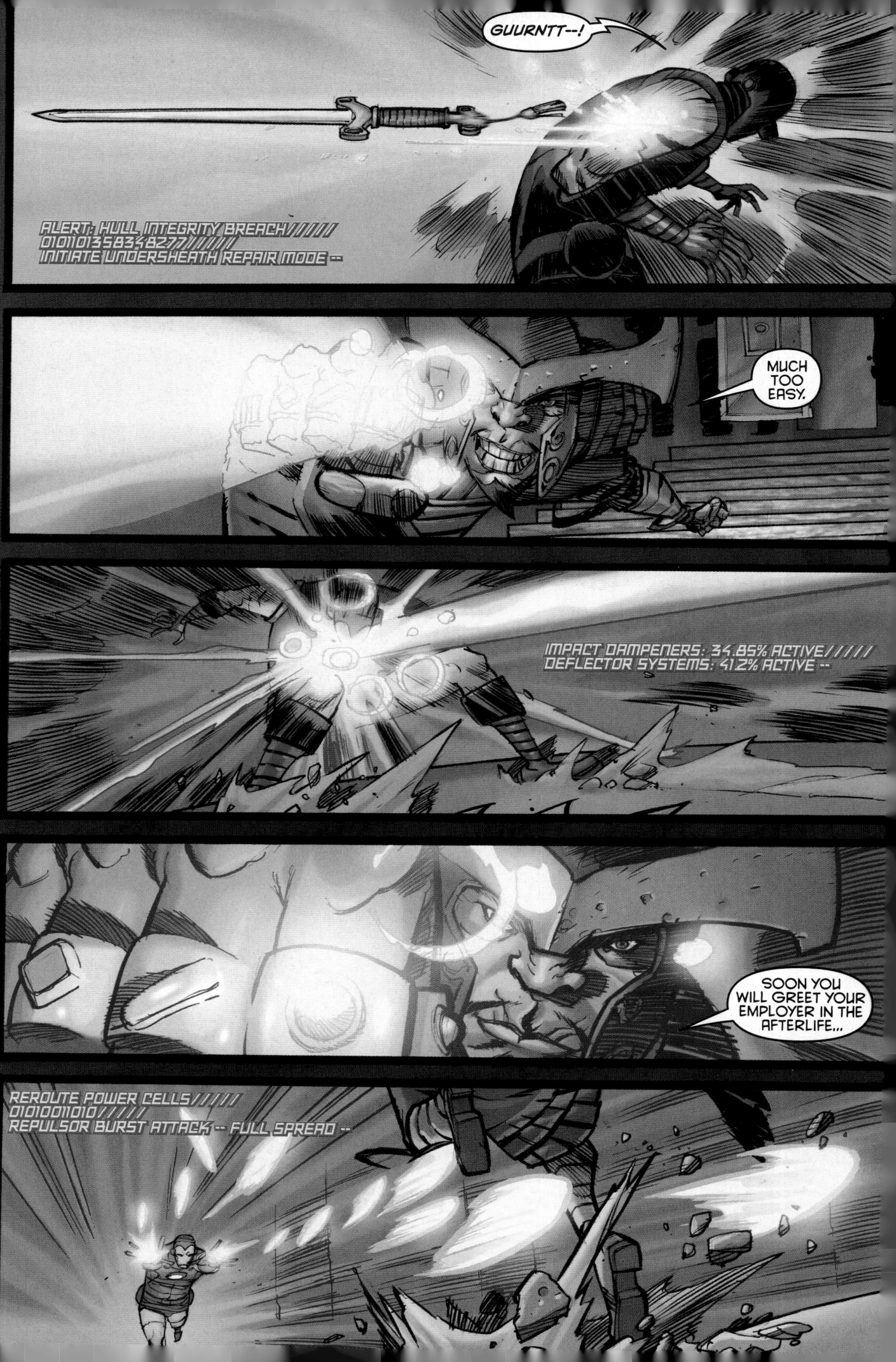
GUURNTT--!
ALERT: HULL INTEGRITY BREACH//////
0101101358348277//////
INITIATE UNDERSHEATH REPAIR MODE --
MUCH TOO EASY.
IMPACT DAMPENERS: 34.85% ACTIVE//////
DEFLECTOR SYSTEMS: 41.2% ACTIVE --
SOON YOU WILL GREET YOUR EMPLOYER IN THE AFTERLIFE...
REROUTE POWER CELLS//////
0101001101O//////
REPULSOR BURST ATTACK -- FULL SPREAD --

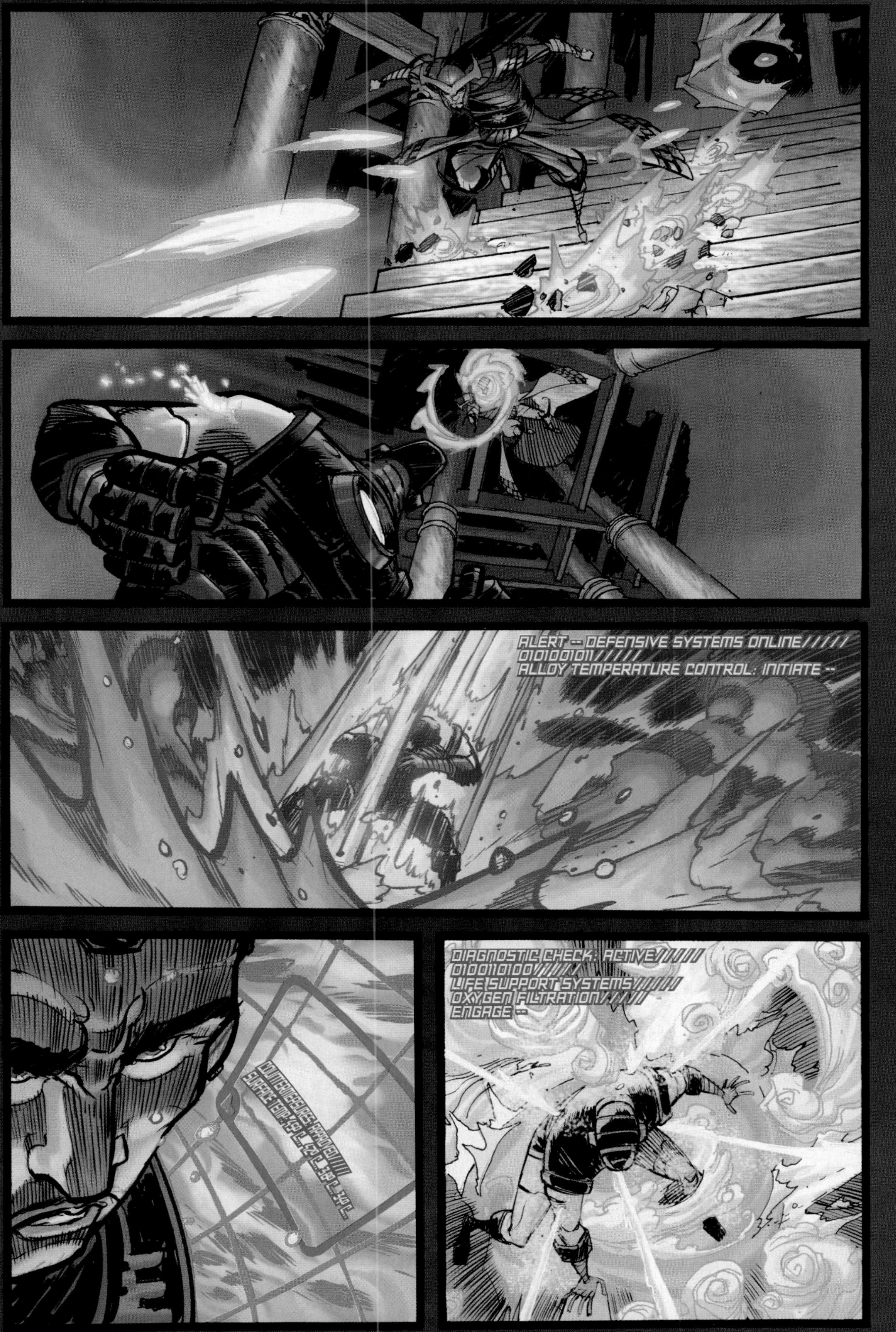
ALERT -- DEFENSIVE SYSTEMS ONLINE//////
0101001011//////
ALLOY TEMPERATURE CONTROL: INITIATE --
COUNTERMEASURES APPROVED//////
SURFACE TEMP: 49°C... 42°C... 38°C... 34°C...
DIAGNOSTIC CHECK: ACTIVE//////
0100110100//////
LIFE SUPPORT SYSTEMS//////
OXYGEN FILTRATION//////
ENGAGE --

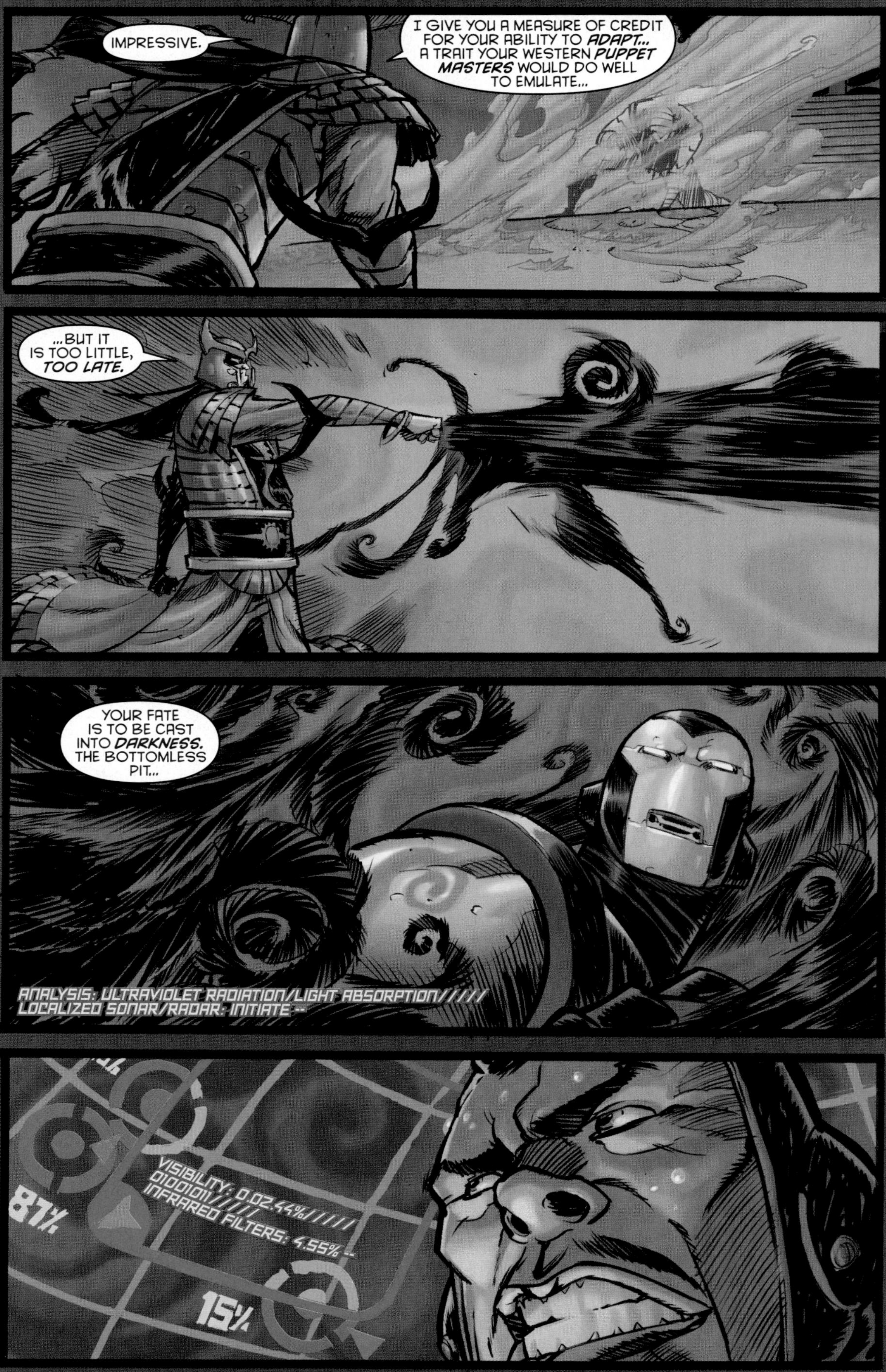
IMPRESSIVE.
I GIVE YOU A MEASURE OF CREDIT FOR YOUR ABILITY TO ADAPT... A TRAIT YOUR WESTERN PUPPET MASTERS WOULD DO WELL TO EMULATE...
...BUT IT IS TOO LITTLE, TOO LATE.
YOUR FATE IS TO BE CAST INTO DARKNESS. THE BOTTOMLESS PIT...
ANALYSIS: ULTRAVIOLET RADIATION/LIGHT ABSORPTION/////
LOCALIZED SONAR/RADAR: INITIATE --
VISIBILITY: 0.02.44%/////
01001011/////
INFRARED FILTERS: 4.55% --
87%
15%

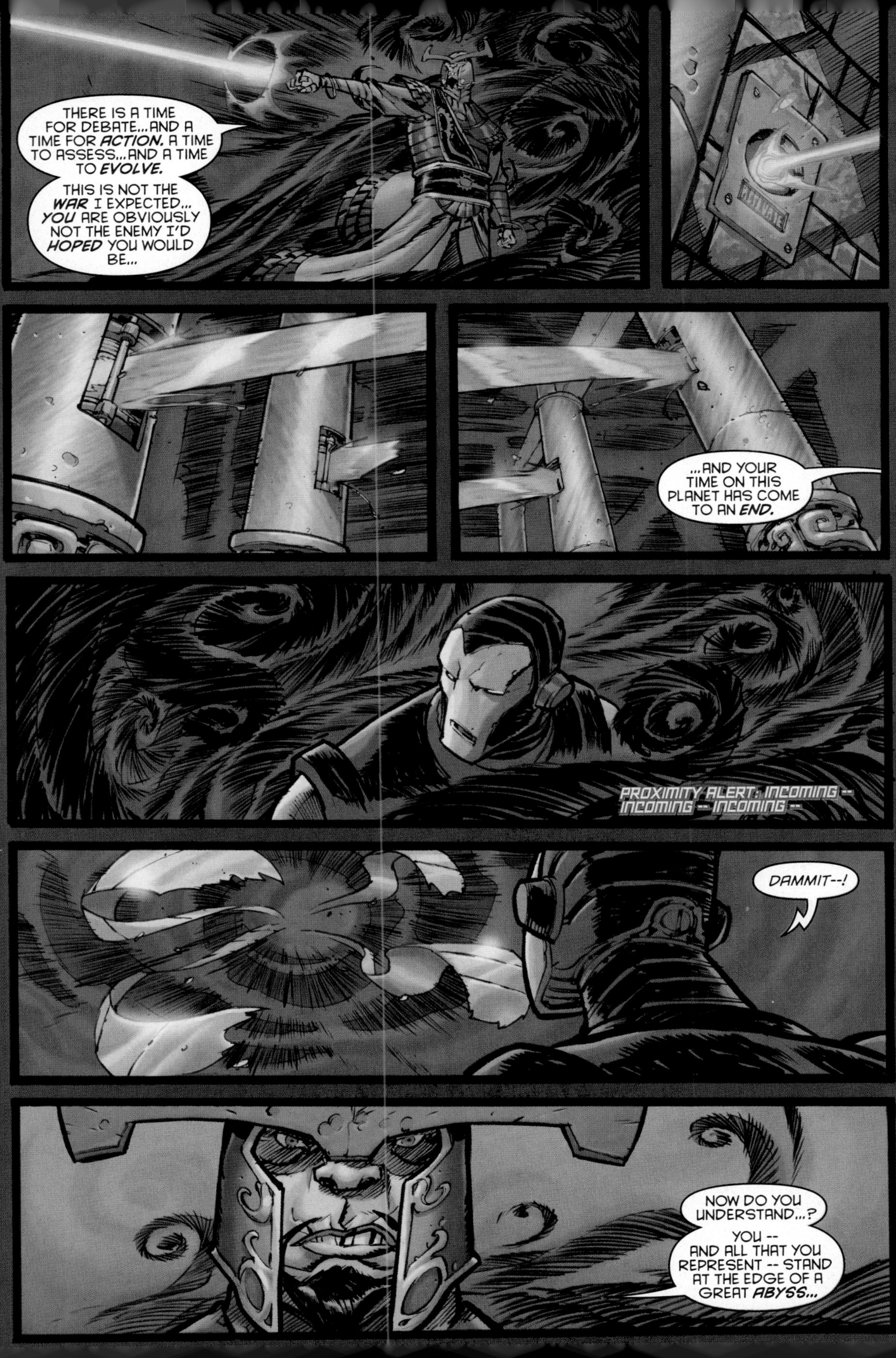
THERE IS A TIME FOR DEBATE...AND A TIME FOR ACTION. A TIME TO ASSESS...AND A TIME TO EVOLVE.
THIS IS NOT THE WAR I EXPECTED... YOU ARE OBVIOUSLY NOT THE ENEMY I'D HOPED YOU WOULD BE...
...AND YOUR TIME ON THIS PLANET HAS COME TO AN END.
PROXIMITY ALERT: INCOMING -- INCOMING -- INCOMING --
DAMMIT--!
NOW DO YOU UNDERSTAND...?
YOU -- AND ALL THAT YOU REPRESENT -- STAND AT THE EDGE OF A GREAT ABYSS...

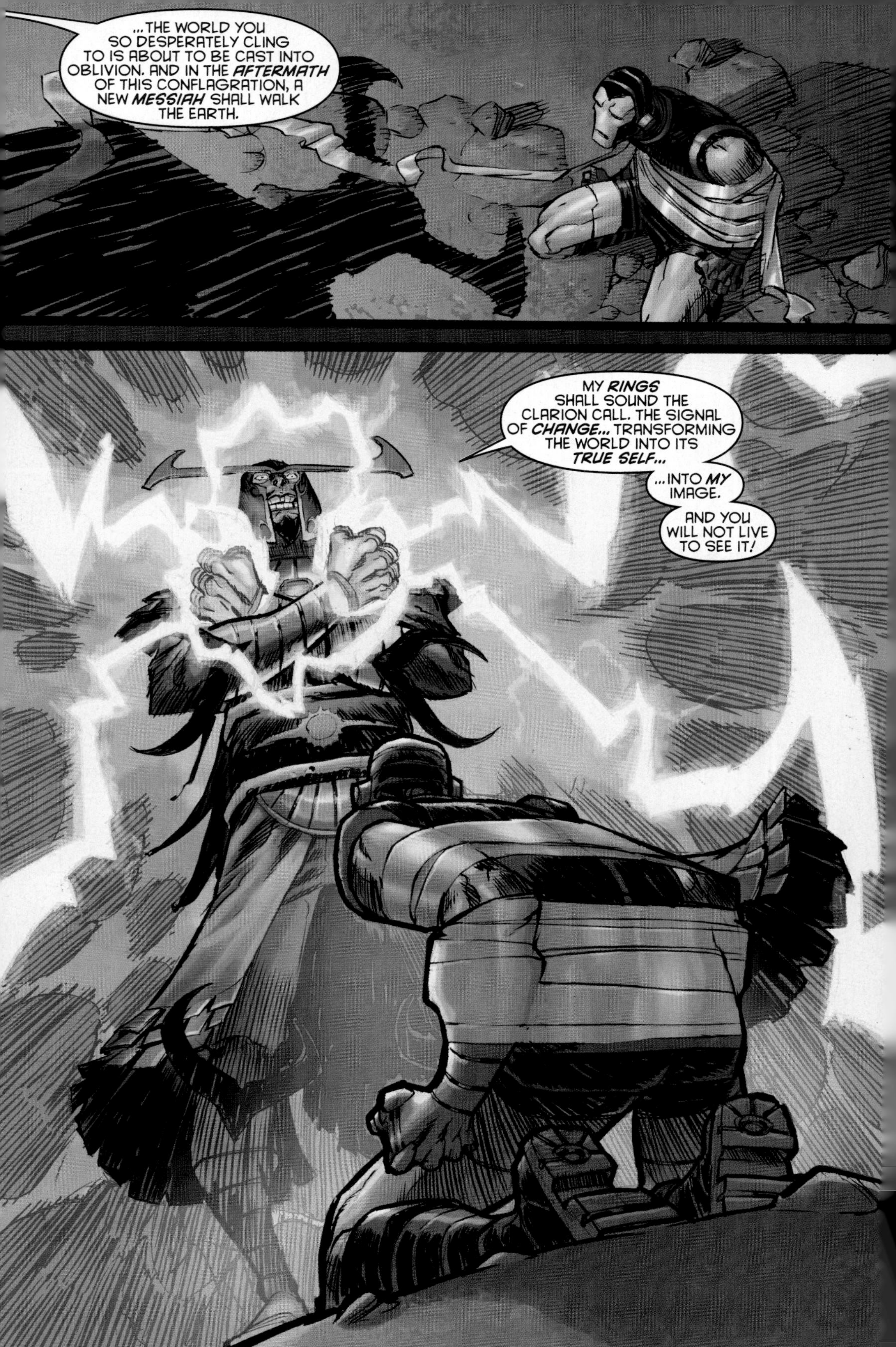
...THE WORLD YOU SO DESPERATELY CLING TO IS ABOUT TO BE CAST INTO OBLIVION. AND IN THE AFTERMATH OF THIS CONFLAGRATION, A NEW MESSIAH SHALL WALK THE EARTH.
MY RINGS SHALL SOUND THE CLARION CALL. THE SIGNAL OF CHANGE... TRANSFORMING THE WORLD INTO ITS TRUE SELF...
...INTO MY IMAGE.
AND YOU WILL NOT LIVE TO SEE IT!

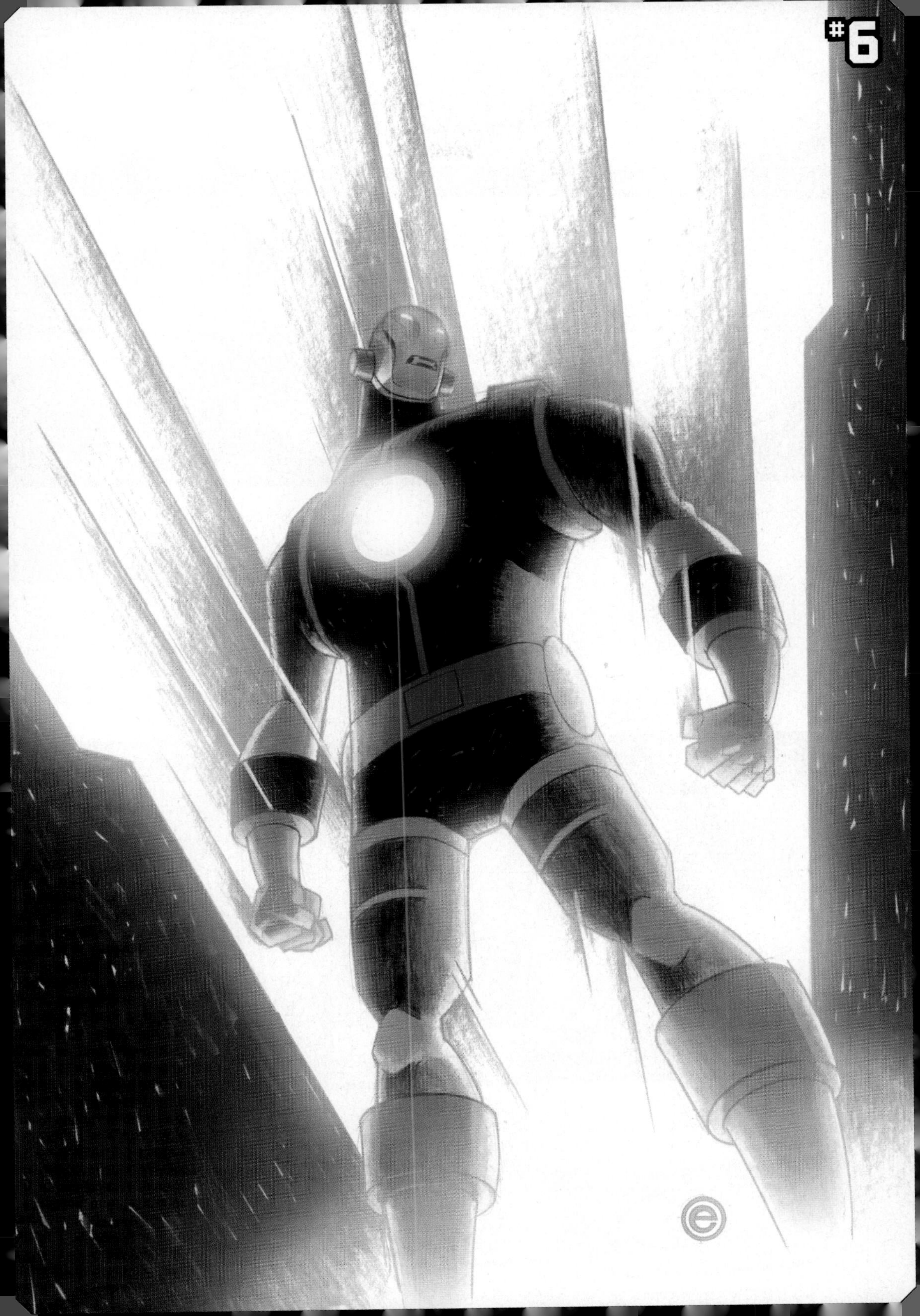
#6

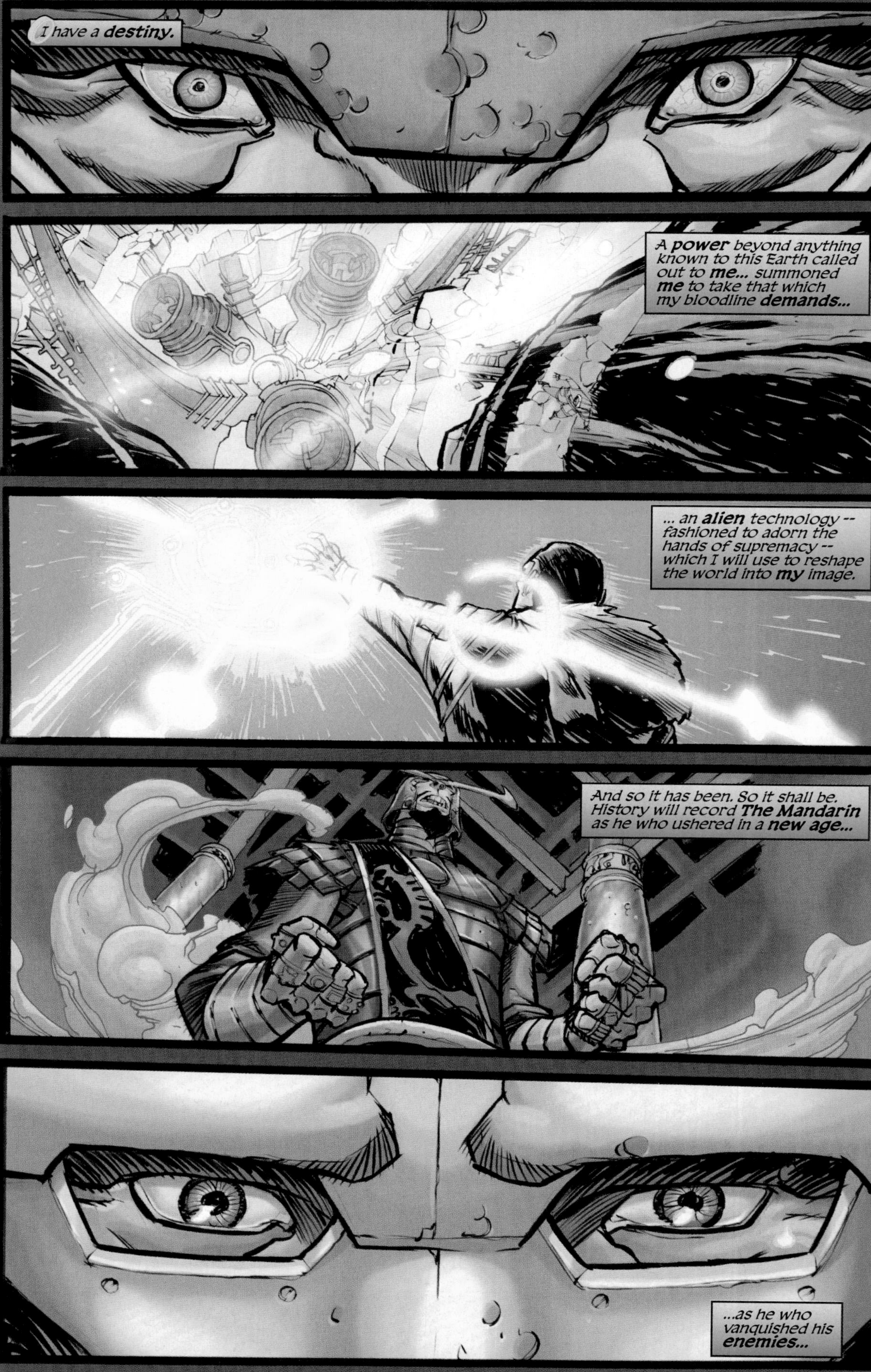
I have a destiny.
A power beyond anything known to this Earth called out to me... summoned me to take that which my bloodline demands...
... an alien technology -- fashioned to adorn the hands of supremacy -- which I will use to reshape the world into my image.
And so it has been. So it shall be. History will record The Mandarin as he who ushered in a new age...
...as he who vanquished his enemies...

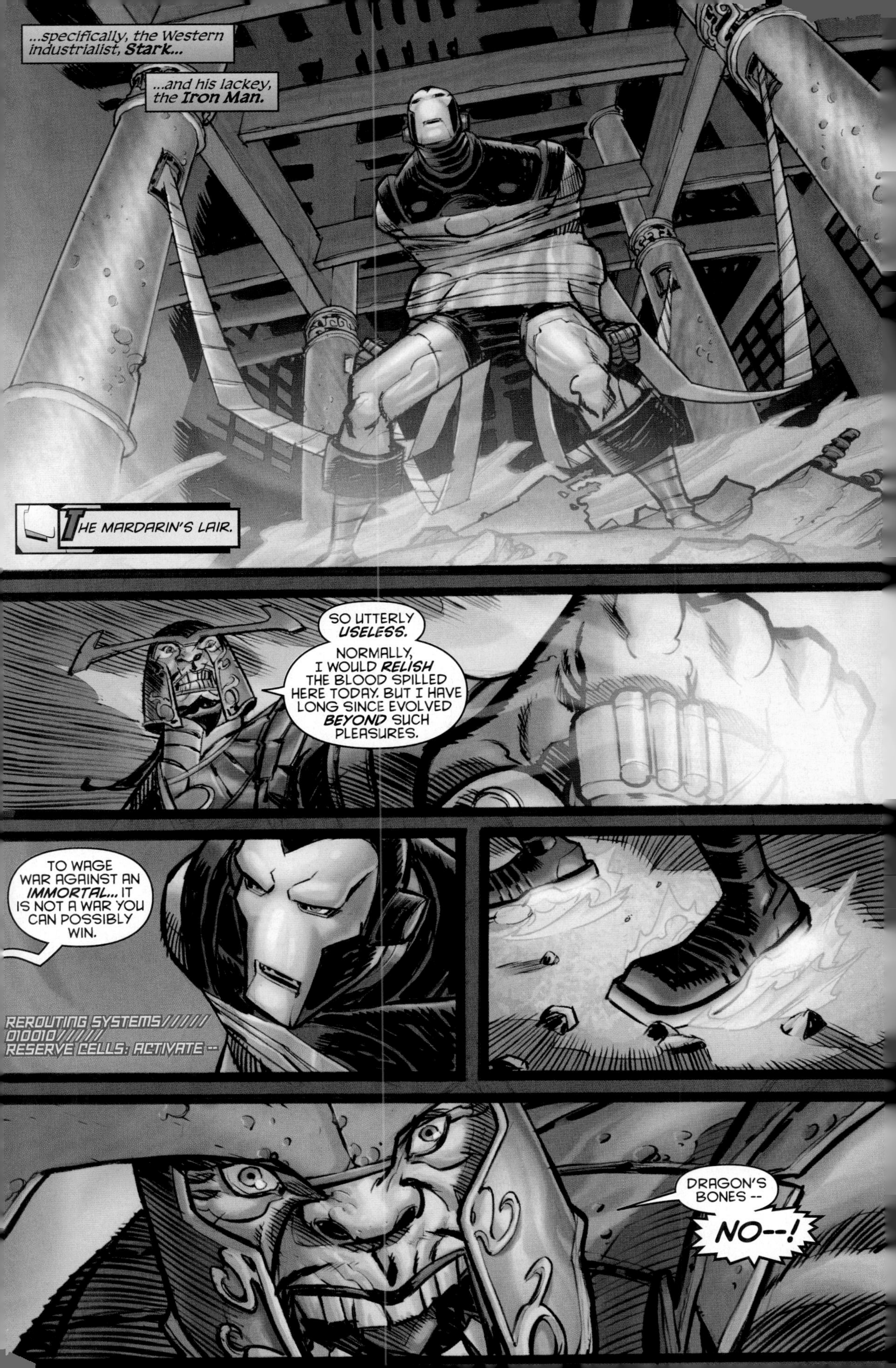
...specifically, the Western industrialist, Stark...
...and his lackey, the Iron Man.
THE MANDARIN'S LAIR.
SO UTTERLY USELESS.
NORMALLY, I WOULD RELISH THE BLOOD SPILLED HERE TODAY. BUT I HAVE LONG SINCE EVOLVED BEYOND SUCH PLEASURES.
TO WAGE WAR AGAINST AN IMMORTAL... IT IS NOT A WAR YOU CAN POSSIBLY WIN.
REROUTING SYSTEMS//////
010010//////
RESERVE CELLS: ACTIVATE --
DRAGON'S BONES --
NO--!

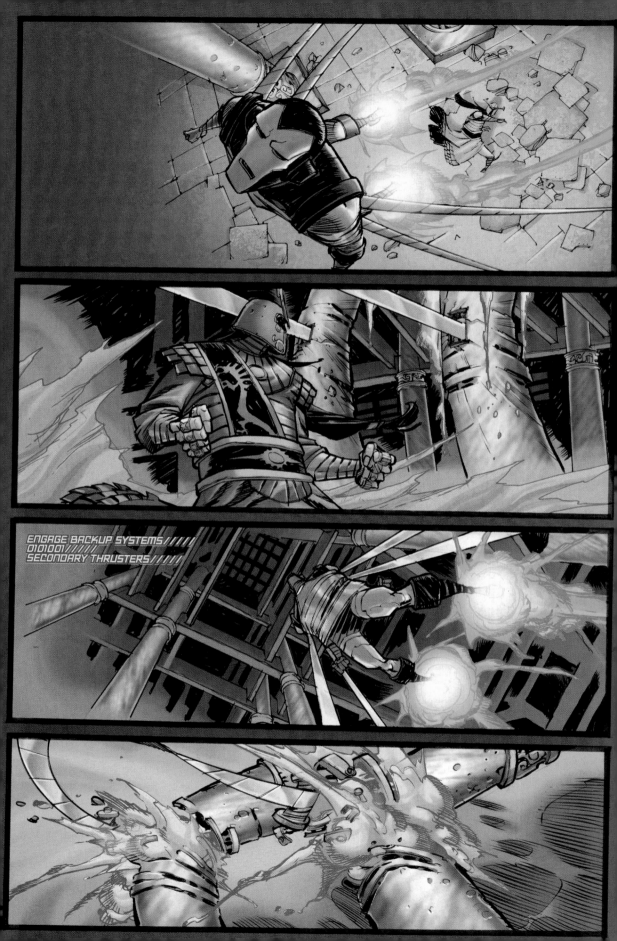

ENGAGE BACKUP SYSTEMS//////
010100I//////
SECONDARY THRUSTERS//////

YOU HAVE MERELY *POSTPONED* WHAT IS FATED TO BE, BUT I WILL CONCEDE *THIS*... EVEN IN THESE *FINAL* MOMENTS --

-- YOU HAVE MADE FOR GOOD SPORT.

INCOMING//////
INCOMING//////
INITIATE: AUTO-AVOIDANCE SYSTEMS//////
010010111//////

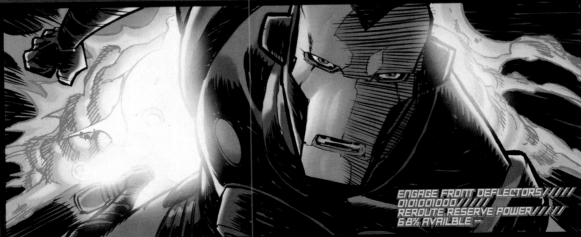

ENGAGE FRONT DEFLECTORS//////
010100100//////
REROUTE RESERVE POWER//////
68% AVAILBLE --

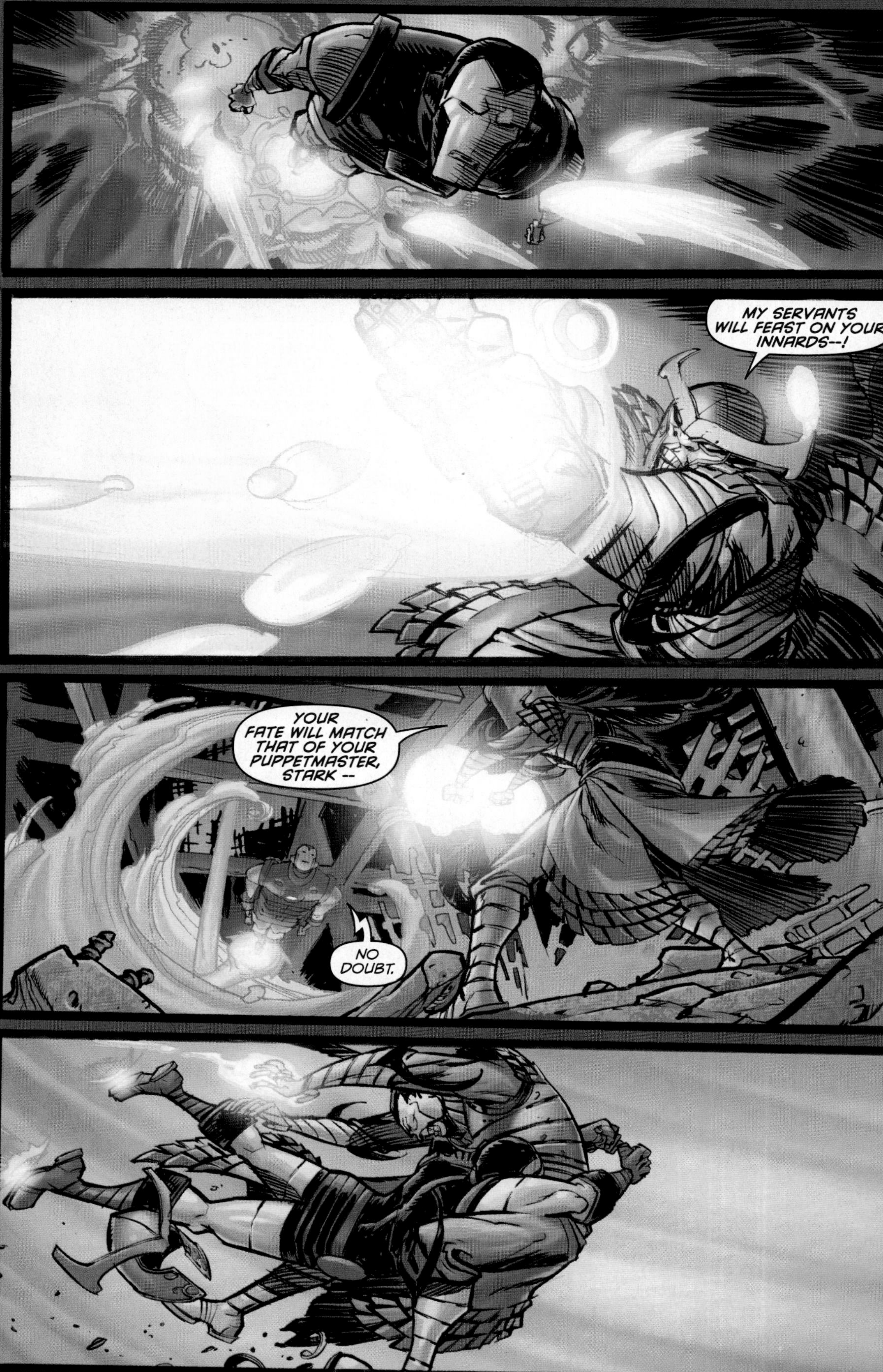
MY SERVANTS WILL FEAST ON YOUR INNARDS--!
YOUR FATE WILL MATCH THAT OF YOUR PUPPETMASTER, STARK --
NO DOUBT.

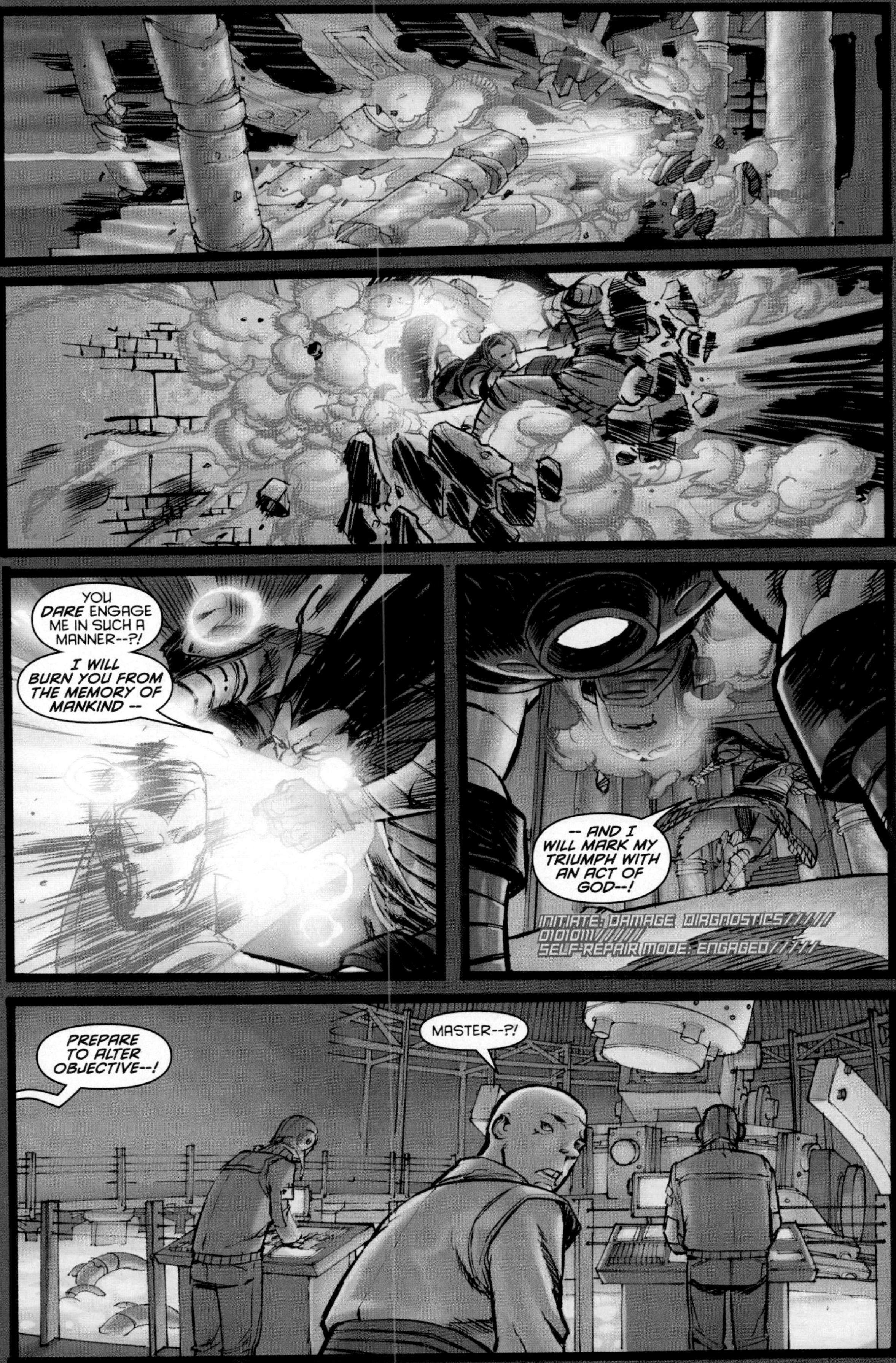
YOU DARE ENGAGE ME IN SUCH A MANNER--?!
I WILL BURN YOU FROM THE MEMORY OF MANKIND --
-- AND I WILL MARK MY TRIUMPH WITH AN ACT OF GOD--!
INITIATE: DAMAGE DIAGNOSTICS//////
01010111///////
SELF-REPAIR MODE: ENGAGED/////
PREPARE TO ALTER OBJECTIVE--!
MASTER--?!

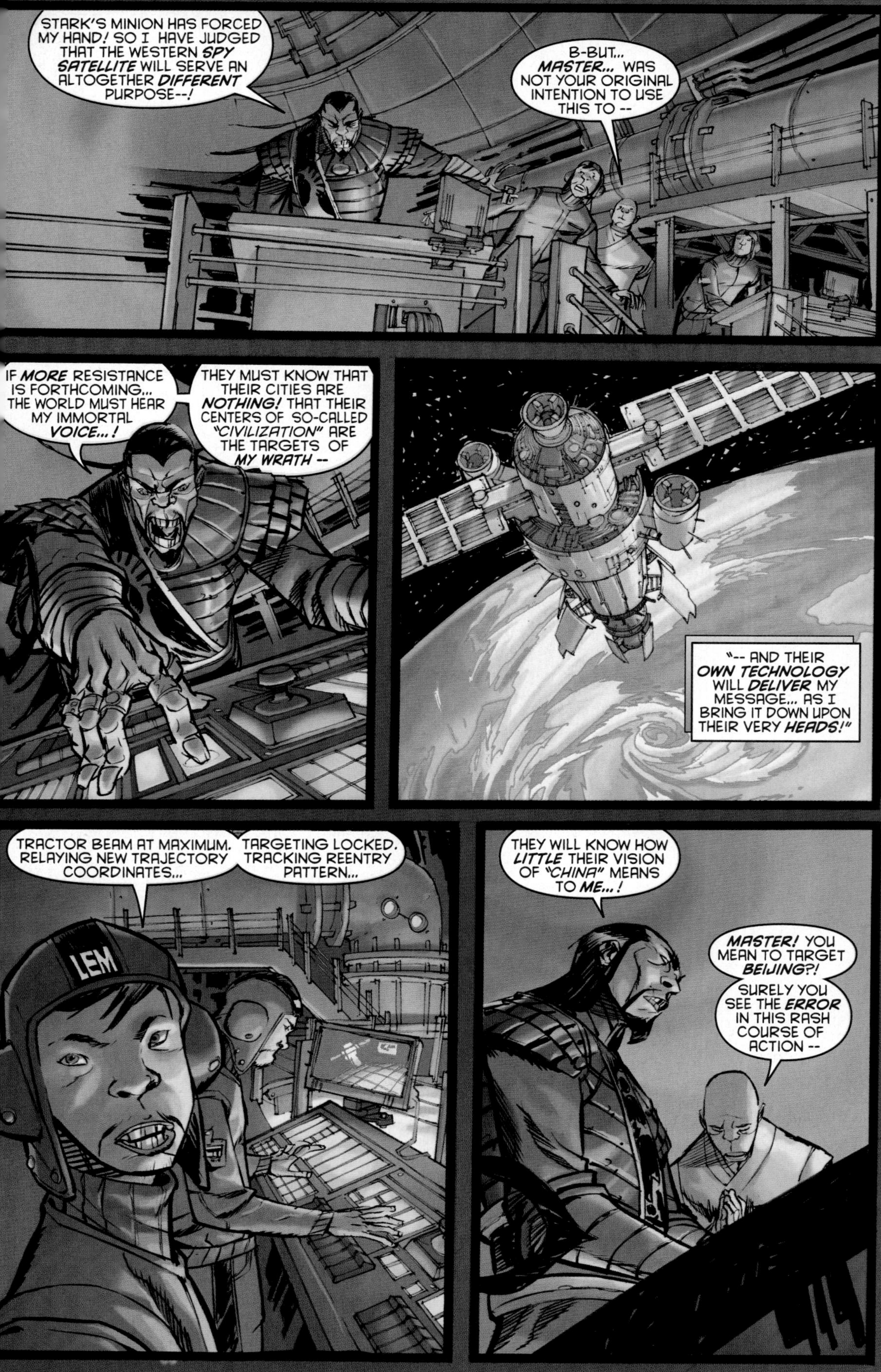
STARK'S MINION HAS FORCED MY HAND! SO I HAVE JUDGED THAT THE WESTERN SPY SATELLITE WILL SERVE AN ALTOGETHER DIFFERENT PURPOSE--!
B-BUT... MASTER... WAS NOT YOUR ORIGINAL INTENTION TO USE THIS TO --
IF MORE RESISTANCE IS FORTHCOMING... THE WORLD MUST HEAR MY IMMORTAL VOICE...!
THEY MUST KNOW THAT THEIR CITIES ARE NOTHING! THAT THEIR CENTERS OF SO-CALLED "CIVILIZATION" ARE THE TARGETS OF MY WRATH --
"-- AND THEIR OWN TECHNOLOGY WILL DELIVER MY MESSAGE... AS I BRING IT DOWN UPON THEIR VERY HEADS!"
TRACTOR BEAM AT MAXIMUM. RELAYING NEW TRAJECTORY COORDINATES...
TARGETING LOCKED. TRACKING REENTRY PATTERN...
LEM
THEY WILL KNOW HOW LITTLE THEIR VISION OF "CHINA" MEANS TO ME...!
MASTER! YOU MEAN TO TARGET BEIJING?!
SURELY YOU SEE THE ERROR IN THIS RASH COURSE OF ACTION --

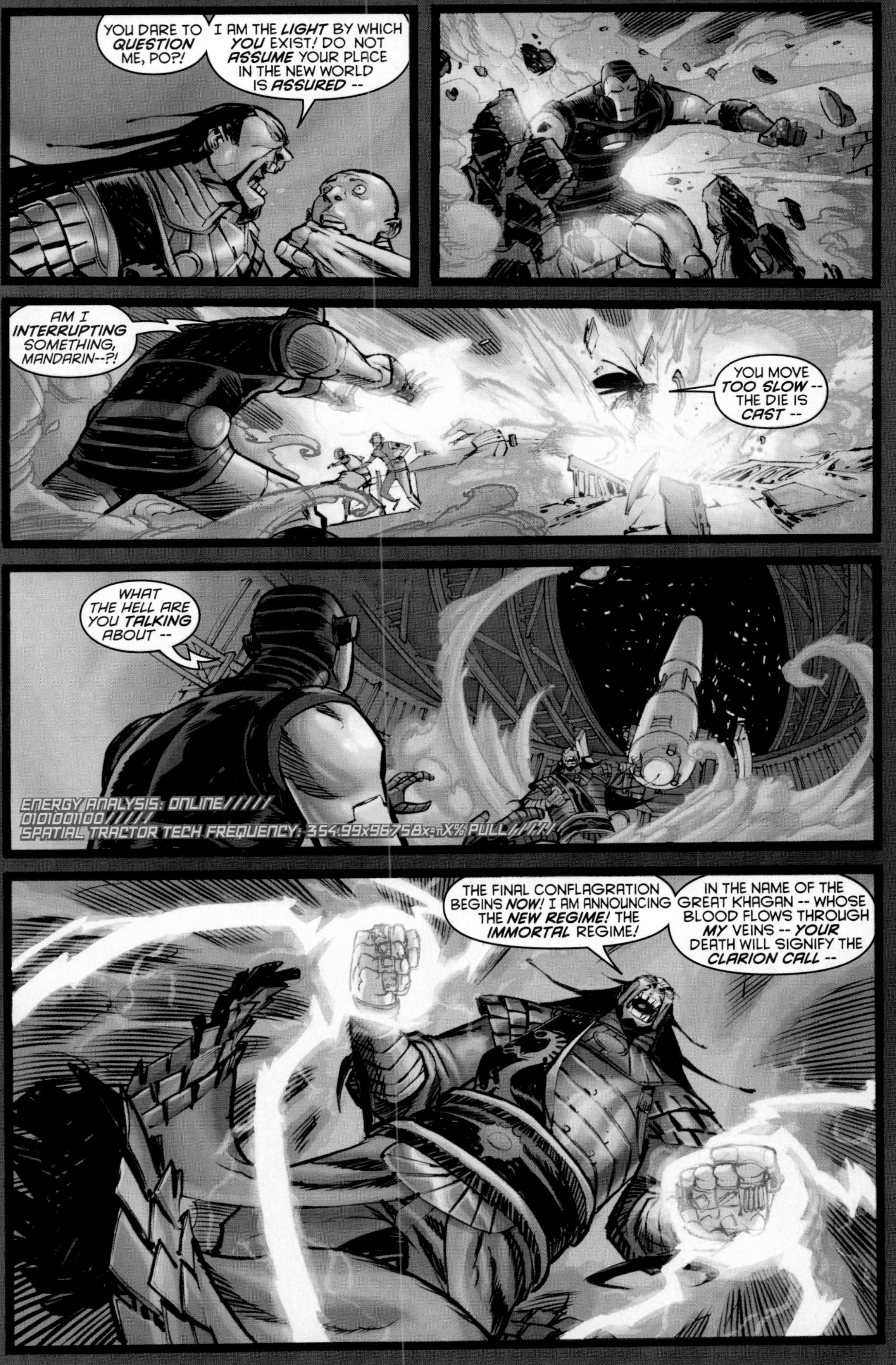

YOU DARE TO QUESTION ME, PO?!
I AM THE LIGHT BY WHICH YOU EXIST! DO NOT ASSUME YOUR PLACE IN THE NEW WORLD IS ASSURED --
AM I INTERRUPTING SOMETHING, MANDARIN--?!
YOU MOVE TOO SLOW -- THE DIE IS CAST --
WHAT THE HELL ARE YOU TALKING ABOUT --
ENERGY ANALYSIS: ONLINE//////
0101001100//////
SPATIAL TRACTOR TECH FREQUENCY: 354.99x96758x=πX% PULL//////
THE FINAL CONFLAGRATION BEGINS NOW! I AM ANNOUNCING THE NEW REGIME! THE IMMORTAL REGIME!
IN THE NAME OF THE GREAT KHAGAN -- WHOSE BLOOD FLOWS THROUGH MY VEINS -- YOUR DEATH WILL SIGNIFY THE CLARION CALL --

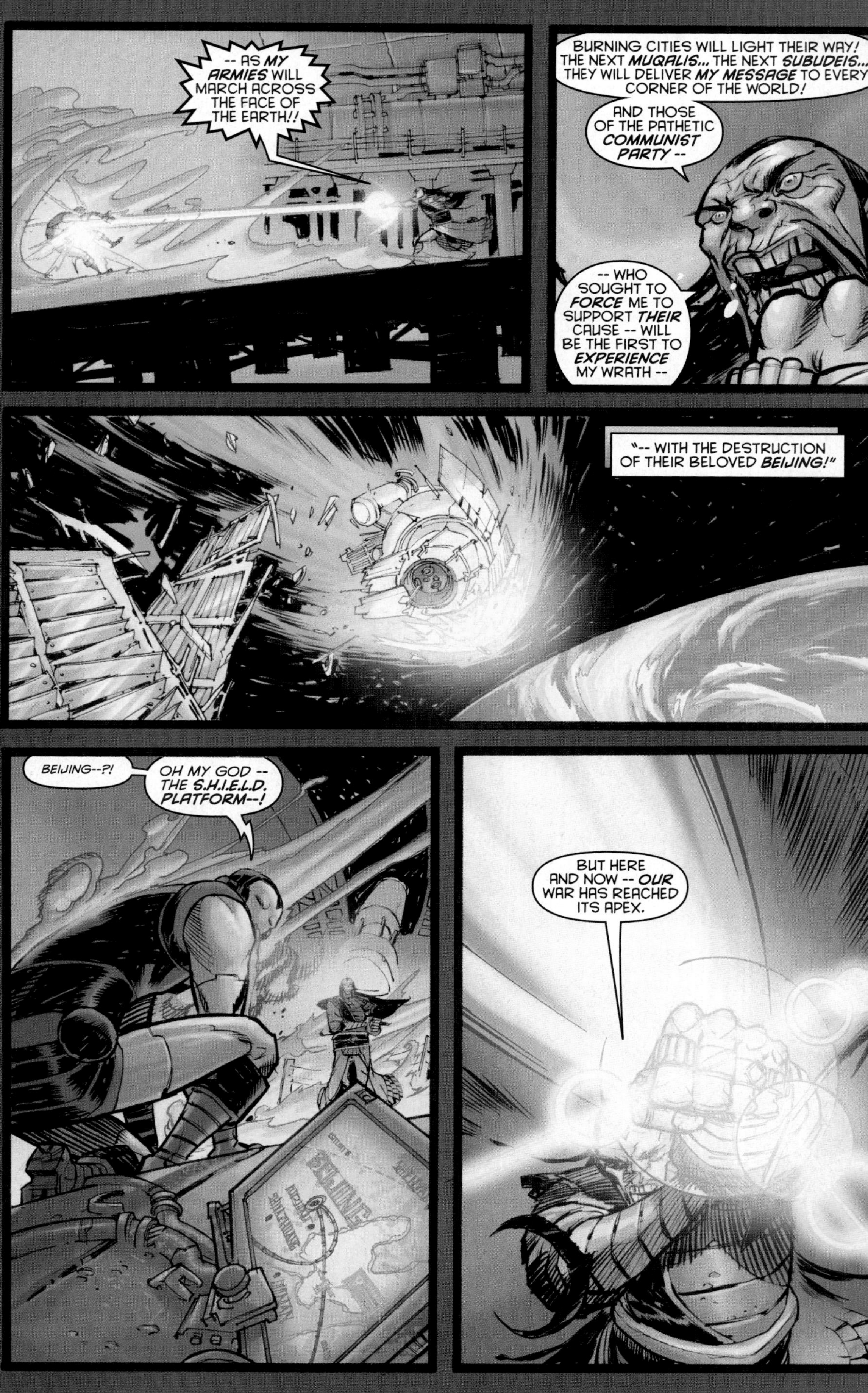

-- AS MY ARMIES WILL MARCH ACROSS THE FACE OF THE EARTH!!
BURNING CITIES WILL LIGHT THEIR WAY! THE NEXT MUQALIS... THE NEXT SUBUDEIS... THEY WILL DELIVER MY MESSAGE TO EVERY CORNER OF THE WORLD!
AND THOSE OF THE PATHETIC COMMUNIST PARTY --
-- WHO SOUGHT TO FORCE ME TO SUPPORT THEIR CAUSE -- WILL BE THE FIRST TO EXPERIENCE MY WRATH --
"-- WITH THE DESTRUCTION OF THEIR BELOVED BEIJING!"
BEIJING--?!
OH MY GOD -- THE S.H.I.E.L.D. PLATFORM--!
BEIJING
BUT HERE AND NOW -- OUR WAR HAS REACHED ITS APEX.

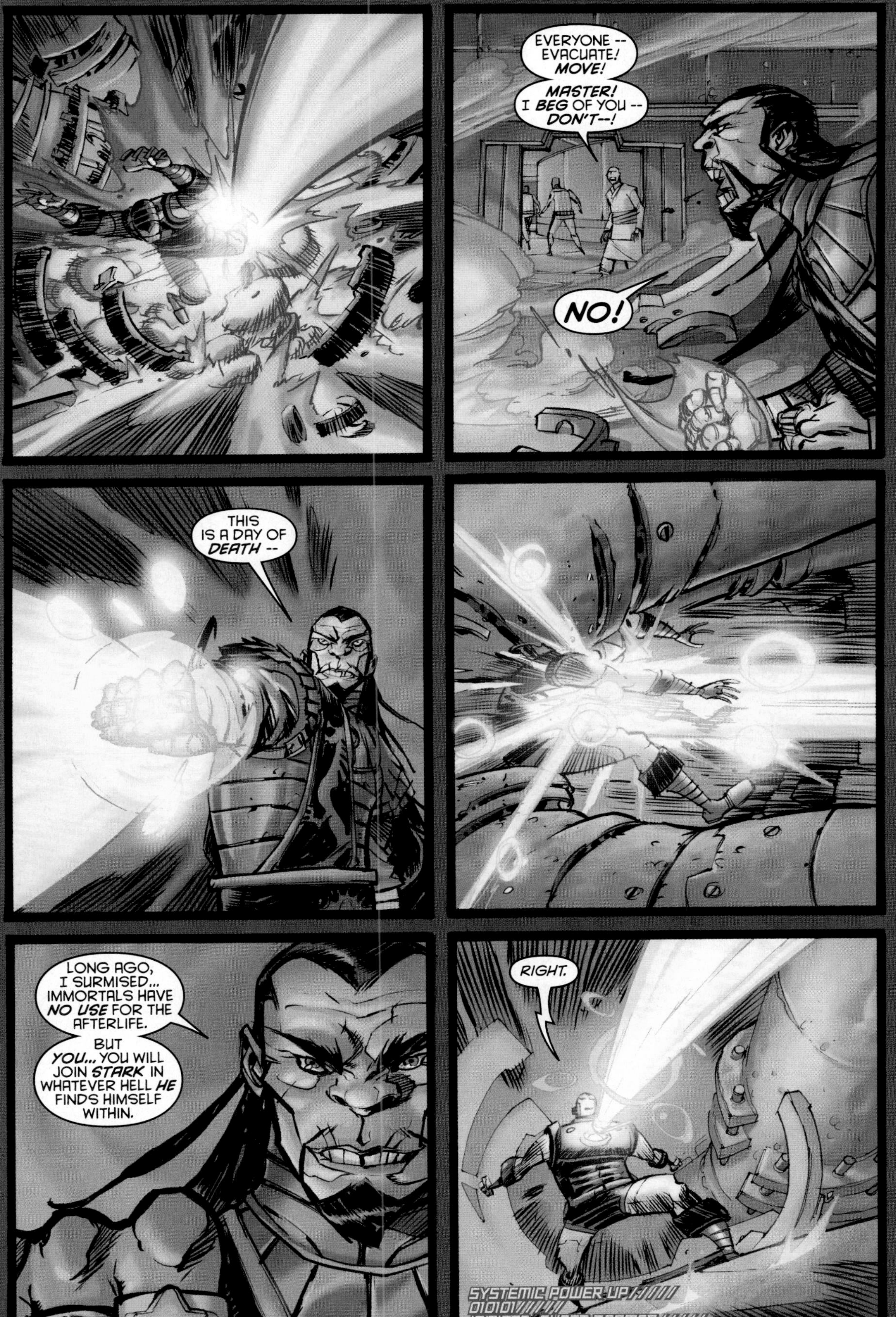
EVERYONE -- EVACUATE! MOVE!
MASTER! I BEG OF YOU -- DON'T--!
NO!
THIS IS A DAY OF DEATH --
LONG AGO, I SURMISED... IMMORTALS HAVE NO USE FOR THE AFTERLIFE.
BUT YOU... YOU WILL JOIN STARK IN WHATEVER HELL HE FINDS HIMSELF WITHIN.
RIGHT.
SYSTEMIC POWER-UP//////
010101//////
INITIATE: CHEST BEAMER//////

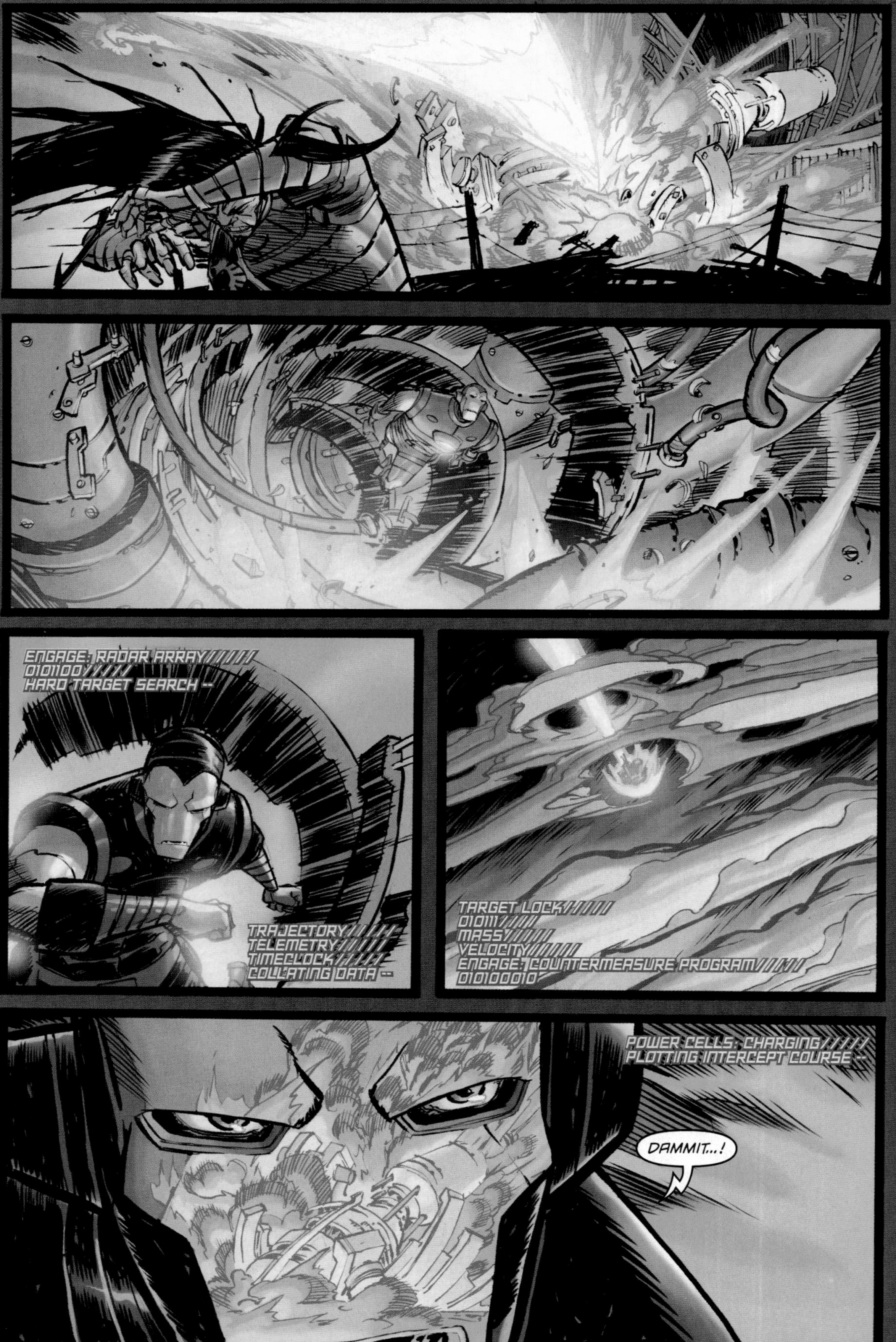
ENGAGE: RADAR ARRAY//////
0101100//////
HARD TARGET SEARCH --
TRAJECTORY//////
TELEMETRY//////
TIMECLOCK//////
COLLATING DATA --
TARGET LOCK//////
010111//////
MASS//////
VELOCITY//////
ENGAGE: COUNTERMEASURE PROGRAM//////
010100010
POWER CELLS: CHARGING//////
PLOTTING INTERCEPT COURSE --
DAMMIT...!

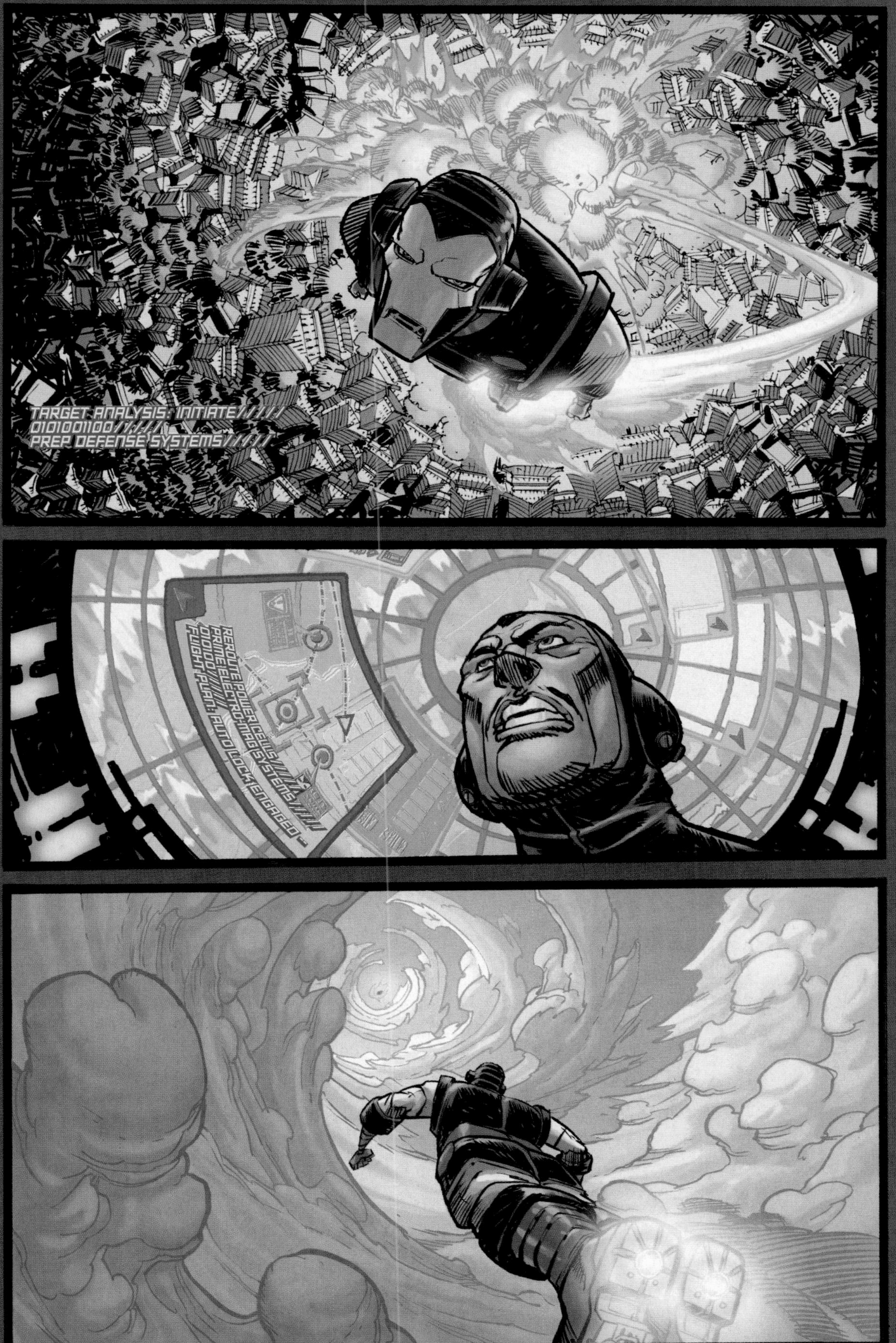

TARGET ANALYSIS: INITIATE//////
0101001100//////
PREP DEFENSE SYSTEMS//////
REROUTE POWER CELLS/////
PRIME ELECTRO-MAG SYSTEMS/////
0101001/////
FLIGHT PLAN: AUTO LOCK ENGAGED

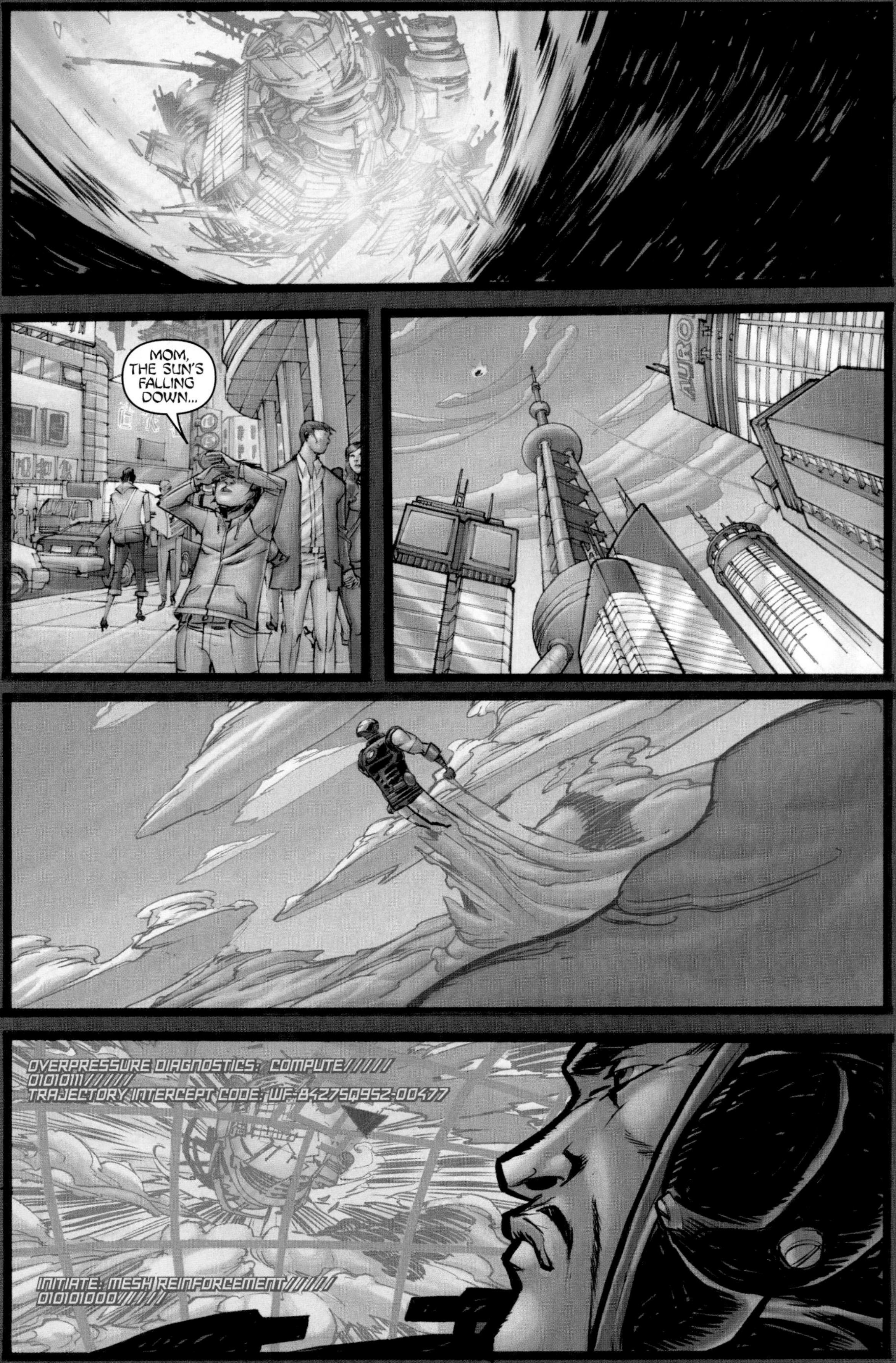
MOM, THE SUN'S FALLING DOWN...
OVERPRESSURE DIAGNOSTICS: COMPUTE//////
01010111//////
TRAJECTORY INTERCEPT CODE: WF-84275Q952-00477
INITIATE: MESH REINFORCEMENT//////
010101000//////

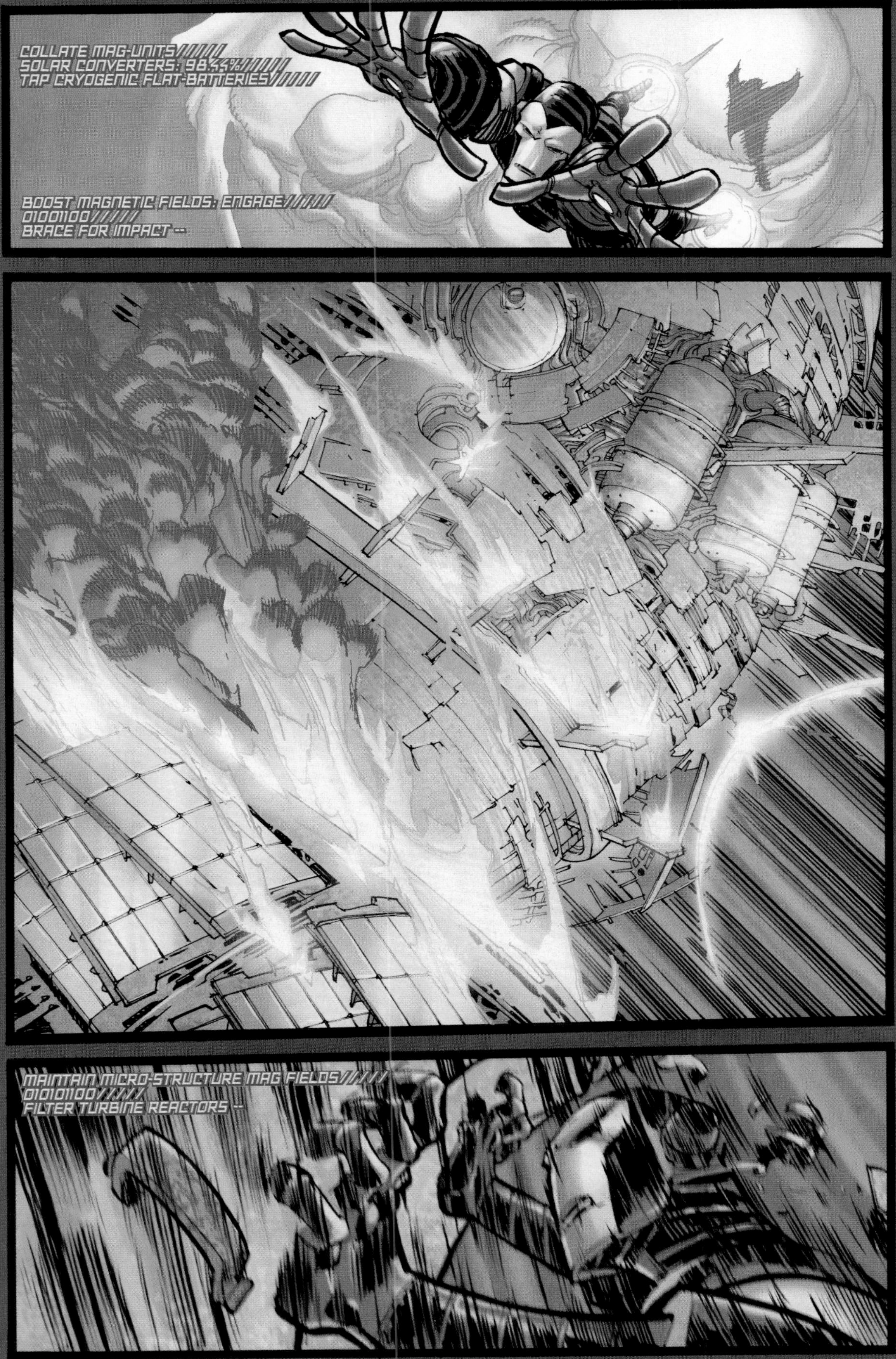
COLLATE MAG-UNITS//////
SOLAR CONVERTERS: 98.44%///////
TAP CRYOGENIC FLAT-BATTERIES//////
BOOST MAGNETIC FIELDS: ENGAGE//////
01001100//////
BRACE FOR IMPACT --
MAINTAIN MICRO-STRUCTURE MAG FIELDS//////
01010100//////
FILTER TURBINE REACTORS --

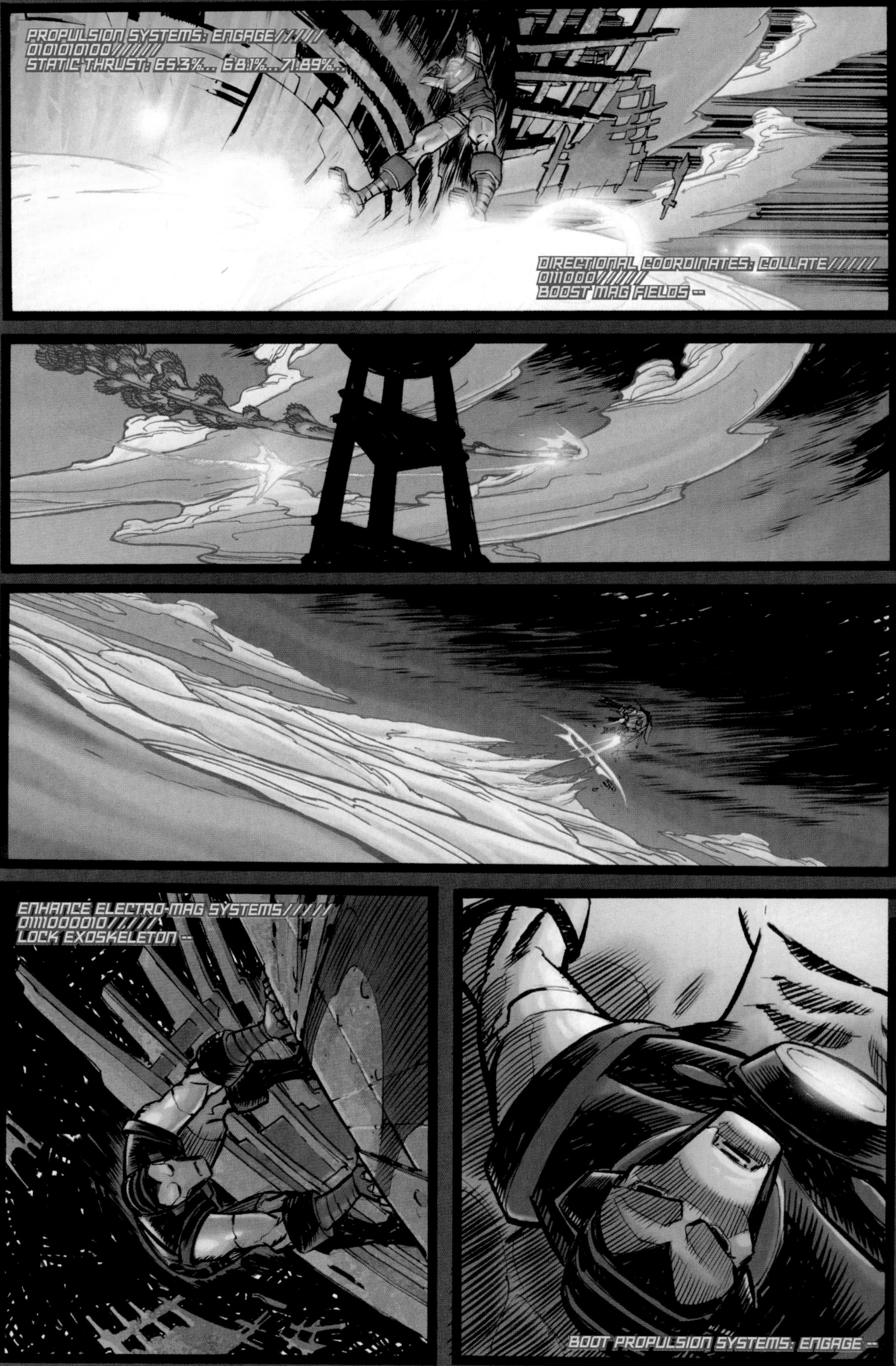
PROPULSION SYSTEMS: ENGAGE//////
0101010100///////
STATIC THRUST: 65.3%... 68.1%...71.89%...
DIRECTIONAL COORDINATES: COLLATE//////
0111000///////
BOOST MAG FIELDS --
ENHANCE ELECTRO-MAG SYSTEMS//////
01110000010//////
LOCK EXOSKELETON --
BOOT PROPULSION SYSTEMS: ENGAGE --

—FULL THRUST/////

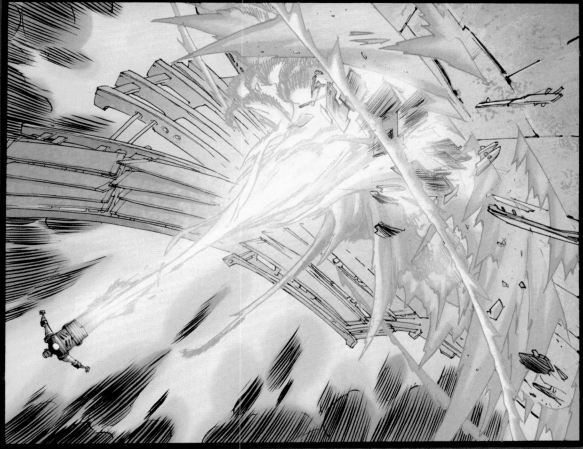

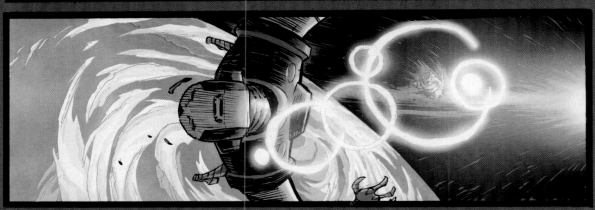

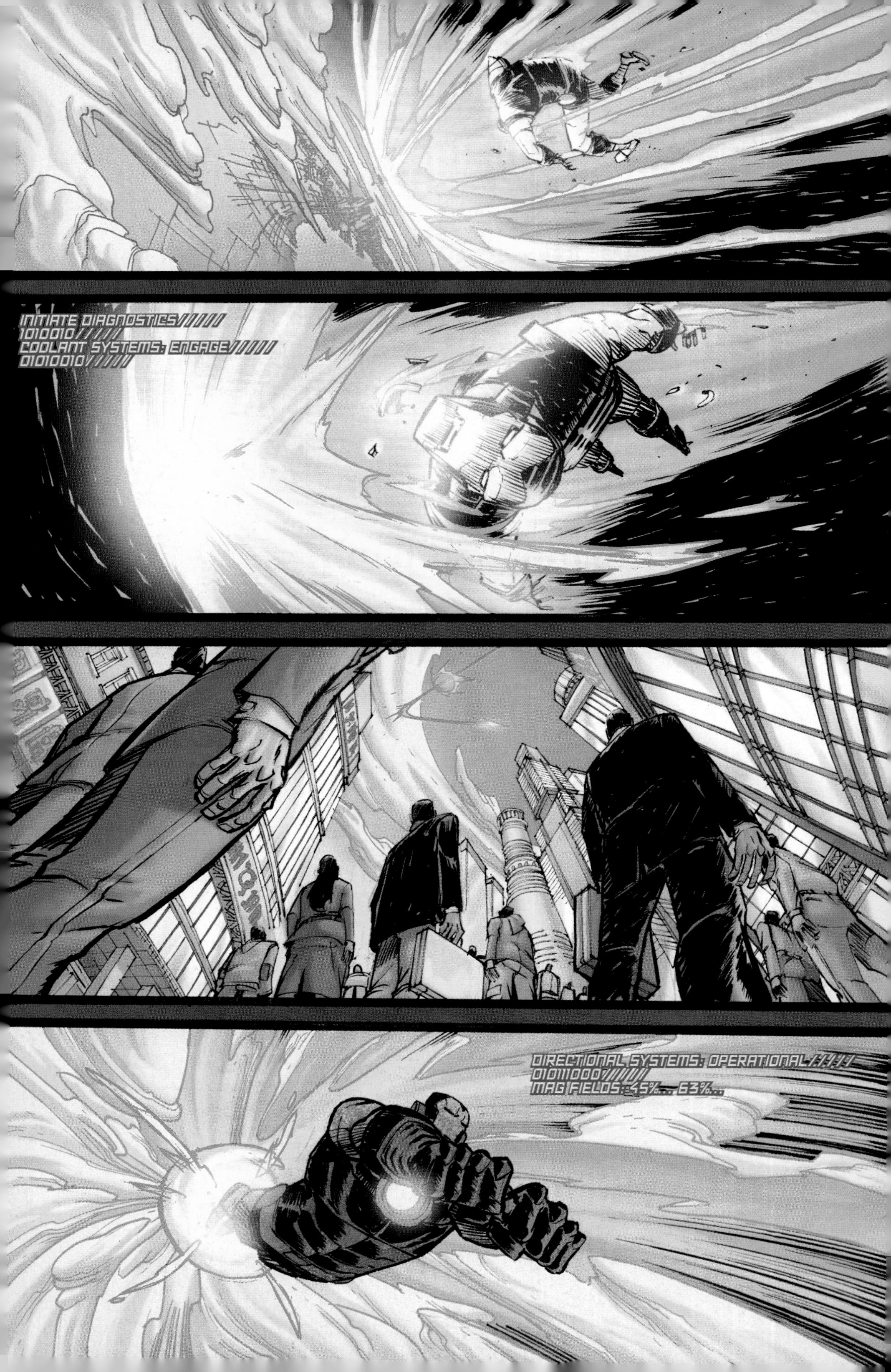
INITIATE DIAGNOSTICS//////
1010010//////
COOLANT SYSTEMS: ENGAGE//////
010100010//////
DIRECTIONAL SYSTEMS: OPERATIONAL//////
010111000//////
MAG FIELDS: 45%... 63%...

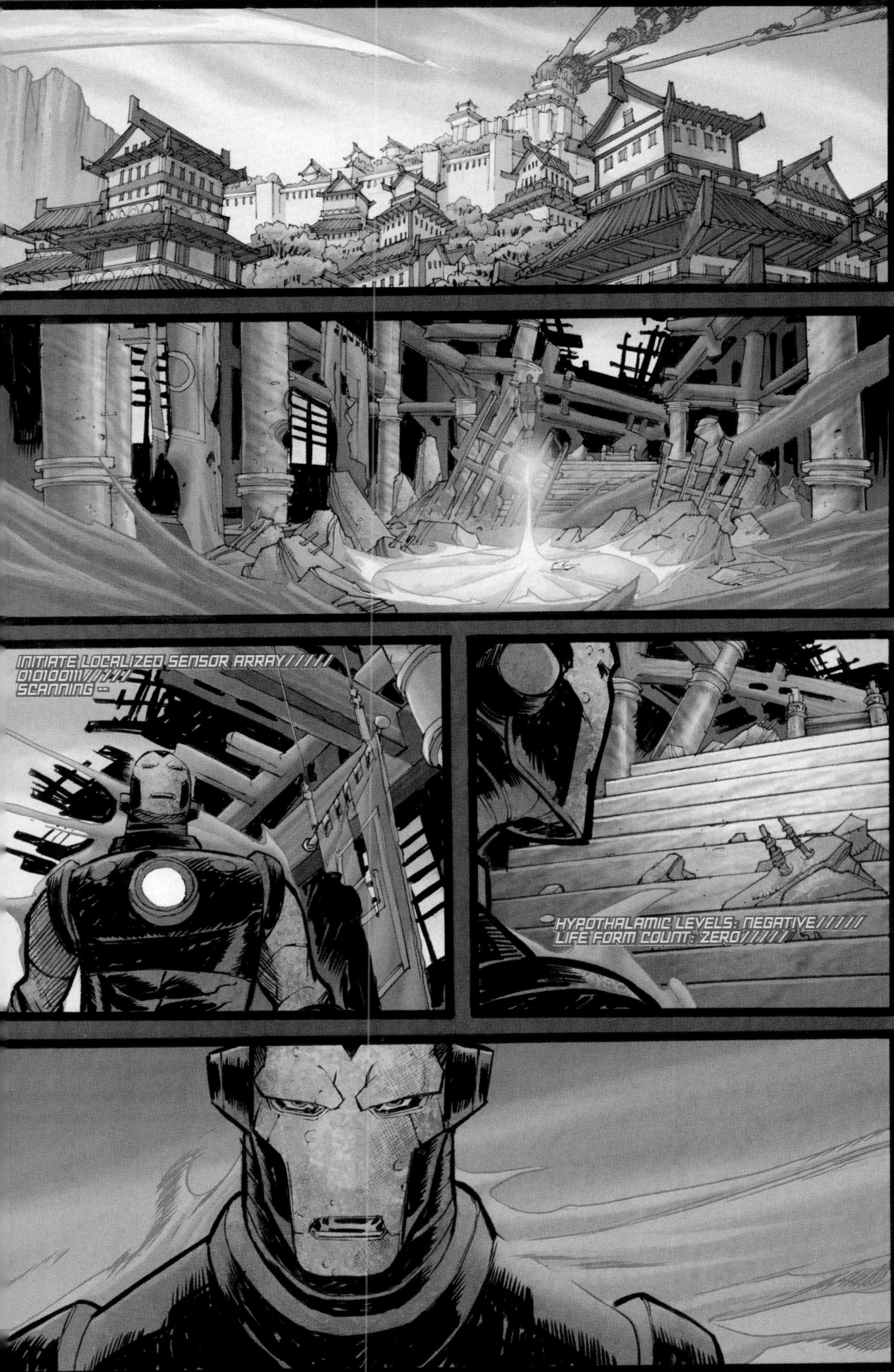
INITIATE LOCALIZED SENSOR ARRAY//////
01010011//////
SCANNING--
HYPOTHALAMIC LEVELS: NEGATIVE//////
LIFE FORM COUNT: ZERO//////

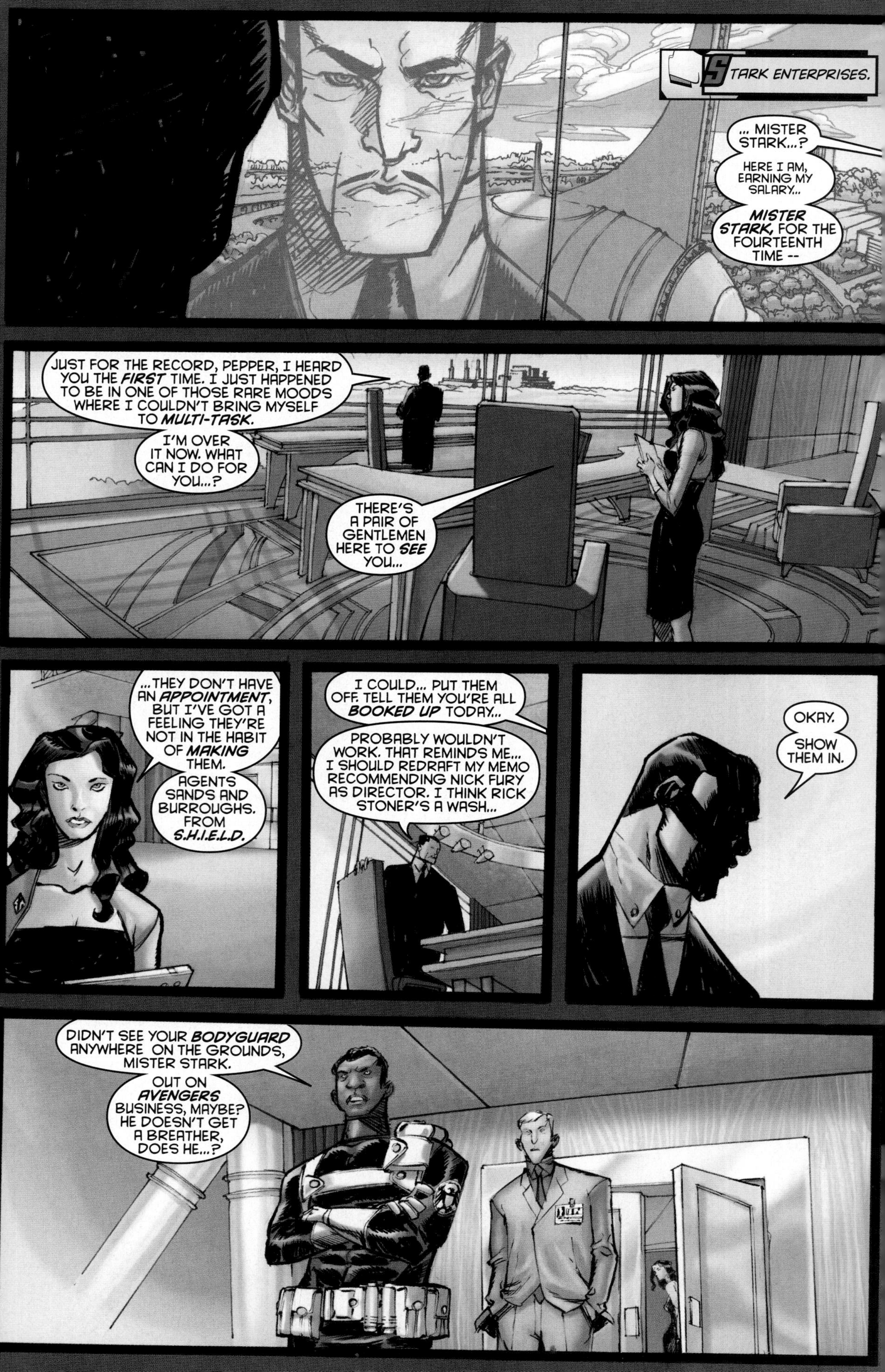
STARK ENTERPRISES.
... MISTER STARK...?
HERE I AM, EARNING MY SALARY...
MISTER STARK, FOR THE FOURTEENTH TIME --
JUST FOR THE RECORD, PEPPER, I HEARD YOU THE FIRST TIME. I JUST HAPPENED TO BE IN ONE OF THOSE RARE MOODS WHERE I COULDN'T BRING MYSELF TO MULTI-TASK.
I'M OVER IT NOW. WHAT CAN I DO FOR YOU...?
THERE'S A PAIR OF GENTLEMEN HERE TO SEE YOU...
...THEY DON'T HAVE AN APPOINTMENT, BUT I'VE GOT A FEELING THEY'RE NOT IN THE HABIT OF MAKING THEM.
AGENTS SANDS AND BURROUGHS. FROM S.H.I.E.L.D.
I COULD... PUT THEM OFF. TELL THEM YOU'RE ALL BOOKED UP TODAY...
PROBABLY WOULDN'T WORK. THAT REMINDS ME... I SHOULD REDRAFT MY MEMO RECOMMENDING NICK FURY AS DIRECTOR. I THINK RICK STONER'S A WASH...
OKAY.
SHOW THEM IN.
DIDN'T SEE YOUR BODYGUARD ANYWHERE ON THE GROUNDS, MISTER STARK.
OUT ON AVENGERS BUSINESS, MAYBE? HE DOESN'T GET A BREATHER, DOES HE...?

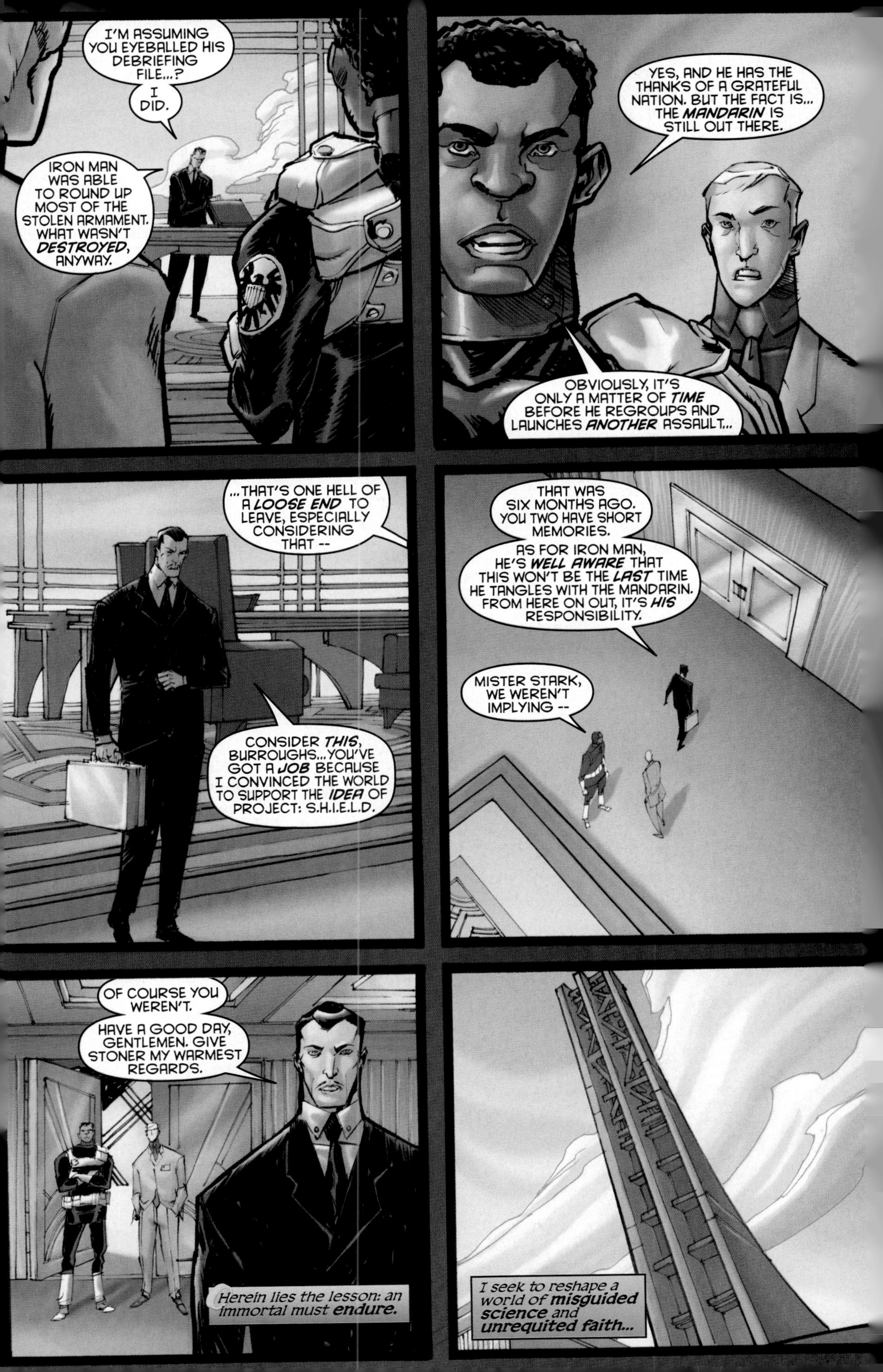
I'M ASSUMING YOU EYEBALLED HIS DEBRIEFING FILE...?
I DID.
IRON MAN WAS ABLE TO ROUND UP MOST OF THE STOLEN ARMAMENT. WHAT WASN'T DESTROYED, ANYWAY.
YES, AND HE HAS THE THANKS OF A GRATEFUL NATION. BUT THE FACT IS... THE MANDARIN IS STILL OUT THERE.
OBVIOUSLY, IT'S ONLY A MATTER OF TIME BEFORE HE REGROUPS AND LAUNCHES ANOTHER ASSAULT...
...THAT'S ONE HELL OF A LOOSE END TO LEAVE, ESPECIALLY CONSIDERING THAT --
CONSIDER THIS, BURROUGHS...YOU'VE GOT A JOB BECAUSE I CONVINCED THE WORLD TO SUPPORT THE IDEA OF PROJECT: S.H.I.E.L.D.
THAT WAS SIX MONTHS AGO. YOU TWO HAVE SHORT MEMORIES.
AS FOR IRON MAN, HE'S WELL AWARE THAT THIS WON'T BE THE LAST TIME HE TANGLES WITH THE MANDARIN. FROM HERE ON OUT, IT'S HIS RESPONSIBILITY.
MISTER STARK, WE WEREN'T IMPLYING --
OF COURSE YOU WEREN'T.
HAVE A GOOD DAY, GENTLEMEN. GIVE STONER MY WARMEST REGARDS.
Herein lies the lesson: an immortal must endure.
I seek to reshape a world of misguided science and unrequited faith...

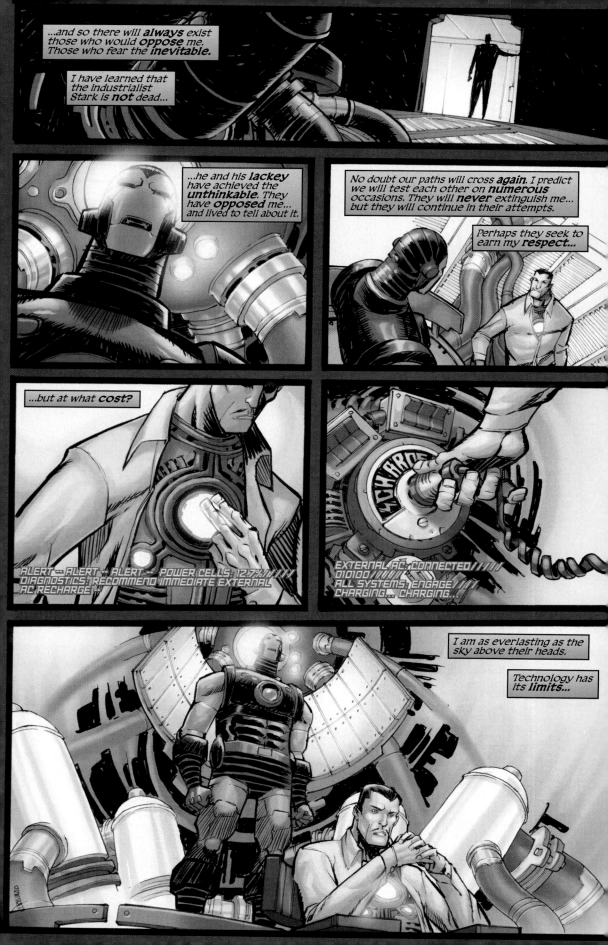

...and so there will **always** exist those who would **oppose** me. Those who fear the **inevitable**.

I have learned that the industrialist Stark is **not** dead...

...he and his **lackey** have achieved the **unthinkable**. They have **opposed** me... and lived to tell about it.

No doubt our paths will cross **again**. I predict we will test each other on **numerous** occasions. They will **never** extinguish me... but they will continue in their attempts.

Perhaps they seek to earn my **respect**...

...but at what **cost?**

ALERT -- ALERT -- ALERT -- POWER CELLS: 12.7% ////// DIAGNOSTICS: RECOMMEND IMMEDIATE EXTERNAL AC RECHARGE --

EXTERNAL AC CONNECTED ////// 010100 ////// ALL SYSTEMS ENGAGE ////// CHARGING... CHARGING...//

I am as everlasting as the sky above their heads.

Technology has its **limits**...

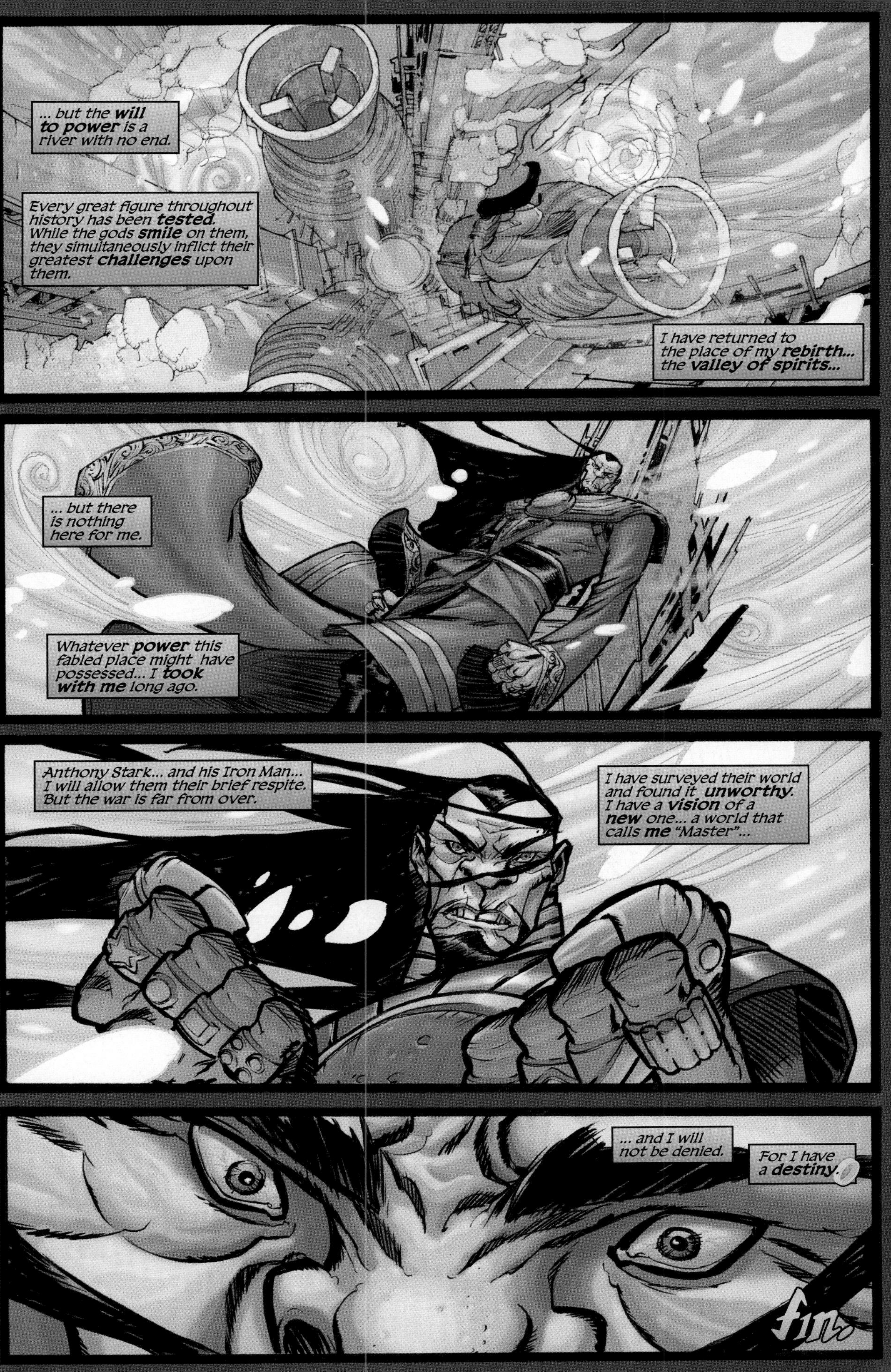

... but the will to power is a river with no end.
Every great figure throughout history has been tested. While the gods smile on them, they simultaneously inflict their greatest challenges upon them.
I have returned to the place of my rebirth... the valley of spirits...
... but there is nothing here for me.
Whatever power this fabled place might have possessed... I took with me long ago.
Anthony Stark... and his Iron Man... I will allow them their brief respite. But the war is far from over.
I have surveyed their world and found it unworthy. I have a vision of a new one... a world that calls me "Master"...
... and I will not be denied.
For I have a destiny.
fin.

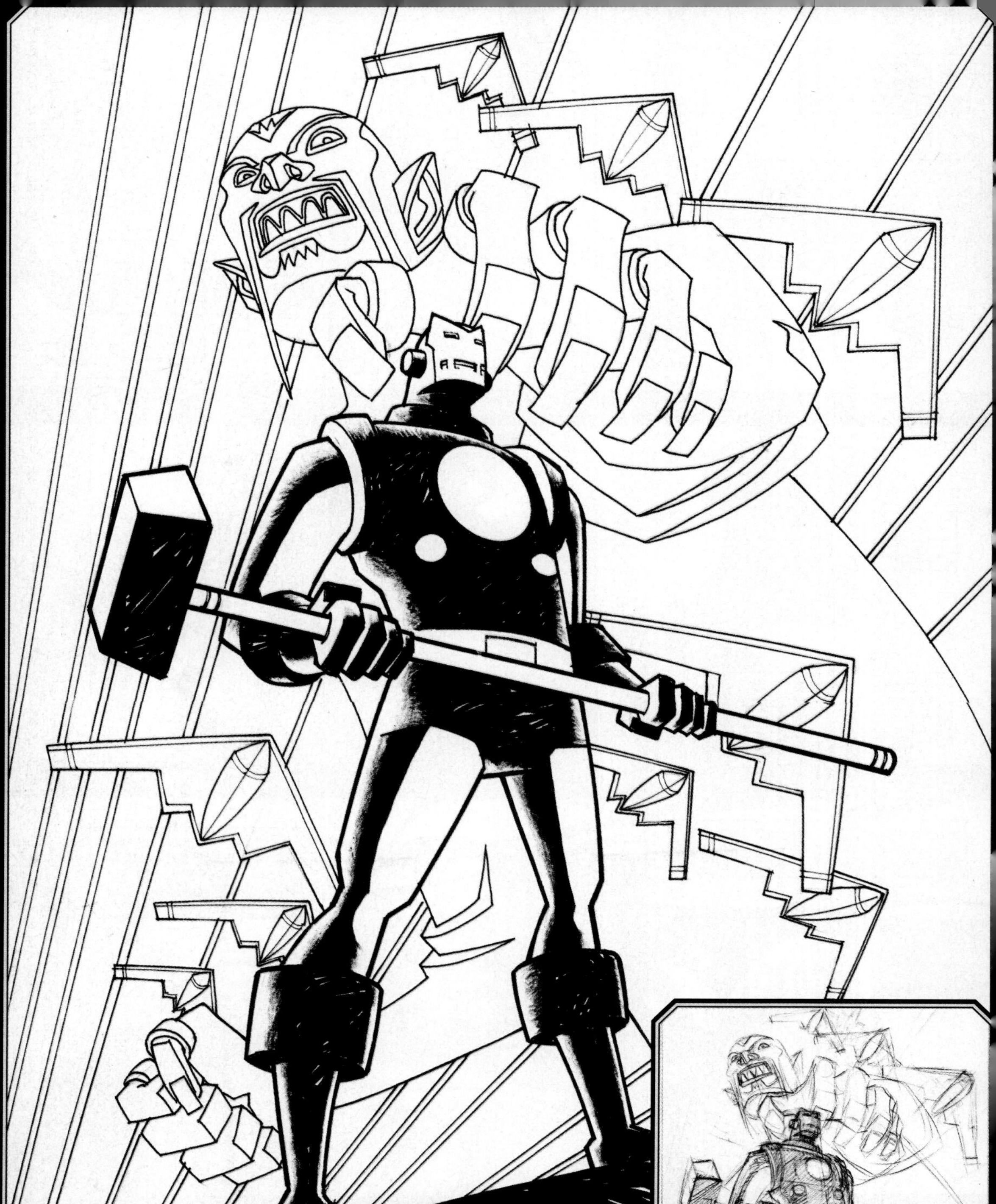

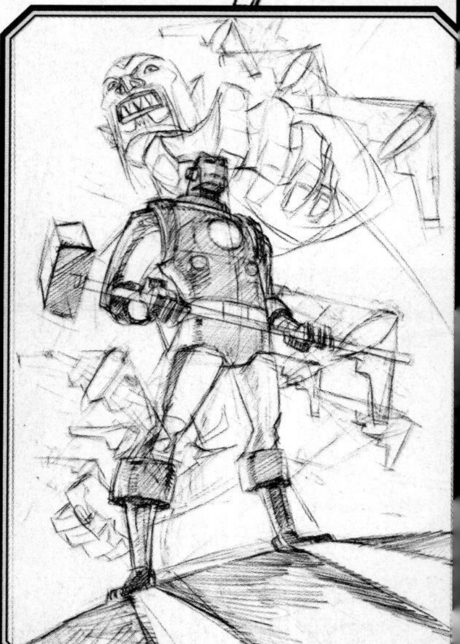

COVER SKETCHES AND INKS BY ERIC CANETE

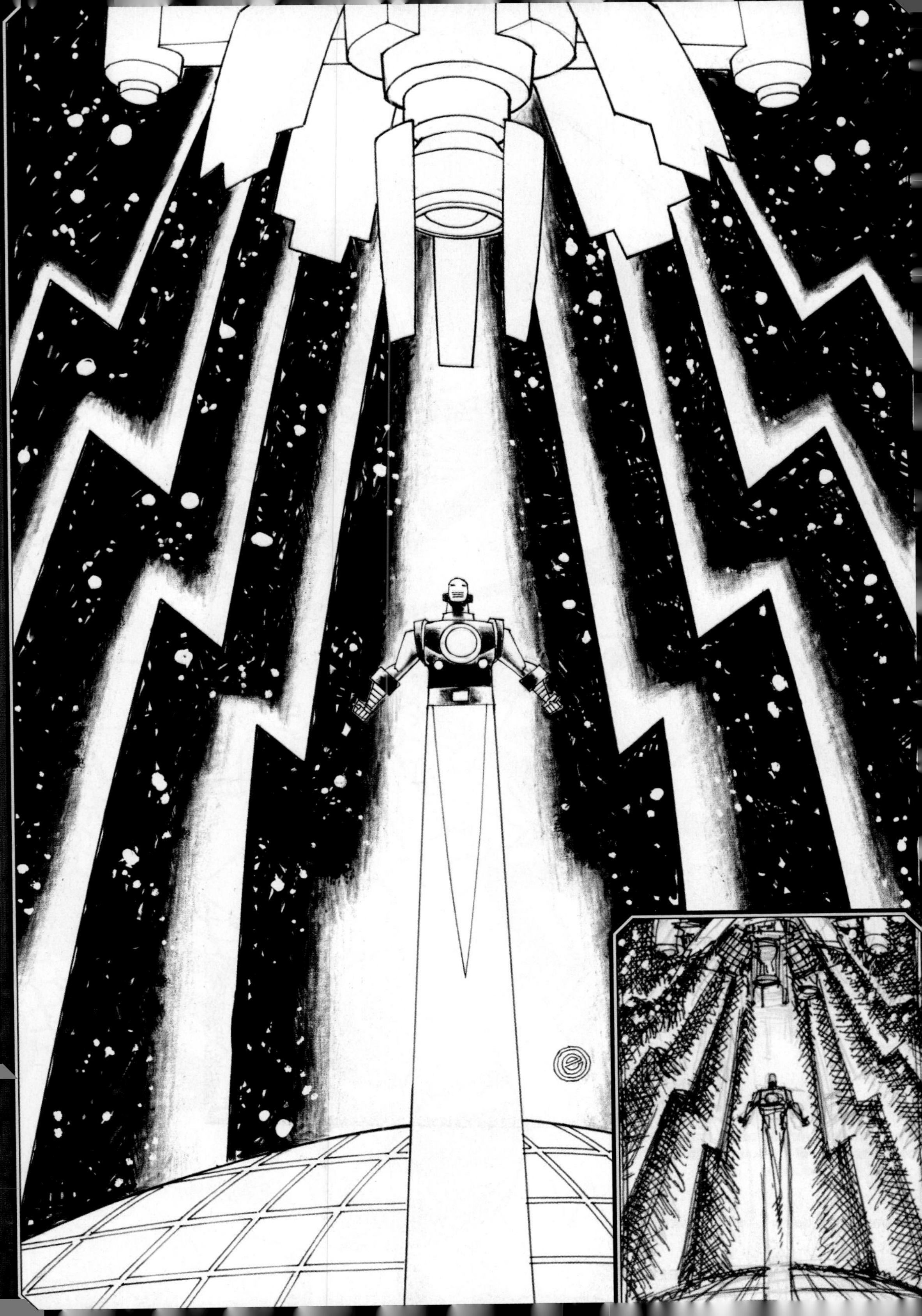

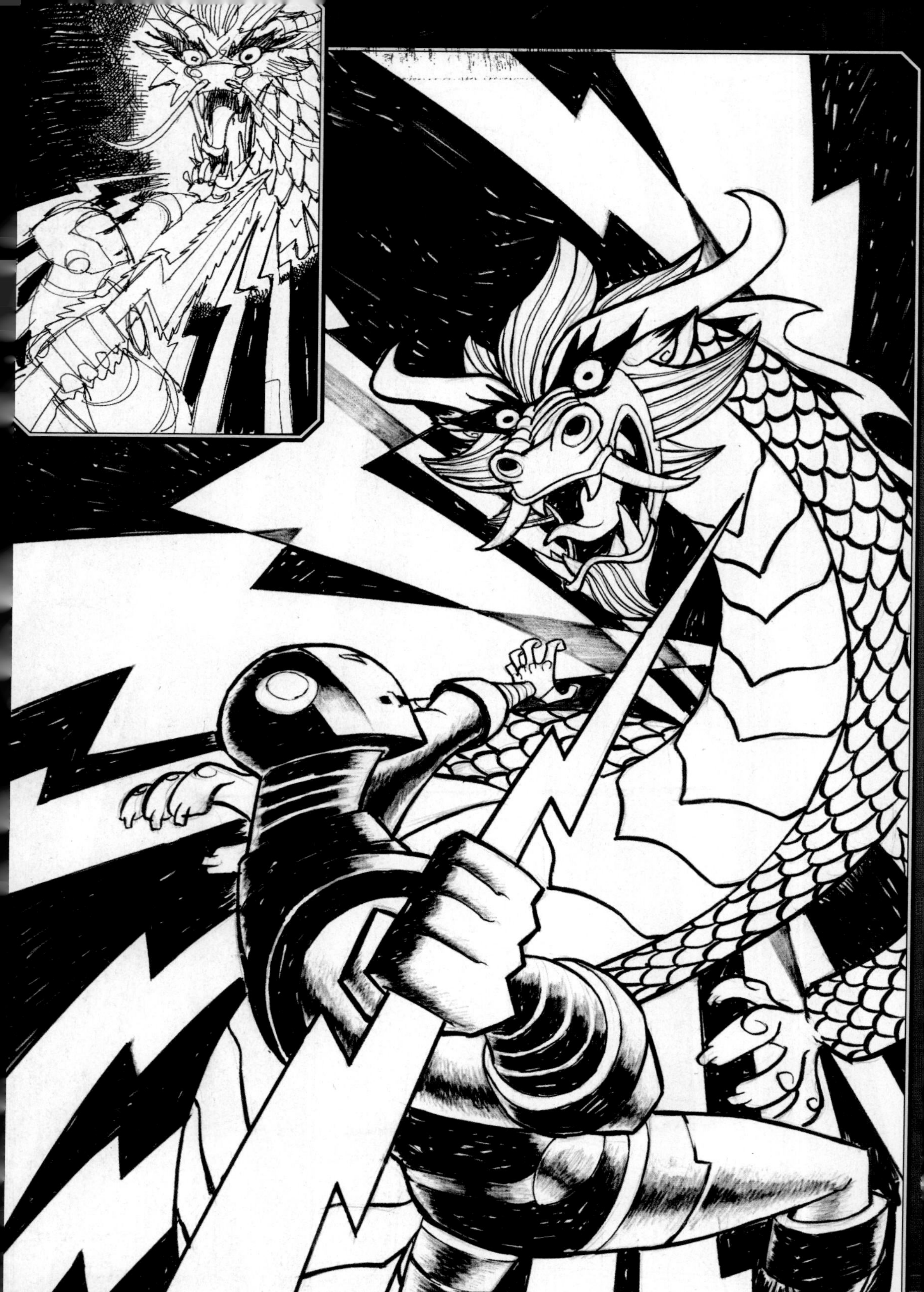